14.99

# BRUCE LEE

*Fighting Spirit*

## BRUCE THOMAS

SIDGWICK & JACKSON

First published 1996 by Sidgwick & Jackson and updated 2002
This updated edition published 2008 by Sidgwick & Jackson
an imprint of Pan Macmillan
20 New Wharf Road, London N1 9RR
Associated companies throughout the world
www.panmacmillan.com

ISBN 978-0-283-07066-2

13

A CIP catalogue record for this book is
available from the British Library.

Typeset by SetSystems Ltd, Saffron Walden, Essex
Printed and bound by
CPI Group (UK) Ltd, Croydon, CR0 4YY

The author and the publishers have made every effort to trace the
copyright holders of illustrations used in this book. In the event that any
have been inadvertently overlooked, please contact the publishers so that
the situation can be rectified in future editions.

#### Picture Acknowledgements:
p1 Getty Images, p2 Getty Images, p3 Everett Collection/Rex Features,
p4 c20thC.Fox/Everett/Rex Features, p5 (bottom) Everett Collection /
Rex Features, p6 SNAP/Rex Features, p7 Everett Collection / Rex Features,
p8 c.Paramount/Everett/Rex Features, p10 (top) The Kobal Collection, p9 (top)
The Kobal Collection, (bottom) Everett Collection/Rex Features, p11 (top & bottom)
Everett Collection/Rex Features, p12 Aquarius Library, p14 Everett Collection/
Rex Features, p15 (top) Hulton Deutsch, p16 The Kobal Collection.

Visit **www.panmacmillan.com** to read more about all our books
and to buy them. You will also find features, author interviews and
news of any author events, and you can sign up for e-newsletters
so that you're always first to hear about our new releases.

*For my mother*

## Acknowledgements

I would like to thank Julian Alexander and Ingrid Connell for their help in bringing this book to fruition.

## Pictures

The author extends his grateful thanks to all the copyright holders who have generously given permission for the illustrations used in this book, including Twentieth Century Fox, Paramount, Golden Harvest, Warner Brothers and the South China Post. Every reasonable effort has been made to clear all of the images used in the book; however if anyone feels that they have been inadvertently overlooked, please contact the author via the publishers so that any mistakes may be redressed and future editions of the book can be amended.

# Contents

# *Introduction*

Those who have read earlier editions of my biography *Bruce Lee: Fighting Spirit* will recognize passages in this book. But there is such a significant amount of new material here that it can be considered to be a new work rather than an updating of the previous one. In the course of researching new material I've taken the opportunity to re-interview several people and correct some mistakes in previous accounts of Bruce Lee's life and work – not only in my own book but also in those of other biographers. I've also taken the opportunity to compile a new photo section.

Many of the new interviews and new material concerns 'the Seattle years', which are often little more than a footnote to Bruce Lee's headlong rush to stardom. But as these were the happiest years of his life I have given them the consideration and detail they warrant. This book also includes a comprehensive new appendix, packed with detailed information and anecdotal material that would have interrupted the flow of the narrative text. This new section also includes references to projects that Bruce Lee set in motion but was unable to complete.

As the years have passed since Bruce Lee's death it has become possible to see more accurately what his legacy is becoming.' In redefining action films he set the stage for a new era of film-making. A film like *Kill Bill* openly acknowledges this by having its star Uma Thurman wear an iconic yellow and black track suit similar to the one Bruce wore in *Game of Death*, as well as lifting dialogue from *Fist of Fury*. Bruce Lee was the driving force behind moving martial arts and martial sport into modern era, and the development of mixed martial arts and 'ultimate fighting' is a direct result of Bruce's application of his 'jeet kune do' philosophy to sports karate, the introduction of full-contact fighting and the cross-pollination of styles.

As an icon, Bruce Lee's worldwide popularity continues to grow. Asian *Time* magazine even placed him on their list of heroes who helped Asia 'from poverty to powerhouse' and from 'imitator to imitated'. His face has appeared on postage stamps throughout the world. At the time of writing there are plans for a Broadway musical about his life, a Hong Kong theme park and, as a prelude to the Beijing Olympics, plans for a 40-part TV series *The Legend of Bruce Lee*.

Bruce always wanted to go beyond the limits and do it faster, longer and higher, pushing the boundaries of what is physically possible for the human body, both through the demands he made on it and via the cutting-edge training methods he employed. He also pushed the limits of his art, being the first Chinese man to reveal the secrets of the martial arts to the West. He even pushed the limits of the martial arts themselves as he rode roughshod over tradition and protocol. Not only did he break the mould of the Chinese stereotype as seen by the Western world, he remade the image of the Asian man through his films and personal life. All of this was underpinned by a philosophy, jeet kune do, which in its ultimate expression reflects the nature of the Tao itself, and so is limitless in its possibilities.

*Bruce Thomas*

# Life and Work

# 1

## Early Years

Grace was an attractive girl, the daughter of a Chinese mother and German father. Raised as a Catholic she had come from Shanghai to the British colony of Hong Kong at the age of nineteen. While accompanying her father on his regular visits to the opera she was taken by its comic singer and actor Lee Hoi Cheun and would make sure she always had a seat near the orchestra where he would be able to see her. Her efforts to gain his attention were not in vain. Hoi Cheun and Grace were soon married and took up residence at 218 Nathan Road in the Kowloon district of Hong Kong.

Hong Kong's Cantonese Opera was more of a music hall than a classical company like the Peking Opera. Although Hoi Cheun wasn't a great celebrity he had an enthusiastic following that enjoyed his dramatic flourishes and he had done well enough to become the owner and landlord of several apartments. Opium smoking was common among the men and Hoi Cheun was fond of saying that he smoked it 'because it helps sweeten my singing voice'. Hoi Cheun was also partial to gambling, and so his cronies, as much as his family, enjoyed his company and generosity.

Bruce was the fourth child born to Hoi Cheun and Grace. The Lees' first child, a son James, had died soon after birth and this had been taken as a bad omen that the spirits were looking on them unkindly and trying to prevent the continuation of the family name. A daughter Phoebe was adopted, after which Grace gave birth to a healthy daughter, Agnes, and a son, Peter.

While these children were lodged with relatives in Hong Kong, Grace was accompanying her husband on the Cantonese Opera Company's tour of the US when she discovered that she was again pregnant. While her husband continued on to New York, Grace stayed in San Francisco.

On 27 November 1940 – according to the Chinese zodiac, the Year of the Dragon – between 6 and 8a.m. – the Hour of the Dragon – at the Jackson Street Hospital in San Francisco's Chinatown, Grace Lee gave birth to another son. To confuse any potentially unfriendly spirits, the child was given a girl's name, Sai Fon (Small Phoenix) and one of his ears was pierced. Grace Lee soon renamed her new son Jun Fan (Return Again) because she had an intuition that he would one day return to his birthplace. On her papers, the supervising doctor, Mary Glover, nicknamed the boy Bruce and anglicized his family name to Lee. The name was remembered, although he was never called Bruce by his family until he enrolled in college, when he was twelve years old.

Early in 1941, a few months after Bruce's birth, the Lee family returned to Hong Kong. The city then was nothing like it is today with its dramatic vistas of steel and glass, Chanel-suited businesswomen and Mercedes limos. This Hong Kong was a seething maze of lanes threading between ramshackle apartment buildings, crowded shops and restaurants where signs projected from every available surface. The lanes were choked with lorries, taxis, pushcarts and rickshaws, all jostling with locals in their traditional suits of long shirts and baggy trousers. Vendors shaded by canopied stalls displayed fruit, fish and rows of shiny hanging ducks. The atmosphere was a complex blend of exotic food and equally exotic rubbish in various stages of decay – a thick stew of smells and an oppressive, muggy heat. The humid conditions soon made baby Bruce ill, and he remained a sickly, skinny child throughout his early years.

The Lees' apartment on Nathan Road was on the second floor

of an old building above some shops. The narrow stairway had no door at street level, so tramps frequently set up home in the entrance. Two sets of strong doors guarded the apartment entrance on the second floor landing, though, the outer doors with thick steel bars and the inner doors containing a peephole.

One of Bruce's most vivid memories of his early years was the occupation of Hong Kong by the Japanese during the Second World War (1939–45). The Lees' apartment was directly across the street from a Japanese military base and Bruce's mother later told the story of how she would find her young son leaning precariously over the balcony, raising his fist to the Japanese 'Zeroes' circling above.

Inside, the apartment was sparsely furnished. The large main room had a refrigerator at one end, a big table in the middle and a series of beds with simple iron frames and hard mattresses against the walls. Beyond this main room were two smaller rooms; one held two double-deck bunks. The other, overlooking Nathan Road, had a veranda containing numerous potted plants and a caged chicken.

In the unrelenting humidity and heat no bedclothes were needed at night. In the mornings there was a constant queue to use the single bathroom, not that bathing did much good as within minutes one would be covered in sweat again. During times of drought, when the water supply was sporadic, the bathtub was kept filled and the chicken had to share the veranda with a makeshift bathing area set up behind some curtains.

When Hoi Cheun's brother died, his widow and her five children were taken in by the Lee family, as is the Chinese custom. Together with a couple of servants and Wu Ngan, an unofficially adopted child, there were sometimes as many as twenty people crammed into the apartment, along with assorted dogs, birds and fish. Bruce's favourite dog was an Alsatian named Bobby who slept under his bed.

It would be a mistake to think that Bruce Lee had an under-privileged background. The rent from his father's properties, along with his income from the opera, meant that the Lees could always afford servants, but despite the fact that his father made good money, Bruce claimed that he never saw any of it. He complained that his father was 'miserly' and Bruce sometimes stole money from him to take friends to restaurants. In reality Bruce's father was not a mean man and was known to have paid medical bills for acquaintances who couldn't afford them.

Bruce's father sometimes took him to the theatres where he was working and it was there that he met Siu Kee Lun, better known to his friends as Unicorn, whose father was also an actor in the Chinese Opera. Although Unicorn was three years older than Bruce, the two boys became friends. They would fight and fence with bamboo swords, with Bruce imitating Errol Flynn in *Robin Hood*. Although Unicorn was older and stronger, Bruce would never admit defeat but would keep on fighting until Unicorn gave up.

Bruce spent much of his early life amusing himself in the streets of Hong Kong. In a busy household he wasn't always missed and his mother generally had to deal with most of the trouble he caused. She paid his school fees every month but would get calls asking why Bruce hadn't been attending. In the end she told Bruce that it didn't matter so much if he didn't like school, but he had to tell her where he was going so that she knew where he was.

'Bruce never changed his character,' said his mother. 'He repeated the same mistakes time after time. I was disappointed with him again and again. Once I asked how he expected to earn a living if he kept on like that and he said, "I'll be a famous film star one day." I scolded him and told him that the life of a famous film star was not as comfortable as he imagined and that their lives were abnormal. I told Bruce, "You can't even behave like a normal person. How do you expect to become a famous film star?"'

But Grace Lee also has fond memories of her son. She recalls how she once saw him looking intently from the window of the house at something down in the street. Suddenly he jumped up and ran out the door. When she went to the window she saw

Bruce helping a blind man across the street. He told her that he just had to go and help the man who looked so sad and frustrated as everyone walked by ignoring him.

It was Bruce's sister, Agnes, who gave him the name that stuck with him for life: Little Dragon. She recalls that even from an early age Bruce knew he was special and was going to make something of his life. She also remembers him having nightmares and sleepwalking. The rest of the family affectionately called him Mo Si Tung (Never Sits Still). It was the perfect description. If Bruce was still, even for a moment, they thought he was sick. The only time he stopped running, jumping and talking was when he disappeared to a quiet corner and became absorbed in a book. He often stayed up half the night reading. His mother believes that this caused him to become near-sighted and from the age of six Bruce had to wear spectacles.

Young Bruce took great delight in playing practical jokes. After starting out with simple gags, like packets of itching powder and electric-shock tricks, his practical jokes became far more sophisticated. On one occasion he rearranged all the furniture in a room to confuse the cleaner. Bruce once told his brother Robert to imagine he was a submarine and look up the sleeve of his jacket as if it were the periscope. As he did so, Bruce fired his depth charge and poured a jug of water down the sleeve, soaking him. Some of his other jokes had an edge to them that wasn't always funny. Once, after Bruce had pushed his sister Phoebe into the swimming pool, she held his head under water until he promised never to do it again. Bruce never went into a swimming pool again after that.

Bruce Lee had begun his acting career at the age of three months, before his parents left San Francisco, in a film called *Golden Gate Girl*. He played the role of a female baby, carried by his father more as a stage prop than anything else. Although Bruce never took formal acting lessons, with his father's help and connections he landed his first proper role at the age of six in the Hong Kong-made film *The Birth of Mankind*. Bruce played a street kid who

9

fights with a shoeshine boy, played by his friend Unicorn. Also when he was six, Bruce played his first role under the name Lee Siu Lung (Lee Little Dragon, the name by which he became known in Asia) appearing with his father in *My Son, Ah Chung*. Bruce was cast as the cute co-star to the top Cantonese film comic, Chow Shui, and played a streetwise kid trying to survive in Hong Kong's sweatshops.

Both in tragedies like *A Mother's Tears* and comedies such as *It's Father's Fault*, Bruce played street urchins and orphans. Later he was cast in roles playing juvenile delinquents and teenage rebels in films that imitated those being made in the US. There were occasional fight scenes and already Bruce began using some of the gestures that would later become his trademarks: the admonishing finger, the thumb wiped across the nose, the brushing down of the jacket sleeves and the slow-burning gaze. Altogether Bruce appeared as a child actor in around twenty pictures, the best known of which was *The Orphan*, a film about street gangs, which was made when he was eighteen. It was the only time he played the leading role as a child actor. Besides making these early films, his greatest influence came from the films he enjoyed watching.

Between 1920 and 1949, Chinese filmmaking centred on the Westernized areas of Hong Kong and Shanghai, whose populations were more cosmopolitan than most of China. Even so, it was a highly stylized cinema strongly based on theatrical tradition. In 1949, director Hu Peng decided to make a film about a martial arts master, Wong Fei Hung, who lived between 1847 and 1924. Up until then most martial arts films were savage tales of revenge with ludicrously exaggerated action in which fighters could leap a hundred feet or fly through the air for a hundred yards doing endless somersaults. But both the director and the leading actor of the Wong Fei Hung movies insisted on realistic action scenes and, for the first time, martial arts were at the heart of the film. Apart from being a master of the hung gar style of kung fu, Wong also practised herbal medicine, and the actor who played him had an uncannily similar background.

The actor Kwan Tak Hing was, like Bruce Lee's father, an actor in the Cantonese Opera. He was a *wen wu* player, which meant that he had to be a martial artist as well as an actor. Like the character he now played, Kwan excelled in hung gar. In addition he knew the Shaolin fighting systems which were based on the movements of various animals. A master of the white crane style, Master Kwan, as he became popularly known, was also a herbal physician and healer.

As this epic series of films progressed – the director went on to make eighty films featuring this character, all played by the same leading actor – Master Kwan became as skilled as the master whose legend he honoured by choreographing superb battles with his main opponent, played by Shih Kien. The young Bruce Lee could hardly have avoided being deeply influenced by these films. During the 1950s and 60s, this series of movies virtually monopolized the market. In 1956, all but four of the year's twenty-nine kung fu pictures featured Wong Fei Hung. Bruce could recite whole scenes of dialogue from films like *How Wong Fei Hung Rescues the Fishmonger*, *How Wong Fei Hung Saved the Lovelorn Monk From the Ancient Monastery* and *How Wong Fei Hung Smashed the Flying Dagger Gang*.

When he was twelve years old, Bruce Lee began attending La Salle College, where most of the students were Chinese Catholics. Although he was in trouble from the start, he was fortunate enough to attract the attention of one of the better teachers, the round-faced, bespectacled Brother Henry Pang. While many of the teachers found Bruce stubborn, wild or lazy, Brother Henry was aware that although Bruce was a difficult pupil he was also very bright, full of potential and needed to be approached differently.

Brother Henry channelled what would now be described as Bruce's 'attention-deficit hyperactivity disorder' into running errands, cleaning the blackboards and opening the windows – chores Bruce did willingly. Even so, he found it impossible to sit still in the classroom and was continually in trouble for causing disturbances. At home Bruce spent many hours reading in bed, and his brother Peter recalls that Bruce already had ambitions to become a doctor, though he showed no interest in biology. It would seem that while he was very interested in learning he wasn't so interested in schooling.

In Hong Kong there was a long history of subjugation under colonial rule and the feelings of resentment towards the British were long-standing. The Chinese hated the British almost as much as they hated the Japanese and Bruce soon became the leader of a school gang with strong anti-British sympathies. At the end of a long and tedious school day, frustrations would be directed against the British pupils of the nearby King George V School. Bruce's gang would gather near the school and heap insults on the British schoolboys walking up the road, or gathered behind the fence in the playing field, until a fight got underway. These fights would continue until one side was beaten or the police arrived. Although the British boys were bigger than the Chinese and won their share of fights, Bruce would never acknowledge defeat or admit that his gang had been beaten fairly.

Phone calls and visits from the police became a regular event in the Lee household and when Bruce's father came home late from the theatre Bruce would pretend to be asleep and hide under the blankets to avoid punishment. More often than not his mother would simply 'forget' to tell his father. To keep out of the way of the police, fights were staged on the flat roofs of apartment buildings, the largest areas of open space to found anywhere in Hong Kong. When a black eye or some other injury made it impossible for Grace to protect Bruce, his father, realizing what was going on, became angry and placed all kinds of restrictions on Bruce's movements, but he wasn't home enough to enforce his rulings. After continuing trouble led to Bruce's expulsion from La Salle, he swept his parents through the headmasters' offices of a number of schools before finally settling, a little, at the exclusive St Francis Xavier College.

\*

Hong Kong in the 1950s was a place suffering from high unemployment, a depressed economy, overcrowding, homelessness and from people simply taking advantage of each other. Thousands upon thousands of Chinese streamed into the city in order to escape the communist regime on the mainland. With nowhere to go, most of them took to living in parks, on the street, in doorways or in shanties that were little more than sheets of board propped up and lashed together. Some squatted on roofs; some camped in apartment building stairwells. The struggle for survival became fierce and anyone with a job worked long hard hours every day of the year simply in order to eat and carry on working.

Though the British government in Hong Kong provided a state education through elementary school, only those who passed the entrance exam for secondary school went further. Those who failed, which was the majority, were let loose to roam the streets, with few opportunities except bad ones. Restless youths became junior gangsters looking for some excitement and a little cash. They organized themselves into gangs and jealously defended their territory, starting with street fights and ending in all-out gang warfare. Since the British police were not armed and had successfully restricted the use of firearms, most fights were either hand-to-hand fist fights or bloody affairs involving knives and machetes, and many neighbourhood gangs were loosely affiliated to a local kung fu school. Although Bruce was from a well-to-do family and attended an exclusive private school, he still felt drawn to the streets, and he formed his own small gang: the Tigers of Junction Street.

William Cheung first met Bruce Lee when an uncle who had friends in the Chinese Opera invited him to attend Bruce's birthday party. Bruce later heard of Cheung's growing reputation as a street fighter who practised a formidable style of kung fu known as wing chun and sought him out to learn more.

Cheung didn't take Bruce seriously, though, and later told *Inside Kung Fu* magazine:

The Tigers were just eight people who got together, they weren't all that tough – they got their fur singed a lot. I told Bruce that because he was a film actor, he shouldn't fight but should look after his appearance.

On a website interview, Bruce's younger brother Robert recalls:

One day when I was at home I heard a knock on the door. I opened it to find Bruce with his head down, looking toward the ground. A few days earlier I'd heard that Bruce was supposed to fight some guy over a disagreement, and as Bruce raised his head I saw that one of his eyes was black and blue. I started to laugh and Bruce said, 'If you think this is funny, you should see the other guy; he has no more teeth.' My mother rushed him into the maid's quarters and put a boiled egg on his eye. The Chinese believe that if you put an egg over a bruised eye it will heal quickly, and she wanted to do anything to help the eye clear up before my father saw. Luckily he never found out about it.

When Bruce came off worse in a gang-related fight he stormed home and demanded to be trained in an effective martial art in order to defend himself against bullies. Although Bruce had been shown some tai chi by his father, the slow flowing movements held little appeal for him. Tai chi is more therapeutic than anything else and needs a great deal of practice before it can be used as an efficient fighting art.

When Grace Lee agreed to give Bruce money for lessons he hunted down William Cheung and asked to train at the same school as him. Only when Bruce persisted did Cheung finally take him to the Restaurant Workers Union Hall on Lee Tat Street, where the classes were held, and introduce him to his master Yip Man. Because Bruce was a celebrity Yip Man was pleased to take him on and he began teaching him on the spot.

The thirteen-year-old Bruce Lee took to wing chun with the kind of obsessive enthusiasm that characterized everything he applied himself to. Yip Man's son, Yip Chun, called Bruce 'fighting crazy'. At first, Bruce was interested in wing chun only for fighting, but under the instruction of Yip Man he began to absorb some of the finer points of the art that he would eventually embrace to devastating effect.

# 2

# The Shaolin Way

In order to understand the full impact and achievement of Bruce Lee's later life and work, it's important to understand the roots from which it grew. Martial art was introduced to sixth-century China by an Indian monk, Bodhidharma – known in China as Da Mo – a member of the warrior caste who had entered the priesthood and then sought to spread the teachings of the Buddha. While crossing the mountains of northern China on foot, he came across the monastery at Shaolin. While there Bodhidharma saw how unhealthy and lethargic the scholarly monks had become. They didn't take kindly to being told this and refused to allow the wandering priest to stay there, so Bodhidharma retired to a nearby cave to meditate. Legend has it that he stayed there for nine years, other accounts say that it was only forty days, but the generally accepted period is three months.

During his time in the cave Bodhidharma helped many of the local people and news of this reached Shaolin. As a result, when he returned to the monastery he was allowed in. Bodhidharma explained to the monks that as the body, mind and spirit function as one, any imbalance in this interdependent system will lead to illness, so he devised a series of exercises designed to extract chi (life force) from the air by moving consciously in coordination with the breathing, in a prototype of what we might now recognize as chi kung.

These exercises also had the effect of reconnecting the monks with the natural world and soon they developed a series of exercises derived from watching the movement of animals, which became the basis of Shaolin kung fu. These 'animal forms' were not only the basis of the method the Shaolin monks used to stimulate and rebalance the body-mind system, they also became a fighting method which they used to protect themselves from bandits while on their travels to market or other monasteries.

The Shaolin way of life flourished for over a thousand years until, in the eighteenth century, the Manchus seized power in China, even though they represented only a small minority of the population. Positions of authority were only open to 'Manchurian candidates', and to keep the Han majority under control, the Manchus imposed severe restrictions on them. The Han males were required to shave their foreheads and wear their hair in a pigtail so as to make them more easily identifiable, while the women had to bind their feet to restrict their movements. There were even limits on the number of knives a Han household could own. Surprisingly the Manchus allowed the continuation of Han monastic life, and as a result the Shaolin monastery became a natural home for dissidents and a hotbed of rebellious plotting.

Because it took eighteen years to train a fully fledged Shaolin martial artist, it was not a realistic method of training revolution-aries to take on the Manchu soldiers. To overcome this the five most knowledgeable elders of the Shaolin temple, who have entered legend as 'the Venerable Five', devised a fighting style to overcome all the other known styles and which was faster to learn. The elders, each a master of his own discipline, pooled their knowledge in order to create, or perhaps reveal, a set of root fighting principles.

The first thing they did was to note the two essential aspects of any martial art: its yin or yang qualities. Firstly there were hard external (yang) styles that tended to commit the body's placement before a kick or punch could be landed. This generated a lot of power but left the practitioner inflexible. Secondly there were the soft internal (yin) styles, where the body's weight and commitment are more adaptable, elusive and spontaneous, but which tend to lack power. The elders reasoned that to get the best of both worlds they needed to develop techniques that could be landed quickly and unpredictably, yet with power.

This new fighting method involved strikes thrown with total commitment, but which could be halted abruptly and instantly re-thrown from another angle. They also determined that this new method would best suit close-range fighting. Long-range kicks and swinging punches from an opponent would be frustrated through a system of jams, straight-line deflecting strikes, simultaneous blocks and strikes and mobile and adaptable footwork patterns. Once in close-fighting range the second aspect of this new method would reveal itself where physical contact with the opponent's limbs would trigger the right moves spontaneously.

The Shaolin elders renamed the hall in which this fighting method was evolved as the Wing Chun hall: wing chun translating variously as 'hope for the future' or 'eternal springtime'. This expressed their hope for the evolution of the Shaolin martial arts as well as their hope of defeating the Manchu rulers.

But in 1768, before this new method could be put into practice, the Manchus raided the Shaolin temple and destroyed it. The only one of the five elders to survive was a nun, Ng Mui. While in hiding Ng Mui continued to refine and develop this new fighting method, calling it wing chun in remembrance of its original intention.

Soon after coming out of hiding, Ng Mui met Yim the daughter of a bean-curd seller in a local market. The nun learned that the girl was having trouble from a local gangster who demanded that she marry him. The gangster had threatened to ruin Yim's father if she didn't comply. The nun listened to the story and then advised a course of action. Knowing that she had perfected a fighting method that was both ruthlessly efficient and rapidly taught, she advised the girl to tell the gangster she would marry him, but only if he could defeat her in a fight. In those days it took several months to arrange a marriage, giving them time to implement Ng Mui's plan, and as Yim was a small, delicate girl, the gangster readily took up the challenge.

At the appointed time, when the fight took place, the burly gangster attacked the young girl with a wild roundhouse punch which she blocked as she made a simultaneous counter strike, knocking the bully unconscious with her first blow. Yim's father asked Ng Mui if she would take care of his daughter and so the girl followed her new guardian to a nunnery. There Ng Mui renamed the girl Wing Chun, knowing that she was to be the future of the art. Yim Wing Chun stayed with Ng Mui until the nun died, then later married a salt merchant and taught him the art. After a further six links in the chain the art passed to Yip Man, who taught William Cheung who introduced Bruce Lee to it.

Yip Man began to learn the art of wing chun at the age of thirteen, but didn't begin teaching it until he was nearly sixty. At the age of thirteen, the young Bruce Lee began training under him. Although he was a mild-mannered and slightly built man standing only five-and-a-half feet tall, Yip Man was a former policeman and cut an imposing figure. He also held definite opinions. He shunned Western clothing, would not pose for publicity photographs and felt strongly that only the Chinese should be taught wing chun. Bruce Lee was attracted to the style because of its economy and directness and its emphasis on developing energy. As he said, it gave the 'maximum of anguish with the minimum of movement'. Where Shaolin kung fu had thirty-eight forms (practice routines) wing chun has only three: the sil lum tao (Cantonese for 'Shaolin way'), chum kil ('searching for the opening') and the deadly bil jee ('stabbing fingers').

Wing chun is based on the principle that the shortest distance between two points is a straight line. For example, it has none of the big circular movements of tai chi. Although there are kicks in wing chun, none is landed higher than the opponent's waist; the emphasis is on gaining position for close-in fighting. All attacks are directed straight at the central axis of the opponent's body, just as it is one's own axis which is defended.

Crucial to the effectiveness of wing chun is the unique training practice of chi sao or 'sticking hands'. The initial objective is to not lose touch with your opponent – you don't push so hard that you move him, but you don't hold back so much that you lose contact, hence 'sticking'. Chi sao is not so much an actual fighting technique as a practice designed to help one develop sensitivity to the shifting balance of physical forces in a fight. This is based on the fact that when two people make a physical connection, an actual point of contact exists. With sufficient practice, it is at this point that any move, or even *intended* move, can be felt instinctively, a response which is called the contact reflex. This is similar to the experience of a fisherman who doesn't have to see the fish nibbling the bait at the end of his line to know he has a bite.

While developing this reflex action to the point where it has become not just second nature but *first* nature, the student passes through various levels of chi sao training. At each stage the student must progress from predetermined moves to random moves until, at the advanced stage, he or she can practise while blindfolded. It's important to understand that while the practice routines of chi sao do not apply to combat situations, the awareness and coordination they develop are essential. Chi sao gave Bruce Lee his first practical experience of the interplay of the energies yin and yang, the active and yielding forces.

Wing chun has one further unique training method in which a wooden dummy representing the opponent is used to simulate almost all conceivable combat situations in 108 practice moves. The wooden dummy also has the effect of toughening and conditioning the hands, the student is able to lock out when striking it, using the kind of power that might injure a sparring partner or cause injury to his or her own joints when working alone.

Every day after school, Bruce Lee headed straight to Yip Man's class, anticipating training by practising his kicks on the trees that he passed on the way. Even after training, Bruce would still thump the chair next to him as he sat at the dinner table at home. Before long William Cheung began to hear complaints from some of the older students who were coming off worse in their training encounters with Bruce. He recalls:

> They were upset because he was progressing so fast. I noticed that even when he was talking he was always doing some kind of arm or leg movement. That's when I realized that he was serious about kung fu.

# 3

## Tiger of Junction Street

A year after beginning kung fu Bruce Lee took up dancing the cha-cha, mainly because of his interest in his partner Pearl Cho, although it also served to develop his balance and footwork. Unable to do anything by halves, Bruce kept a list of over a hundred different dance steps on a card in his wallet. Along with fellow wing chun student Victor Kan, Bruce spent many evenings at the Champagne nightclub at Tsimshatsui, where they went to dance and admire the talents of the resident singer Miss Fong Yat Wah. A sharp dresser, Bruce insisted on ironing his own clothes. As he left the apartment each evening, he paused for a moment in front of the mirror to check his hair and flash the confident smile that never failed to charm the girls.

His first serious girlfriend was Amy Chan, who later became famous in the East as film actress Pak Yan. Whenever Bruce had any money he would take her dancing, and on their dates, he would by turns make her laugh hysterically and scream with frustration. In private, she found him to be a good-hearted person who was always willing to help his friends, but as soon as they were joined by anyone else, Bruce turned into a chauvinistic show-off.

Hawkins Cheung had also begun training with Yip Man in

1953 and he and Bruce soon struck up a friendship. Speaking to *Inside Kung Fu* magazine, Cheung recalls:

> We started learning wing chun because of its reputation against other systems. But while learning the first form we felt frustrated. We said, 'Why do you have to learn this? How can you fight like this?' Everyone wanted to learn it quickly so that they could move on to the sticking hands exercises. The single sticking hands exercise was no fun and the younger students wanted to get through that even quicker. When we finally got to the double sticking hands exercise, we thought, 'I can fight now!' If you could land a punch on an opponent you felt proud and excited. 'I can beat him now,' was the first thought. That was our character – everyone wanted to beat his partner first and be top dog. Egos ran wild and everyone wanted to be the best.
>
> The Old Man always told us, 'Relax! Relax! Don't get excited!' But whenever I practiced chi sao with someone, it was hard to relax: I became angry when struck and wanted to kill my opponent. When I saw Yip Man stick hands with others, he was very relaxed and even talked to his partner. Sometimes he threw his partner out without having to hit him. When I did sticking hands with Yip Man, I felt my balance being controlled by him when I attempted to strike. I was always off balance, with my toes or my heels off the ground. I felt my hands rebound when I tried to strike him, as if he used my force to hit me, yet his movement was so slight, he didn't seem to do anything, it was not a violent movement. When I asked him how he did it, he said, 'Like this,' and he demonstrated the movement which was the same as the practice form.

Bruce Lee was going through the same experience: trying to master a physical technique, while confronting emotions like fear and anger, and rigid mental attitudes. The challenge was to persevere. He wanted to learn how to fight and he found it hard to follow Yip Man's advice, which was to practise the form often and do it more slowly. Yip Man even suggested that Bruce stop doing sticking hands at all for a while.

Bruce still wasn't secure about his new skills and often used to carry a concealed blade or steel toilet chain as a weapon, although he didn't use them often. Most of his street fights involved ripped clothes and bloody noses from blows landed by hands and feet.

Leung Pak Chun, who was one of the Tigers, says:

> One day one of us was beaten up by a gang from Kowloon. Bruce and the others went off to get revenge. At first, Bruce approached them as if to talk it over, but when he got close enough to the two biggest ones, he hit them without warning.

These two turned out to be the family of a local Triad and William Cheung's father, a high-ranking policeman, had to step in and mediate to prevent trouble escalating.

Bruce's sister Agnes says, 'He began to get into more and more fights for no reason at all. And if he didn't win, he was furious. Losing, even once in a while, was unbearable for him.'

'You never had to ask Bruce twice about a fight,' said his younger brother Robert. Part of the responsibility for this also lay with Yip Man who, besides teaching relaxation and calmness, advised his students not to take everything on trust but to go out and test the system.

Despite Bruce's innate aggression, the seeds of understanding were beginning to take root, and a there was a depth of questioning that went beyond the brashness of his youth. Bruce even surprised himself by taking Yip Man's advice to stop training for a while and spend some time contemplating the principles his teacher was trying to instil in him. Why was form so important? And what did that have to do with flowing with the events around him?

As he would do throughout his life, whenever Bruce wanted to calm his fiery nature and reflect, he would walk by the water or through the rain. Now he spent time walking beside the harbour, as far away from the city's bustle as he could get. Thinking about it over and over was no use – that would just drive you crazy. Suppose he could grow an extra head; would that increase his capacity to understand? No, it was a matter of using the form he already had more efficiently. Would he be a better fighter if he had four arms and four legs? If there were humans like that, he thought, then perhaps there might be another way of fighting!

As he stood at the water's edge, Bruce's thoughts turned to the fish swimming in the deep as the possibility of a new way of approaching things dawned on him. Just as the reflections of clouds passed across the surface of the water, so he was able to see his own thoughts and feelings pass across his awareness. He wasn't without feelings or thoughts but somehow, here, now, he wasn't so bound up in them. The real challenge was whether he could find this sense of self when he was fighting and when more powerful emotions were involved. Bruce leaned down over the water and punched at his reflection. For a moment the water yielded to the force, parting and splashing away, but the instant he withdrew his hand, the water flowed back into the gap. As the reflected image took shape again, his face smiled gently. Nature had taught him something, not only about itself but about his own nature. And right at that moment there was no separation between the two.

Bruce was soon to experience a new kind of conflict. When jealous juniors found out that he had German ancestors, they put pressure on Yip Man to stop teaching him, knowing that Yip was a staunch traditionalist who believed the art should never be taught to Westerners. Yip Man's affection for Bruce and respect for his efforts caused him to refuse the other students' demands. Soon people threatened to leave the school and no one would train with Bruce, so he left of his own accord. At first he trained with one of Yip Man's senior students, Wong Sheung Leung, and sometimes he would intercept Wong's other students and tell them their teacher was sick and there was no class that day, so they would go home and he would gain some private instruction.

At St Francis Xavier some of Bruce's restless energy was channelled by a teacher called Brother Edward, who encouraged

Bruce to enter the 1958 Boxing Championships, which were held between twelve Hong Kong schools. Brother Edward, an ex-boxer himself, says of Bruce, 'He was tough but he wasn't a bully as some people think.' Bruce used to train for the approaching contest every weekend with William Cheung, and by sheer force and determination he blasted his way through the preliminaries, leaving three opponents knocked out in the first round. In the final he faced an English boy, Gary Elms – from rival school, King George V – who had held the title for the past three years.

In the ring, Elms had a classical boxing style. Bruce got into trouble almost immediately, and under some pressure in the corner he began swinging wildly. Despite the fact that boxing gloves are not the best aid to the trapping skills of wing chun, Bruce began to use some of the blocks he'd learned and countered with the continuous punching and two-level hitting he'd been working on. He was pleased enough with his third round knock-out win to note it in the fight diary he kept.

Meanwhile, the street fights continued, along with contests against other schools, and Bruce's mother had to make frequent visits to the police station. In one such fight, the wing chun students fought the choy li fut students on the roof of an apartment building on Union Road in Kowloon. According to Wong Sheun Leung it was Bruce who made the challenge. Wong recalls him as a hot-head who often caused trouble and showed no respect for the seniors of other styles, though he insists he wasn't the delinquent some have portrayed him to be.

Bruce's fight was set to last two rounds, each two minutes long, with Wong as the referee. The fighters took up their positions and almost immediately Bruce's opponent, a boy named Chung, attacked with a punch that Bruce palmed away. The next punch caught Bruce in the eye, shaking him up, and he reacted with a flurry of punches that fell short. He closed the distance but his blows were too wild and he was again hit on the nose and cheek. At the end of the first round Bruce sat in his corner, somewhat discouraged; his eye was swelling, his nose was bleeding and he hadn't managed to land a single effective strike of his own. Bruce told Wong that he wanted to quit, worried that he wouldn't be able to hide his injuries from his father, but Wong persuaded him to go on.

As the second round opened, Bruce steadied himself and took a more determined stance, then feinted a couple of times and scored a straight punch to Chung's face. As Chung gave ground, Bruce pursued him, hitting him repeatedly until he went down and others intervened. Bruce was elated and held his arms aloft. The victim's parents went straight to the police and Mrs Lee was obliged to sign a paper promising to take responsibility for Bruce's good conduct.

Bruce had managed to stay in school largely by coercing other pupils to do his homework for him. Realizing that he stood more of a chance of going to jail than college, Grace Lee suggested that Bruce claim his right to American citizenship before the option lapsed on his eighteenth birthday. At first Bruce wasn't keen on the idea of emigrating, but his father rapidly warmed to it.

Bruce told Hawkins Cheung that he was going to the US to become a dentist, but said he intended to earn money by teaching kung fu. Cheung reminded him that he only knew wing chun up to the second form, along with forty of the movements on the wooden dummy. Despite this, Bruce considered himself to be the sixth-best exponent in their style, but he took note of Cheung's comments and felt it might be a good idea to have a few showy moves under his belt before he left. To learn these he went to see a man called Uncle Siu, who taught northern styles of kung fu. Bruce took Siu to a local coffee shop and struck a deal with him: over the following month Siu would teach him some of his moves, and in return Bruce would give Siu dancing lessons. They began at seven one morning, with Siu leading Bruce through two northern-style kung fu forms, a praying mantis form and another called jeet kune or 'quick fist'. But Siu got the worst of the deal. He expected Bruce to take three or four weeks to learn the forms but Bruce mastered them in just three days, before Siu even got going with the basic cha-cha steps.

Bruce had retained his friendship with Unicorn throughout their youth and they both became child actors. The two appeared together in Bruce's first full-length film *The Birth of Mankind*, with Unicorn playing a shoeshine boy and Bruce a street rascal who fought with him. Run Run Shaw, the head of the Shaw Brothers studio, which employed Unicorn, now asked Bruce to sign a contract with them. Bruce told his mother he wanted to accept the offer, but Grace Lee somehow managed to persuade him that his best chance of making something of his life would come from finishing his education in the US. But before he left he managed to become the Crown Colony Cha-Cha Champion of 1958.

Prior to leaving Hong Kong, Bruce had to apply to the local police station for a certificate to clear him for emigration. There he found that both he and Hawkins Cheung were on a blacklist of local troublemakers. Over-dramatizing the issue, Bruce phoned his friend, 'We're on a known gangster list,' he said. 'I've got to clear my name, and while I'm there, I'll clear yours too.'

Whatever efforts Bruce made, however, resulted, a few days later, in a policeman calling at the Cheung household to ask questions about 'gang relations'. Rather than settling matters, he'd succeeded in stirring up even more trouble. In the end Mr Cheung Senior had to pay to have his son's name wiped from the record, so he could go to Australia to attend college.

The day before Bruce left for America, he went to say goodbye to Unicorn. He told his friend he felt his father and his family didn't love him or respect him. He felt that he had to achieve something in life, conceding that his mother was right, and if he didn't take this opportunity, he might end up in real trouble.

Bruce's younger brother Robert recalls, 'One evening Bruce came to my room with a suitcase in his hand. He put the case down and for a moment looked at me with a sad expression. He didn't say anything, then he picked up the case, turned and left. I guess that was his way of saying goodbye.'

As he was leaving, Bruce's mother slipped a hundred dollars into his pocket, while his father gave him fifteen. Bruce picked up his bags, but as he left the room his father called him back. As Bruce returned, his father suddenly waved him away again: he was enacting a Chinese tradition. Because he had made this gesture, even though his son was going far away, he would return to attend the father's funeral. Quietly and a little disappointed, Bruce picked up his bags and continued on his way.

# 4

## Return to San Francisco

Bruce Lee fulfilled his mother's expectations and lived up to his
Chinese name, Jun Fan, by returning to the city of his birth. In
April 1959 he made the twenty-one-day Pacific crossing to San
Francisco. Although he was booked on board the Presidents Line
ship as a third-class passenger, he soon found that most of the fun
was to be had in first class and contrived to spend most of his
time there by giving dancing lessons. Neat and bespectacled, he
looked more like a young Clark Kent than the hot-headed
troublemaker who'd had to leave Hong Kong in a hurry. Back in
his cabin, he considered what might happen once his 115 dollars
had been spent. As the ship docked, there to meet him were Mr
Quan Ging Ho, an official of the Cantonese Opera and family
friend, and his sister Agnes, who was a guest of Mr Quan's.
Bruce's parents had arranged for him to lodge with Mr Quan
while he settled in and, so they hoped, made plans to complete
his education.

Mr Quan thought that getting Bruce to give dancing lessons
would be a good way for him to meet people and earn some
money, and his first few weeks were spent on trips around the
Bay Area doing just that. Bruce had taken up Mr Quan's suggestion and put together a dance and wing chun routine that was

both entertaining and technically difficult and which he could perform in Chinese or English. This helped bring in students for his dance classes, for which he charged a dollar per session. On weekends Bruce would do this at the Victory Hall, and it was at one of these Saturday dances that he met Bob Lee, the brother of James Yimm Lee, a man who was later to play a big part in his life.

On 19 June, Bruce got a phone call from his father, Hoi Cheun, who was in New York for three weeks performing with the Cantonese Opera. The following week Bruce flew to New York, where he was warmly greeted by his father as if all the troubles of his youth had been set aside. Hoi Cheun was pleased to learn that Bruce had renewed his US citizenship which was now good for another seventeen years.

For the first few days of his visit Bruce hung around backstage during rehearsals, but he soon grew restless and started asking if there were any kung fu teachers in Chinatown. One of Hoi Cheun's friends, Jao Ju Yin, said that there was a very skilful praying mantis master, Gin Foon Mark, who taught over on East Broadway, about eight blocks from the theatre. Hoi Cheun said that he'd heard of him, but had also heard that Mark only taught privately sponsored members in a closed school because he thought that many people would want to learn the art for the wrong reasons. This only made Bruce more interested and he persisted until it was decided that 'Uncle Yong', the owner of one of his father's favourite restaurants, would accompany Bruce to the school to try and get him an introduction.

After several minutes of persistent knocking on the door of a nondescript old building, the door opened slowly to reveal a sweat-drenched student who glared uninvitingly at the two callers. Uncle Yong explained their business and the student replied that sifu Mark was busy teaching a class but invited them to follow him inside. (Sifu translates both as 'instructor' and 'father' and so carries the meaning of 'elder teacher'.) Sifu Mark's office was like an old apothecary's, with acupuncture charts on the wall and shelves lined with jars of herbs, some containing the liniment known as dit da jow (literally 'hit wine') which was used to heal sprains and bruises, harden bones and strengthen sinews in kung fu Iron Palm training.

At the end of the class the master came up to greet them. As Bruce shook his hand he got a shock: sifu Mark's hand was so soft and flexible it felt like gelatin. There were no calluses or hard ridges, only soft supple flesh. He was baffled that a master of tiger claw and eagle claw kung fu should have such hands. The master asked about Bruce's experience and Bruce told him about his time training in wing chun under Yip Man in Hong Kong. As he questioned Bruce, Mark assessed his character, and after a few minutes his face softened. 'Maybe you'd like to stay and watch a class?' he said.

The main teaching hall was large, about 35 feet by 100 feet. Classical Chinese weapons – butterfly knives, staffs and swords – lined the walls, along with images of venerated masters from the past. At the far end of the hall incense burned on an altar. At the end of the class Bruce remarked as diplomatically as he could that his wing chun training had been more intense, causing sifu Mark to respond, 'Not many people understand this rare system. The power in the techniques is hidden.'

In order to prove his point, Bruce asked if he could spar with one of the students, but every one of his attacks was blocked before it reached its target. He had to swallow his pride when he found out that the student had been training there for less than a year.

Gin Foon Mark explained to Bruce that praying mantis is a style that relies on generating internal energy rather than using muscular strength and, as in wing chun, this was achieved by the practice of chi sao, or sticking hands. He added that the techniques rely on practising this to the point where eventually the hands react as if they had eyes and a mind of their own. The hands should be always alive, with each limb acting independently of any other limb in a relaxed and continuous flow, never mentally rigid or emotionally tense.

Sifu Mark then touched on the secretive art of dim mak, or

'death touch', the technique of striking acupuncture points with a view to disrupting the energy flow and causing damage rather than stimulating them to encourage healing and balance.

Bruce began to realize that this man had something to offer that he wouldn't find anywhere else and he blurted out, 'Sifu Mark, will you please accept me as your student for three weeks?' The master replied, 'You come here tomorrow night. Don't eat before training. The club dues are fifteen dollars.'

Sifu Mark realized that Bruce hadn't got the traditional jing mo costume, so allowed him to train in his street clothes. The first thing he did was change Bruce's wing chun stance in which the toes are turned slightly inwards so that his feet were parallel, then he showed him how to integrate his body force into a punch without winding up beforehand. What impressed Bruce time and again was how sifu Mark's hands felt so soft and supple to touch but like solid steel claws when he fought. At dinner that night at the Bo Bo restaurant, Bruce's father joked to the guests that his son smelt like a Chinese herb shop. Bruce's arms were stained dark brown from fingertip to elbow with linament.

Bruce absorbed everything he was shown, so sifu Mark decided to accelerate his training to the level of the student he had sparred with on his first visit. He introduced Bruce to the principle of 'borrowing the opponent's energy', stating that a fighter must have a mind and body that are fluid in expression and actions, so they fit the opponent's tactics like water flowing into a gap. That way the mind and body are free to respond instinctively. Bruce remembered Yip Man talking about these ideas in Hong Kong, but only now was he beginning to grasp their full significance and potential.

While he was in New York Bruce's mother Grace asked the Chows – family friends in Seattle – to take Bruce in. Bruce spent the last morning of his visit to New York with this father discussing plans to move to Seattle before Uncle Tong drove him to the airport.

Back in San Francisco, Bruce was joined briefly by his older brother Peter, who recalled how Bruce would yell out in his sleep, punching and kicking out and flinging the covers from the bed. Bruce's stay in San Francisco was only a brief one. He was joined on the flight to Seattle by Peter, who then caught a connecting flight to Wisconsin, where he was going to attend the university.

Like Bruce's father, Chow Ping had been a member of Hong Kong's Cantonese Opera company, but due to illness he'd found himself stranded in New York following the United States' declaration of war in 1941. There he met his future wife, Ruby, who nursed him back to health. The couple later moved to Seattle, where they opened a restaurant. Ruby Chow was a tough and independent woman. Not only had she flown in the face of tradition by divorcing her first husband in order to marry Ping, she had gone against the advice of all her friends and opened the first Chinese restaurant outside of Seattle's Chinatown. There she established herself as one of the most influential people in the local community.

Ruby Chow acted as a go-between for the Chinese, sorting out problems with the police or immigration authorities and advising them on personal or money matters. She regularly took new arrivals from Hong Kong into her household where she provided temporary lodging and food in return for casual work until they found their feet in the new country. As far as Ruby Chow was concerned, Bruce Lee was going to be no different to any of the others who passed through. She did, however, go to pick him up from the airport.

By the time Ruby Chow's Cadillac turned on to Minor Avenue and stopped outside the restaurant, the domestic arrangements were already in place. Bruce would have his own room on the third floor and work as a junior waiter, except during busy shifts when he would also double as a busboy. After lugging his bags up three flights of stairs he was shown into a tiny room containing nothing more than a single bed, a small dresser and a bare lightbulb hanging from the ceiling. No sooner had he dropped his luggage than he was put to work.

Life in Seattle came as a rude awakening for the young Bruce, who had thought he was going to be the Chows' house guest while attending school. He'd never seen his name on a work schedule before, and being the most recently recruited member of staff, he was also the lowest in the pecking order. Working as a waiter made him miserable. He wasn't exactly a natural at taking orders and there were daily complaints from customers about his attitude. His treatment of the other waiters and kitchen staff wasn't much better. In his first few weeks at the restaurant Bruce got a harsh lesson in how Westerners treated Asians.

At the time most Westerners had a strongly stereotypical image of the Chinese, personified by Hop Sing, the Chinese houseboy in the TV series *Bonanza*. Bruce had seen the same attitude in Western tourists in colonial Hong Kong and resented it as much there as he resented the spineless subservience of his co-workers here. The waiters, who had been there many years, had long since accepted their lot in life, but when a customer snapped his fingers at Bruce or called him 'boy', he would plant his feet shoulder width apart, cross his arms over his chest and tilt his head slightly to one side while he glared at them through narrowed eyes.

Bruce's relationship with Ruby Chow quickly became hostile. Ruby expected to be shown respect and wasn't used to being shouted at by one of her junior waiters, telling her she was taking advantage of him. In truth, Ruby and Bruce were both forceful personalities and neither was going to give way to the other.

Unsurprisingly, Ruby Chow doesn't remember Bruce Lee fondly:

> If I can't say anything good about anyone, I'd rather not talk about it ... I took care of him for four years. I raised five children and I treated him like a second son. He was just not the sort of person you want your children to grow up like; he was wild and undisciplined, he had no respect. Lots of martial arts people are insecure; martial arts are supposed to be to defend people, but he used them to be aggressive.

The insecurity he felt kept Bruce in a constant state of inner conflict and defiance; he was a time bomb waiting to explode. Back in his room he would lie back on the small bed, staring up at the bare lightbulb hanging from the ceiling. It was the last thing he saw at night and the first thing he saw in the morning, and when he couldn't sleep, he would stare at the faint image of the bulb in the dark space above him. Even when he did sleep he tossed and turned restlessly, seemingly at war with the unknown forces holding him back.

In the middle of one fateful night all of this came to a dramatic climax as Bruce fought with what he later described as 'a black shadow', which held him down for several minutes. Insisting that he'd been wide awake throughout the entire episode, he reported that the effort of resisting defeat left him drenched in sweat. Over the years, journalists and scriptwriters have turned this event into a wild tale about a 'demon' or a 'curse', or simply dismissed it as a nightmare, so much so that it has become one of the most cheapened and distorted incidents of Bruce's life, and one that needs to be put into its correct perspective.

As a significant event in Bruce's life, it deserves some serious consideration, and when events have played themselves out we will return to it later to see what a powerful undercurrent was stirring there.

As a result of his intense development as a martial artist, Bruce was rapidly stirring up the inner changes that accompany such a way of life. Bruce's sister Agnes relates how he sleepwalked regularly from childhood and his brother Peter recounts how Bruce fought in his sleep. That night, it would seem that he wasn't fighting a ghost but was being brought face-to-face with aspects of his own personality which he had previously been reluctant to acknowledge. He underwent an intense confrontation with his own unconscious self in which all the contradictions in the hidden side of his nature were made apparent to him. It was a confrontation that may well have *felt* as if he were fighting a dark force – attacking him from outside.

The psychologist Jung represents this archetypal force as 'the Shadow'. The Shadow has many aspects, but its main characteristic is that it personifies the contents of one's personal unconscious in a symbolic way. That is to say, the Shadow gives life and personality to the hidden layers of the mind – just as they can also be found in the symbolic events of dreams, myths and legends. Like these images, the Shadow can be human, animal or supernatural in appearance and sometimes has dark or dangerous qualities.

There are both constructive and destructive sides to the Shadow. On the destructive side, it often represents everything a person doesn't wish to acknowledge about him- or herself. On the constructive side, the Shadow may represent hidden positive influences. According to Jung, the Shadow is both instinctive and irrational, but it's not necessarily evil, even though it might appear to be. It can be both ruthless in conflict and empathetic in friendship, and it is important as a source for learning how to accept and integrate the more problematic or troubling aspects of one's personality.

The Shadow may appear in dreams and visions in various forms and may act either as an adversary or a friend. The Shadow's appearance and role depend greatly on the experiences of the person concerned, because it develops in the individual's own mind rather than being a figure common to everyone. According to Jung, the Shadow can sometimes overwhelm a person's actions: for example, when the conscious mind is shocked, confused or paralysed by indecision. Interactions with the Shadow in dreams may shed light on a person's state of mind; for instance, conflicting desires or intentions, or perhaps a combination of driving ambition, resent- ment at doing a lowly job and gnawing homesickness.

On the night in question, Bruce Lee experienced, in the most direct way possible, the reality of the famous saying that the martial artist's greatest opponent is himself. That night, Bruce did not fight a ghost or a demon but was brought face-to-face with aspects of his own personality that he'd previously been unaware of: his anger, cockiness and insecurities.

On the positive side, once these aspects or negative feelings are acknowledged and the blocked energy is released, all the energy can now be directed to more positive purposes. For Jung, the goal was to bring the dark to light and to bring them both into a harmonious balance, as symbolized by the yin-yang emblem.

Soon after this incident Bruce embarked on a deliberate course of self-improvement. Because he hadn't completed his education in Hong Kong he made that his priority, aiming to gain a high school diploma that would make him eligible for admission to the University of Washington the following year. Edison Technical Vocational School wasn't too far from the restaurant, and on 3 September 1959 he enrolled and began attending classes three weeks later.

In his room at Chow's, Bruce used the radio as a way of practising his English pronunciation and slang expressions by imitating the DJs. He also worked at his handwriting skills, refining the elegant, flowing style that became so instantly recognizable and practising signing his name for hours until it had the symmetry he wanted. Any extra money that he made from tips in the restaurant or that his mother occasionally sent him was spent on new clothes.

One evening, after Bruce saw one of his workmates, another Chinese busboy Chinn Wah Min, leave Chow's in a shiny blue Chrysler, Bruce quickly sought him out and asked how he could afford such a nice car on his restaurant wages. Min replied that he worked part-time stuffing leaflets at the Sunday edition of the *Seattle Times*, because the newspaper customarily hired Chinese people to do the job. It wasn't long before Bruce got a job there, even though it meant getting up well before daylight to do it.

In a letter dated 16 May 1960, Bruce Lee wrote to Hawkins Cheung, telling him that he was still practising his kung fu and was thinking about having a wing chun wooden dummy shipped from Hong Kong. The letter continued:

At present, I'm still going to the Edison High School and will be graduated this summer. I plan to go to the University next year, that is, in 1961. Well! I still don't know what I'm going to major in, but when I find out I'll write to you again. Now I find out that all those stuff [sic] like cha-cha are just for killing time and have little fun out of it and that study always comes first. Yes, that's right; your own future depends on how well you have studied. Now I am really on my own, since the day I stepped into this country. I didn't spend any money from my father. Now I am working as a waiter for a part-time job after school. I am telling you, it's tough boy! I always have a heck of a time!

After his duties Bruce used to practise alone in the Chows' parking lot. Running through the wing chun forms not only gave him a connection with Hong Kong, the movements also had a calming effect on his psyche. When he resumed his workouts as intensively as he'd performed them in Hong Kong he noticed a change in his attitude and he became more cheerful and approachable. After his solo practice sessions he used to take a daily walk to explore the surrounding districts, and loved walking in the cool drizzle by the water's edge, stopping and talking to the elderly Chinese practising tai chi in Volunteer Park.

# 5

## *A New Beginning*

At Edison Tech, Bruce quickly became known as the guy who did that Asian martial arts thing. By the end of the third school week, in late September, the teaching staff asked Bruce if he'd give a martial arts demonstration at the annual Asian Day celebration at Capitol Hill. One man who saw a notice about the coming event was James DeMile. As former heavyweight boxing champion for the US Air Force who now did most of his fighting on the streets around Capitol Hill, DeMile was intrigued enough to turn up for the display.

In his neat dark suit and thick round glasses Bruce hardly looked like a fighter as he told the small crowd they were about to see something that had always been kept secret in China. The effect was heightened by Bruce's Chinese accent, which made his 'r's sound like 'w's. As he ran through various kung fu animal forms, it looked like anything but fighting and the audience grew restless. Suddenly Bruce became still and his gaze settled on James DeMile. 'You look like you can fight,' said Bruce. 'How about coming up here?'

DeMile looked every inch the fighter he was and couldn't have been too worried as the young man beside him, who weighed 140 pounds and stood only 5 foot 7 inches, explained that he was about to demonstrate a simple fighting system devised by a tiny Buddhist nun. Bruce turned to DeMile and invited him to attack.

DeMile fired out a straight right, intending to send the upstart's head sailing over the crowd, but Bruce blocked the punch easily while countering with his own punch, which stopped a whisker away from DeMile's nose. From then on, no matter what DeMile tried, Bruce was able to counter his every move. The contact reflex he'd honed from years of sticking hands practice worked automatically every time.

DeMile was used to street fights in which his first move was to break someone's leg. He wasn't used to losing a fight, let alone being made to look helpless. The demonstration continued without mercy, ending when Bruce knocked his knuckles against DeMile's head and asked if he was at home. Later James DeMile swallowed his hurt pride and, responding like a martial artist rather than a brawler, he asked Bruce to teach him some of his skills.

Also in the audience that day was Jesse Glover, an African-American judo black belt and Northwest Judo Champion who discovered to his delight that he and Bruce Lee were attending the same school. Glover suggested that he swap his judo knowledge for lessons in wing chun, and he also told Bruce about his good friend and roommate Ed Hart, a boxer who practised judo with him. Bruce suggested they start an informal martial arts group to work out together and pool their experience. Later Jesse Glover contacted his friend Skip Ellsworth, who decided to join the group; he outweighed Bruce by a good thirty pounds and towered seven inches over him. In the last week of September, the group had its first meeting at Jesse and Ed's apartment.

One of Bruce's first students in Seattle was John Mitsules, who briefly roomed with Bruce; in his autobiography, *The St. Ann's Kid: A Seattle Memoir*, he writes:

> Part of a person's training with Bruce focused on understanding their own value. He told people that they were special and held meaning in this world. I think Bruce was very good at assessing levels of self-confidence and determining what kind of support people required.

You could not convince a person his feats were real by description only – he was like watching a deft magician. You always wondered how he could be so graceful, quick and powerful at the same time. Once people saw him in action they became believers. He would take on four guys effortlessly. You could feel the force in the air when his punches came close to your nose in practice ... To show off, he would do push ups with me lying on his back. I weighed 200 pounds at the time.

As the size of their class increased, they decided to start holding their training sessions on a patch of land on the corner of Maynard Avenue and South Lane Street, near the centre of Chinatown. Bruce knew that working out in public would increase the chances of attracting more interest, and new followers included LeRoy Garcia and Doug Palmer.

Doug Palmer, who now works as an attorney in Seattle, kept a diary which recalls the experience of meeting Bruce:

I saw him give a gung fu demonstration during a street fair and was mesmerized by his blinding speed and obvious power, by his lithe fluidity and his perfectly executed moves imitating the praying mantis and other forms. The brother of a friend of mine was taking gung fu lessons from him and I mentioned that I'd like to learn too. A week or so later, in the middle of a crowd milling around outside the Buddhist temple, I felt a tap on my shoulder. When I turned, a handsome Chinese man a few years older than I stood facing me with a hooded expression. 'I heard you wanted to see me,' he said. I introduced myself and said I was interested in learning gung fu. He shrugged noncommittally, then told me where they practiced. 'Come by and watch sometime,' he said. 'If you're still interested, we'll see.'

Twice a week, until I left for college, I worked out with the class, sometimes in a backyard or, through the winter, in a garage. The class was small, made up mostly of men older than Bruce. Many of the students were proficient in judo; I had boxed for a number of years. All of us were enthralled by a form of martial art that seemed the ultimate in efficiency and deadliness ... No one had heard of gung fu then. Comedians had a lot of fun with it – 'Is that like egg fu yung?' One of my high school teachers, a hulking ex-football player, asked me if it would 'stand up to a good ol' Minnesota haymaker.'

Bruce not only began to develop his students' balance, speed and positioning through the wing chun practice forms, he also gave them an insight into its origins by telling them the history of the Shaolin temple, and the line that stretched from Ng Mui and Yim Wing Chun through to his own teacher Yip Man. He explained that there were no showy kicks, spins or board breaking, like in karate. The most impressive move, he said, is over in the blink of an eye, so fast that the opponent doesn't see it coming, and in it the body's entire chi is released in one explosive instant.

Teaching in open public spaces, Bruce soon knew who was a casual observer and who was genuinely intrigued. If they looked serious he would saunter up and engage them in conversation, and this was how he met Taky Kimura, who stood for two hours attentively watching one of Bruce's demonstrations in an athletics field. Takauki Kimura was a Japanese-American who'd been held in an internment camp during the Second World War, where he'd taken judo lessons from a fellow internee. Taky explained that Jesse Glover and James DeMile were regular customers in his supermarket and, knowing that he would be interested, Jesse and Jim had told him about the incredible young martial artist they had got to know.

Bruce had Taky square off in a fighter's pose and then, in a flurry of rapid-fire strikes, he shot out a dozen or so punches that stopped within an inch of their target.

'Man that was fast!' exclaimed Taky.

In one of the many phone conversations I had with him, Taky Kimura, a softly spoken, likeable man who still runs his supermarket business in Seattle, recalls how he met Bruce Lee:

They told me I just had to go and see him. I'd seen martial artists in Japan who were older and more experienced, so I didn't see how a young kid could be any better, but they kept insisting. I went down to a training session being held on one of the playing fields near the university, and as soon as I saw what he could do I asked if I could join their club, although it was his thinking that impressed me more than his speed and power.

There was a small group of us: Jesse Glover, Jim DeMile, Ed Hart and Doug Palmer. We used to work out in parks or anywhere there was an open space. I worked out with Bruce quite a lot by myself and he would encourage me to socialize with him, but I was already taking time off work to train, and besides, I was twice his age.

At thirty-eight years old, Taky was a sad-eyed man whose confidence had taken many knocks. Bruce was only eighteen and restless with ambition, yet the two warmed to each other and a close friendship developed.

Remember, Jesse Glover was black and James DeMile had ethnic origins. There were a couple of white guys, but most of us were from minorities. I was brought up in one of the few ethnic families in our neighbourhood and we encountered a lot of prejudice . . . I couldn't get served in restaurants, couldn't get a seat on a bus. I tramped the streets for six months, looking for a job. It destroyed my whole sense of being a person. Fortunately I didn't take to drink under the whole stress of it all. Finally, I had to say, 'Am I a man, or what?' and get a grip.

Later I married a Caucasian woman, who loved me and treated me like everyone else. Bruce would say to me, 'You're just as good as they are.' Then he would say, 'Jesus, Taky! You dress like an old man; you look like you're sixty. Get yourself some clothes.' He didn't only build me up physically, he built up the emotional and mental aspects, and I got myself back.

Bruce was pleased to discover that Taky's family business was only a few blocks from the Chows' restaurant. It was much bigger than he'd pictured, with a sizeable basement and large parking area, so it made sense to move the class there. In return, Bruce used to chase away people who'd been using Taky's parking lot for free while they shopped elsewhere.

Although Bruce was capable of deep and genuine insight in one moment and great humour the next, he could explode with anger almost without warning. There was a guy called Eddie Pearce, who used to hang around outside the store. I befriended him and he became almost like my younger brother. Eddie had a bad stutter and Bruce occasionally used to stutter when he talked, although in his case I think it was due to difficulties with the language rather than a speech problem. When I introduced Eddie to Bruce, Eddie began stuttering and I saw Bruce tense up and his fists begin to tighten, thinking he was being mocked. Once Eddie realized what was going on he quickly tried to explain, 'I–I–I really d–d–do stutter.' Which only made the problem worse and I had to step in.

Bruce was a very intense young man and more than once there might have been trouble if I hadn't been there. One Sunday afternoon, Bruce and I were driving through Seattle, being followed by a motorcycle cop. We drove on, stopping at every red light for four or five blocks until the cop pulled us over. 'You guys are having a really good time, driving at twenty-nine in a thirty-mile-an-hour zone.' The cop was trying to stir something up; it was a discriminatory thing. I could feel Bruce tensing up and I know that if I hadn't been there he would have gone for him.

James DeMile recalls an occasion when Bruce and his friends were strolling through Chinatown when they saw a young Chinese girl being harassed by some men in a car. Bruce walked over to the driver's door and told the guy to cut it out. As the guy leaned out of the window to threaten him, Bruce snapped a backfist into the man's face, busting his nose before the car sped off.

As the group of friends trained at the back of Taky's supermarket, Bruce would sometimes become serious and start lecturing them. This meant only one thing: there was a girl around. As Bruce's lecture continued, Jim DeMile would try to slide away. It was DeMile's misfortune to look more menacing and murderous than any of the other guys, and if there was a girl Bruce wanted to impress, he was the natural choice for a demonstration: 'Now what I do in my system is . . . Ah, Jim!'

James DeMile doesn't believe that Bruce set out to teach intentionally:

> It was more like he was saying, 'Here's what I have to offer, you take it. In the meantime, I'm going to be training and developing myself.' Fortunately, I absorbed a tremendous amount of his philosophy and technical skill because I was interested. I also became more focused and aware of myself and more in control of my movements. It helped in my evolution as a person and in my confidence. Meanwhile, Bruce was changing as he developed more flow, more energy and more intensity. His time in Seattle was one of experimenting with various stances and techniques to overcome his limitations.

Bruce also began training with his students one-to-one at their homes. Unsurprisingly, he discovered that none of them were the same. Some were coordinated, others were slow; some were smooth and fluid, others were aggressive and forceful. But since all of them were much bigger and physically stronger than him, Bruce had to use every bit of his experience to subdue them. This private training turned out to be a double-edged sword, though, as he wondered how much he could reveal to a student before they would become a threat to him. He wanted them to do well . . . but not too well.

In Hong Kong, Bruce had fought with people his own size, but now he was faced with opponents who were seventy pounds heavier and six inches taller than him, what he called 'trucks rolling in'. Bruce knew that if he was ever hit by someone like DeMile, or even worse by someone at a public demonstration he would be hurt, and so would his reputation. It wasn't simply a matter of pride; it was a matter of survival.

As Bruce's nucleus of students showed real signs of improvement, privately he intensified his own training, increasing the number of push-ups, sit-ups and body-strengthening routines he did. He adapted the wing chun stance so that it looked more like a boxer's crouch and began mixing in some of the praying mantis techniques he'd learned back in New York. The group also began asking more questions about the background of martial arts and Bruce realized he needed to spend more time in the library searching out texts on Chinese philosophy.

After an impromptu demonstration at a social gathering, Bruce met a Japanese-American girl named Amy Sanbo who, like Taky, had been held in an internment camp during the war. She wasn't bitter about the experience and was a lively, intelligent, ambitious girl who planned to become a writer and dancer. If anything, Bruce felt slightly intimidated by her and felt obliged to tell her about his time as a child star before announcing that he was once a cha-cha champion in Hong Kong. She told him she couldn't understand why he didn't pursue a career as a dancer instead of one in martial arts.

Whenever Bruce and Amy were out together it was usually Amy who was the listener. She would force a chuckle at some of his off-colour jokes and then tell him that although he was fond of quoting philosophy, he didn't always practise what he preached. While Amy showed compassion for those who were less fortunate, Bruce's opinion was that anyone who was in a hole could get out of it if they wanted to. Most of the time, however, their talk was about kung fu and Bruce's ambitions for the future.

As Bruce and his group of students grew closer, they began to talk openly about their relationships, personal problems and needs. Although Bruce never said anything about his poor financial situation, except to say that he thought his job at Chow's was below his natural station in life, Jesse Glover made an off-the-cuff remark that Bruce should begin charging a fee for his teaching, just as a lawyer, doctor, accountant or other professional would. Jesse reckoned that a lot more people might take advantage of what Bruce had to offer, so Bruce sent his students out on a word-of-mouth PR exercise to spread the news that a new kung fu school would soon be opening.

On 27 November 1960, while they were celebrating Bruce's twentieth birthday at the Tai Tung restaurant, Jesse Glover suggested that to get things moving the regulars would each pay him four dollars a week. In the meantime, because there were no funds for advertising, they would attract new students by holding more classes in public, in parks, gyms and recreation centres. Without a car, though, Bruce was finding it more and more difficult to get around Seattle to different venues, not to mention taking Amy on a date.

Taky Kimura offered to help: 'I was happy to take him on his dates, because he was doing something for me, but my family wasn't so happy when I had to get up at 2a.m. to go and collect him.'

Whenever Taky arrived to pick up Bruce and Amy from a party he would likely find Bruce performing one-finger push-ups or demonstrating some kung fu technique. When Amy accused him of being a show-off he said he was only doing it to see if he could attract new students, but Amy felt ignored. Bruce wouldn't talk about her ambitions to be a writer and dancer; all he wanted was for her to support him. He told her that he wanted to become wealthy and independent, and to do that he needed someone beside him he could trust.

Bruce Lee had difficulty understanding that not everyone shared his ambitions or abilities. He could be an impatient teacher and would show a move only once or twice, so if you didn't catch it, it was unlikely to be repeated. He thought that if he could do it, so could anyone else. Taky Kimura was one of those who couldn't always keep up. He told Bruce that he was quitting, adding that it was easy for the teacher, but not the student. Bruce replied that Taky had the talent but refused to recognize it. As Taki explains: 'I was working twice as hard as the other guys because I was older than them. One day I was looking out of the corner of my eye to see if I was making any impression on Bruce. Of course he knew exactly what I was doing and I heard him say to one of the others, "He'll never make it." That hurt me to the bone. But because I'd always been a quitter in the past, it drove me to try that much harder and, even though I was clumsy, I think he saw that I was dedicated and sincere about what I was tying to do. After that he started to work with me, taking me aside and showing me lots of extra things. The next thing I knew, he was grooming me to be his assistant.'

As Bruce's time at Edison was coming to an end, he reckoned that a car of his own would make a perfect graduation present to himself. During the last weeks of term, LeRoy Garcia gave Bruce driving lessons and was astonished that Bruce, who was so skilled and coordinated in kung fu, was the complete opposite when it came to driving. Even so, he passed his driving test and on 2 December 1960 he graduated from Edison Tech with the certified high school diploma that would gain him entry to the University of Washington the following March. He celebrated by spending $100 on a beaten-up white Chevrolet Corvair.

In January 1961, after watching local programming on KCTS Channel 9 public television, Bruce Lee decided to ring the station with a view to presenting a kung fu demonstration. The station had already had a call from another kung fu teacher, Fook Young, and the producers suggested a collaboration. Bruce rang Fook and they discussed a presentation. Bruce then began rehearsing the senior students and contacted a local seamstress, Mrs Mei Wong, to sew some Chinese kung fu uniforms for him.

By now Bruce had also made inroads into more formal teaching by holding classes at a community gym on Yesler Terrace. He designed a flyer and had several hundred mimeographed at the centre advertising that a martial arts demonstration was scheduled there for 14 February. It would be a dummy run for the TV presentation, starting with some wing chun forms, then some sticking hands, followed by the practical application of some of the techniques. On the evening around thirty people turned up. Only one of them seemed unimpressed with the performance, a Japanese karate black belt named Uechi – a fellow student at Edison who objected to Bruce's continual downgrading of karate – who continually interrupted Bruce with his own opinions on the subject.

The following week Bruce and his students put on their display at the TV station, and a week later the station manager invited them to do a short series, which was filmed over three separate occasions. As a result of the publicity a raft of new students enrolled, bringing in fees of a hundred dollars a month, three times what Bruce was making at Ruby's restaurant. Bruce wrote to Yip Man in Hong Kong saying that he was spreading the word about wing chun and explaining that he was still trying to get someone to send him a wooden practice dummy.

In March 1961, Bruce enrolled at the University of Washington and found he had to balance going to classes with doing homework, teaching his own classes and working at the restaurant. At the university, Bruce initially enrolled in subjects that were compulsory or of immediate practical use to him, such as English, American History, Mathematics and Humanities. But with a strong intuition of where he was now heading, optional courses that attracted him were in Theatre Speech and Speech Improvement. Over the years that he would spend at the university, he would also take courses in Drawing, Composition, Social Dance, Chinese Philosophy, Chinese Language, the Far East in the Modern World, General Psychology, the Psychology of Adjustment, Personal Health, Business Management and Leadership. He also began to seek out self-help books on the development of potential, 'making luck' and positive thinking.

Bruce had only been at the university a matter of weeks when he had a chance encounter on the library stairs with the karate man Uechi, who'd also moved there from Edison. He shoved Bruce and called him a show-off.

'You want to fight me, man?' Bruce replied.

'Yeah,' retorted Uechi. 'You need a lesson! Let's do it in the main gym so everyone can see you get your ass kicked.'

'No. You want to fight me, we'll do it on my terms,' said Bruce. 'We'll fight at the YMCA handball court on Sunday night, six o'clock.'

At the appointed time they both turned up, along with a small crowd of spectators filled with anticipation.

'You challenged me, right?' Bruce asked Uechi.

'Yeah.'

'That's all I wanted to know.'

Jesse Glover was appointed referee and makeshift rules were established. There would be three rounds of two minutes. But first Uechi disappeared for ten minutes to go and change into his traditional white karate gi with its black belt. Bruce was in his street clothes, since he wasn't there to represent any particular style of fighting.

Uechi returned, went through a warm-up ritual of snapping out a few punches and then looked at Bruce.

'Are you ready?'

Jesse broke the following silence with the instruction to start. For a few seconds the two fighters circled cautiously. Bruce took up a wing chun stance. Uechi adopted a deep karate forward stance, then switched to a cat stance and snapped out a front kick to Bruce's groin. Bruce parried the kick and instantly closed in with a rapid series of straight punches before Uechi could get any counters going. Uechi never managed to land another blow as Bruce drove him to the ground. As he fell to his knees, Bruce kicked him in the face and Jesse Glover ran in to stop the fight. The karate man reappeared a week later, telling his friends that he'd been involved in a minor car accident.

Taky Kimura recounts, 'It lasted about ten seconds. Bruce was quite generous about the whole business. Rather than embarrass the man in front of his friends, he just let it go at that. Later, the guy became a pupil. Bruce showed a lot of class; he didn't hold a grudge, he let him in and just moved on.'

By June 1961, Bruce was making plans to open a formal school and began looking around Chinatown for suitable premises. After several attempts he realized the only option was to accept a dilapidated but affordable basement which could be spruced up. He designed a red and gold yin-yang emblem, painted it on a poster board and put it up in the entrance. He paid the thirty-five dollars for a business licence and the first Jun Fan Gung Fu Institute opened.

In the meantime, Bruce's relationship with Amy had reached a complete impasse. Bruce asked Taky's advice, telling Taky he was thinking of proposing to Amy but wasn't sure that she'd accept. 'If it's meant to be, it'll happen naturally,' said Taky.

# 6

## The Circle Grows

At the end of Bruce Lee's first university term, his grades averaged B plus. In the summer recess the institute continued with its public demonstrations and core students noticed that Lee's teaching was changing yet again. There were now more praying mantis-like techniques, more kicks and other longer-range strategies, as well as more calisthenics.

When the new term started, one of Bruce's favourite haunts became the campus library, in particular the Chinese philosophy section, where he made page after page of notes on the teachings of Confucius, Sun Tzu, Lao Tzu and other great scholars and prophets. Soon various maxims and aphorisms written on cards started to appear pinned around the walls of the institute. 'Adaptation is like the immediacy of the shadow adjusting itself to the moving body,' read one.

'He was a unique young man,' says Taky. 'He could turn his personality from one segment to another. One minute he would be telling us a raunchy joke, the next he would be talking about Zen and Taoism. He was very flexible and could change depending on who he was talking to.'

'Just as in his childhood, Bruce was still fond of practical jokes,' Doug Palmer recalls. 'One of the guys in the class was an optometrist and Bruce had a whole bunch of contact lenses made. One pair had red veins in them, and he used to put them in and goof around. He would stumble into a restaurant and be led up to a table by one of us, then fumble for a menu, pass his hands across the page and start ordering in Chinese while one of us interpreted.'

Bruce celebrated his twenty-first birthday in November 1961 with nothing stronger than root beer. Christmas that year came a week early for him as the long-awaited wooden dummy finally arrived from Hong Kong. He wasted no time in unpacking it and soon had it assembled in the small back yard below his room at Ruby Chow's. Now he could make up for lost time, practising blocking and striking its hard wooden limbs and trunk. By the end of the day, Bruce decided that he would keep this new piece of equipment a secret, knowing that it would help him regain his edge. After working with it for a while, he nicknamed the dummy Bodhidharma.

One humid May evening in 1962, while the Seattle World's Fair was in full swing, Bruce was visited in his basement school by a group of people led by Wally Jay, who introduced himself as a judo and ju-jitsu instructor from Almeda, California. Jay said he and his students were on a goodwill tour of judo clubs in the northwest and he had dropped in on Bruce because the mother of one of his students had once taken cha-cha lessons from him. 'It wasn't hard to find you,' said Wally. 'Your reputation is growing; everyone seems to know who you are.' A broad smile crossed Bruce's face.

Like Wally Jay, Bruce had a strong intuition of when someone knew what they were talking about through their technical vocabulary and body language and both soon recognized each other's authenticity. Wally volunteered one of his students, who happened to be his most senior student and the biggest and strongest among them, to perform a demonstration with Bruce. They faced off and Bruce beckoned the student forward. As fast as the barrage of attacks came, Bruce reacted instinctively and immediately with multiple blocks and counterattacks. The judo man's strikes had travelled barely halfway to their target before they were deflected.

Wally was impressed, realizing that Bruce was just playing and could have easily finished the student off. Diplomatically, Wally eased any tension by shifting the subject to talk of the rest of his tour, but Bruce had noticed something Chinese about Wally's features and interrupted to ask about his ancestry. Wally was quick to confirm Bruce's observations and the conversation took a new direction. They agreed that most Westerners still thought the Chinese were good at ping pong, and that was about it. As Wally left it was clear that a friendship had begun.

That weekend Bruce called Amy and told her about this meeting, but she wasn't interested in judo, ju-jitsu or kung fu. When Bruce asked her if she'd like to visit the World's Fair and the Space Needle she turned the idea down flat. She kept bringing up the subject of Bruce's car.

'What's wrong with my car?' he asked.

'Don't you think you should get a newer one?' she said.

Amy was letting him know that his old Corvair, with its dents and faded paintwork, was not the kind of car she intended to be seen in. If success was measured that way, Bruce had to admit he still had some way to travel.

James Lee – the Oakland kung fu teacher whose brother Bob had taken a dancing lesson from Bruce – had a friend named Allen Joe who happened to be travelling to Seattle for the World's Fair. 'Since you're going,' said James, 'why don't you check him out?' Allen Joe tracked Bruce Lee down to Ruby Chow's restaurant. He waited till late in the evening and was sitting there drinking a Scotch when Bruce showed up dressed 'real sharp'. Bruce was feeling good, having just received a letter containing $150 from his mother in Kowloon.

Allen Joe mentioned James Lee and he and Bruce began talking kung fu, eventually moving to the back lot where Bruce showed him a practice form on the new wooden training dummy. Not to be outdone, Allen showed Bruce his classical moves. Without smiling, Bruce told him they were no good and to try them on him. For the best part of an hour Allen tried every move he could on Bruce but ended up 'flying all over the place'. 'I was really impressed,' said Allen Joe. 'He was so smooth that everything I had learned seemed stiff and clumsy in comparison.' At four in the morning they parted on good terms.

Bruce now decided to keep one Sunday free exclusively for Amy. During their Sunday dinner at the Bush Garden, he was convinced that this was the right time to propose to her. Holding Amy's hands across the table he told her how much she meant to him, and how he wanted her to be the person behind him, ensuring his success, then he asked her to marry him. The reaction wasn't the one he was hoping for. In fact, she was aghast. She replied that this was the last thing she wanted, but Bruce kept trying to convince her. He pictured himself as the head of a chain of kung fu schools, independent and wealthy, with Amy there to share it all. Choosing her words carefully, she said that they were too alike ever to be married and that she didn't want to sacrifice her own ambitions, which were just as important to her.

At the group's next Sunday gathering at the Hong Kong café in Chinatown, Amy was noticeably absent. It seems Bruce had taken her words to heart, though, because at the end of a nine-course meal he announced that he was getting rid of the old Corvair and treating himself to a new car as a birthday present to himself, then after dinner he took everyone to the Varsity Theatre to see *The Seven Samurai*.

The following weekend Bruce sold the Corvair for $50, which he put towards the $625 he paid for a 1957 Ford Fairlane, bought from a small ad in the *Seattle Times*. The car ran well, had no dents and the paintwork was clean, and it amused him that the black and white colour scheme made it look like a Seattle Police car. He thought that even if it wasn't good enough for Amy, there would be plenty of co-eds on the campus who wouldn't mind being driven around in it.

Just as Yip Man had done, Bruce introduced a ranking structure to the institute. Because of Taky's help and sincerity Bruce promoted him to assistant instructor and gave him the rank of si hing, meaning 'older brother'. There were now about fifty students; some were regulars and some only showed up from time to time, but all were paying customers and this kept him solvent.

In addition Bruce was now getting more and more offers to perform demonstrations, assisted by Taky, Jesse and the other seniors.

'I was with Bruce at some of his demos and he would put away some big guys,' says Taky. 'But his strength wasn't plain brawn. He used to tell us this story about an old lady whose house caught on fire. Her most precious possession was a piano which was on one of the upper floors. Without stopping to think about how she was going to do it, she carried the piano out of the house to safety. Later, it took four men to lift it. Bruce could call up and harness that kind of energy at will. His power came from a tremendous base of internal energy, which he knew how to bring out.

Jesse Glover explains, 'What Bruce could readily demonstrate at the drop of a hat was based on a great many factors other people didn't possess. Few people had the physical background to make Bruce's ideas work. What Bruce presented to the public was only the tip of the iceberg. One of the requirements for learning these arts is intensive practice spread over the appropriate time period. You can't learn them overnight and you can't learn them without effort. In order to successfully use any of Bruce's ideas, you had to develop more than a little of Bruce's skill.

'There were several factors that made Bruce the way he was. First was his ability to take something complex and render it down to its basic essence. Second was his natural speed and ability to imitate any movement he saw, even if it was only once. Third was the motivation that drove him to higher levels; the fear of being beaten and the desire to be the best – the fear that he might meet someone with his own ability but who was bigger and stronger – and the fact that if he was the best, such a thing couldn't happen.

'During the first two years that I knew him, Bruce Lee was a split individual who could rave about the attributes of various martial arts during one conversation, only to put them down in another. During this period in the early 1960s, Bruce travelled around California and the West Coast, as far as Canada, to look at and talk to kung fu masters. Whenever they permitted him to watch or showed him some technique, Bruce quickly saw how he could make them more efficient, something that seldom endeared him to the host. A series of these encounters began to make him think that much of what was being taught was ineffective.

'Bear in mind that during this period Bruce was training forty or more hours a week. He was approaching his peak time of development and his actions reflected the great gains he was making. The better he became, the less regard he had for tradition and he said so whenever he had a platform to speak from, and he could back his words with actions.'

Bruce Lee made an equally powerful impression on one of the students of Garfield High School, where he was an occasional guest lecturer. He arrived one day, looking cool with Amy Sanbo on his arm, to give a talk on Chinese philosophy. He didn't even notice Linda Emery, an athletic girl of seventeen, but she was taken enough to ask the girl beside her who he was. Her friend, a Chinese-American girl named Sue Ann Kay, replied that Bruce was the guy who was teaching her kung fu.

During one busy evening training session Taky took a call from James Lee in Oakland. Allen Joe had given an impressive report on Bruce and James now asked if Bruce would like to come down to Oakland and teach a few classes. A week or so later Bruce set off. He had difficulty reading the American roadmaps – he wondered if his 20/400 vision might be getting even worse – and would occasionally get lost on the coast road, but after nearly sixteen hours and 810 miles, the 'police car' arrived in Oakland.

Bruce eventually found James Lee's house and was made welcome. Naturally enough, all conversation was about martial arts and Bruce discovered that James was the author of several books on the fighting arts of the Orient, karate and kung fu. Bruce asked why he'd chosen to spell it 'kung fu' rather than the traditional Cantonese 'gung fu'. James replied that since most

Americans didn't know Chinese pronunciation he felt that his spelling would make it more accessible and marketable in the US. Bruce was most interested in James's *Modern Kung Fu: Iron Poison Hand Training*, which explained methods for developing stronger hands. The following morning James invited Bruce to see his garage, which was full of all kinds of innovative training equipment he'd welded together himself. Every sort of spring-loaded apparatus imaginable was mounted on the walls and beams of the garage.

Bruce told James how impressed he was that a Chinese-American like himself had become so physically developed, as normally Chinese men had slender frames and little muscle bulk to work with. James replied that body conditioning was only half of it, proper diet and nutrition were just as important. He explained that muscles, when exercised, needed to be taken to the point where they actually tore or shredded, and protein was needed for their rebuilding and growth. But he also added that, once started, such a regimen had to last a lifetime. On that understanding James offered to help Bruce, saying that he could probably increase his 135 pounds to 150 or maybe 160 pounds, without sacrificing any speed or flexibility with the increase in bulk. However, he didn't want him to get so obsessed with the idea that he was tempted to take chemicals or steroids. James warned him never to get into that stuff unless he wanted testosterone imbalances, liver ailments, kidney failure and the like. 'It will kill you with a very slow, agonizing death,' he warned.

As Bruce returned to Seattle, he smiled to himself. He sensed a kindred spirit in James, who he felt as if he'd known all of his life. Over the years, it was the kind of deep friendship he would forge with very few.

# 7

## *Yin Yang*

During the long drive back to Seattle, Bruce worked out the format for a book he intended to produce in collaboration with James Lee. There would be something about the history and philosophy of kung fu, along with photographs of various techniques, featuring himself with his senior students. As soon as he got to Seattle, he drove straight round to the institute to start work on it.

When Taky arrived that evening Bruce had already compiled a stack of notes. Bruce told Taky of his plans to write a book that would serve as an introduction to his art for Americans who weren't familiar with kung fu in general, explaining that he couldn't go too deeply into things without losing the reader. Even so, he wanted to include something about the esoteric background to his art.

Bruce recalled how Yip Man had once told him, 'Instead of opposing force with force, a kung fu man defeats his opponent by accepting his flow of energy and borrowing his force. In order to reconcile oneself to the changing movement of the opponent, a kung fu man should first understand the true meaning of yin yang.'

Now that Bruce was older and had experienced that philosophy directly at the hands of the praying-mantis master Gin Foon Mark in New York, he reasoned that the philosophy of the yin yang symbol, which was the symbol of his institute, would be the best place to begin. By early November he had settled on a structure for the book, and a title: *Chinese Gung Fu: The Philosophical Art of Self-Defense.* Unusually for him, he decided to stick with the traditional 'gung fu' rather than the modern variant 'kung fu' as he felt that this would add an authentic edge. On his daily visits to the University of Washington campus library, Bruce began to compile his notes about the nature of yin and yang.

Every phenomenon in the world can be explained by the interaction of two primal forces termed yin and yang. Yang represents the creative masculine element – heat, light, sound, activity, heaven, infinity and so on – while yin represents the receptive feminine element – coolness, darkness, stillness, earth and the finite. Yin and yang are not concrete realities but a way of representing the flow and flux of energy that lies behind every process in existence.

Nothing is yin or yang except in relation to other things or processes. They are *relative* forces. For example: an iron ball is yang compared to a rubber ball, which would be yin. But a rubber ball would be yang compared to a ball of butter. And a ball of butter would be yang compared to a raindrop, and so on.

Yin and yang are neither cause nor effect. When I say heat makes me perspire, the heat and the perspiring are just parts of one process in which one could not exist without the other, like light and shadow or sound and echo. The interaction of yin and yang is also seen in the way a bicycle is made to work. Both pedals cannot be pushed at the same time: one has to be pushed while the other is released, then vice versa.

This concept of two complementary forces is used to explain the way in which nature creates the sustaining energy of all existence, the breath of life, or chi. This can be understood if one imagines combining fire (yang) and water (yin) to produce steam. The resulting vapour is almost invisible, but when contained and channelled it has great force. The Chinese symbol for chi is an iron pot of hot rice whose steam is lifting up the heavy lid.

Chi permeates the entire universe; it is the vital energy of every living being. In terms of the human body, it is the flow of energy governing muscular movement, the process of breathing, the regulation of the heartbeat, the functioning of the nervous system, in short, all physical, mental and emotional processes. What Western medicine attributes to separate circulatory, endocrine, digestive, muscular and nervous systems, the Chinese have traditionally viewed as interrelating, and an understanding of the flow of chi is the basis of all the Taoist arts, including the martial arts, philosophy and medicine.

In martial arts, the moment of stillness before the arm punches is yin, but as the arm shoots out to strike, it becomes yang. In the wing chun training exercise of chi sao (or 'sticking hands') the student has to apply the same principles of pressure and release that are used to power a bicycle. In attempting to feel the force and intention of his opponent's moves so as to neutralize or counter them, the arms must be soft and sensitive enough to register small changes without being limp, but firm and resilient enough to withstand pressure without being rigid. As the attacks and counters flow, only the one who continues to change and adapt spontaneously, without thought and effort, will prevail.

In a neatly typed fifteen-page essay that Bruce Lee compiled in the university library, he wrote:

> The application of the principles of yin and yang in gung fu are expressed as the law of harmony. One should be in harmony with, not rebelling against, the strength and force of the opposition. When A uses strength (yang) on B, B must not resist him back with strength, but instead yield to him with softness (yin) and lead him in the direction of his own force. When A's force reaches its limits the yang will change to yin and B can then take him in this unguarded moment and attack with force (yang).

In effect, this strategy is very much like the children's game, stone, scissors and paper. If A presents 'stone', then B wraps it in 'paper'. If A present 'paper' then B cuts it with 'scissors'. If A presents 'scissors' then B jams them with 'stone'. The kung fu man flows into the appropriate moves as quickly and naturally as water filling a pot, as instinctively as the reflex of removing a hand from a hot stove, or as automatically as the way we sign our own name. Later, the skill and sensitivity developed allow the student instinctively to counter his opponent's moves at the speed of reflex action.

At a certain point in training this sensitivity may even move beyond a purely physical skill to become a psychic faculty, in which you may also become sensitive to the opponent's emotions and thoughts to such a degree that you experience his intention to attack at the same time as he does, or even before.

After conferring with James Lee in Oakland, Bruce set out to do the necessary work on the layout and photographs, which he planned to shoot in Ruby Chow's parking lot, explaining that he and his colleagues would wear traditional jing mo gung fu uniforms; Bruce would wear a black one and his student would wear grey. James was surprised by the fact that Bruce, who was always progressive in his approach, had decided to do this, but nevertheless suggested they met up again at the Christmas break to put the finishing touches to everything. Bruce was already planning a trip back to Hong Kong the following summer to research an even more ambitious follow-up project: *The Tao of Chinese Gung Fu*.

On his second trip to Oakland over Thanksgiving, Bruce and James's time together was spent working on the book and training. Bruce told James that there were essentials that had to be understood before he could begin the journey to mastery, elements such as guarding the body's centre line – an imaginary line running through the core of the head and torso – and the principle of the immovable elbow. Bruce confessed that what he knew of the more advanced forms of wing chun he had not learned from Yip Man, who kept his students on the basics for years, but from the information he'd managed to prise out of senior students like William Cheung, as well as through spying on advanced classes. 'Anyway,' he added, 'the hardest part of learning is actually learning how to learn it. Once you can concentrate your mental energies, it's a piece of cake.'

In return James initiated Bruce into techniques for breaking wooden boards with his bare hand – 'One hundred miles an hour in, one hundred and ten miles an hour out!' said James – despite the fact that Bruce had always claimed he was unimpressed by such things.

James wrote a short introductory section for Bruce's book, which included these remarks:

> I was really impressed when in friendly sparring matches with Mr. Bruce Lee, I couldn't penetrate or land a telling blow or kick, even when he was blindfolded, once his hands are 'sticking' to mine. I have paid the Mr. Bruce Lee a sincere compliment by changing all of my gung fu techniques to his methods. When he demonstrated his type of striking, which is based on inner energy, I found it much more powerful than the power I had developed from Iron Hand training. The superiority of his gung fu is more refined and effective than that which I have learned in all my past years. Since his striking power is generated from the waist and mind, I maintain that the power to break bricks is not the true test of actual application of energy in real combat.

Aside from the philosophical discourses in his book, Bruce included theories on combat that were just as direct:

> Fighting is not for sport, it's for real. When someone is trying to roll you over like truck, you don't have time to play around. You've got to hit and run before the cops arrive ... Speed is more important than power ... It's about being first with the most that wins ... If the opponent can't see you, he can't hit you. And if he can't hit you, he can't hurt you ... The first move should be a succession of rapid-fire strikes to the eyes.

On one free evening during his stay Bruce asked James to drive him into San Francisco because he wanted to see the Jackson Street Hospital where he'd been born. And on the evening of Bruce's birthday, James and his wife Katherine arranged a surprise party for him at the Lantern Chinese restaurant with a specially made cake decorated with a yin yang symbol and twenty-two candles. Among the guests were Wally Jay and Allen Joe. The following day, as Bruce made ready to leave, James handed him several bottles of dit da jow hand-conditioning medicine as an early Christmas gift.

On 17 December Bruce got the early Christmas present he wanted more than anything, with the news that 1,500 copies of his book were printed, bound and boxed in Oakland. Bruce couldn't wait for them to be shipped up to Seattle, and at midnight, immediately after work, he drove straight down to James Lee's, leaving an irate Ruby Chow with a large gap in her busy Christmas work rota.

On the drive Bruce reflected on how his parents had wanted him to succeed in a world where a good education meant everything. But he also reasoned that even with a degree, he would still want to be doing the things he was doing, and he could certainly do that without the distraction of working at Chow's, along with all the homework assignments and the newspaper job eating into his teaching time. He began thinking that his studies and his job might have to take second place, and that nothing should stand in the way of his martial arts goals.

# 8

## Summer in Hong Kong

In the summer of 1963, Bruce Lee was planning a trip back to Hong Kong and hoping to tell his family that he and Amy Sanbo were to be married. In the three years that he and Amy had been dating Bruce had proposed and been turned down several times. He made one final attempt, hoping to clinch it by offering her a ring that had once belonged to his grandmother. Bruce knew that Amy had been offered a job in New York, so he was pushing her into marrying him or turning him down for good. Amy turned him down for the last time and then disappeared from his life. For a while he tried unsuccessfully to locate her.

At the same time Bruce got a letter from the draft board and they were not at all keen to let him leave the country where his American citizenship had made him eligible for military service. In the end Bruce asked his English professor Margaret Walters to write a character reference, assuring the draft board that he was an honourable man. Although his life in the States had been shadowed by the disappointment of Amy walking out, Bruce had no intention of leaving its shores for good.

That summer, the Lee household in Nathan Road consisted of Bruce's mother and father, his sister Agnes, brother Robert, a cousin, an aunt, a servant, dogs, fish . . . and the chicken living on the veranda. Bruce's friend and student Doug Palmer had studied Chinese at college and he jumped at the chance when Bruce invited him to come along on the visit home. One evening, as the family sat around the table, Doug Palmer was introduced to the subtleties of the language.

In his extensive notes written during this trip, Palmer recalls:

Cantonese, the Chinese dialect predominant in Hong Kong, is a tonal language. Sounds which are otherwise identical can have a radically different meaning with a different tone. By then, I could speak Mandarin, which has four basic tones, reasonably well. But Cantonese has seven and, for me, the differences were sometimes impossible to hear.

One night, the family sat around the dining table playing a simple game which consisted of rolling a die with the figure of a different animal on each face. Whoever was quickest to yell out the correct animal after the die was rolled advanced his marker. One of the animals was a shrimp, pronounced 'haai' in a low tone. In the excitement of the game my voice would rise and I found myself shouting 'hai' with an even higher pitch every time the shrimp was rolled. The ladies of the household thought this was most amusing and giggled each time. Finally, Bruce took me aside to explain the difference in tone between the word for 'shrimp' and the word for 'cunt'.

Bruce and Doug found no shortage of things to do that summer. They swam at the beach, went to the movies, visited amusement parks, ate in restaurants or simply soaked up the atmosphere and energy of the bustling streets. Bruce also got Doug Palmer involved in his practical jokes. One of his targets was the Hong Kong police, who were quite corrupt at the time and, along with the British soldiers, were the people Bruce disliked most. Bruce selected a Chinese policeman wearing a red bar on one of his sleeves, signifying that he spoke rudimentary English. Doug recalls:

Once we spotted one of the cops with a red bar, my job was to walk up to him and ask if he could tell me the way to the Canton Theatre. Since there was no Canton Theatre, but there was a Canton Road, the cop would invariably ask, in heavily accented English, 'Canton Road?'

'No!' I'd say, I was supposed to meet a friend at the Canton Theatre and, thereupon, I would launch into a nonstop monologue of doubletalk.

Each time the confused cop would repeat 'Canton Road?' I would give another burst of doubletalk.

Finally, I would demand loudly, in Cantonese, 'What the hell are you mumbling about?'

At that point, Bruce would stroll up helpfully and ask what the problem was. I would explain that I was looking for the Canton Theatre. Bruce would say that he was going that way and would accompany me and we would walk off, leaving the cop with an even more confused look on his face.

One night Bruce was returning home to Kowloon on the Star Ferry when two street punks goaded him. He endured their comments and ignored them, but after the ferry docked, they continued to follow Bruce and insult him. Finally he spun round and snapped out a low straight kick to the nearest punk's shin. The second one quickly backed off. While Bruce left it at that and continued home. When he heard about the incident, Bruce's cousin Frank, who was a few years older, shook his head in disbelief and laughed: 'A few years ago, he would have beaten them both up.'

Bruce also took delight in faking fights with Doug in front of a crowd of onlookers:

We practiced our routine: two roundhouse swings from me, which he blocked with his forearms, then a stiff uppercut to my stomach, which I had to make sure I'd tightened in time. We would time it so that we'd emerge from an elevator, arguing loudly, then swing into our skit in front of the crowd waiting for the elevator.

I'm not sure whether Bruce's sense of humor was Chinese or uniquely his own. He used to act like a geek and let a street punk goad him, then when the punk swung, Bruce would block it awkwardly and snap at the punk's groin, incapacitating him with a blow that appeared to be an accident. As the punk rolled in pain, Bruce would cover his mouth with his hand and titter effeminately, then walk off.

'A person can accept getting beaten by someone who is stronger or bigger than he is,' Bruce would explain, 'but if he thinks he's been beaten by a fairy, he'll be pissed off for the rest of his life.'

While in Hong Kong, Bruce continued with his serious training and sought out Yip Man, taking Doug along only to watch and cautioning him not to let on that he knew any kung fu.

Although he had kicked over the traces in the States, teaching gung fu to anyone who was interested, without regard to race and to the consternation of many people in Seattle's Chinatown, he was not ready, out of respect for his teacher, to 'come out of the closet' in Hong Kong.

Yip Man was a smiling man with a twinkle in his eyes, slight and getting on in years, but still fit. He and Bruce would practice sticking hands in his apartment at the top of a highrise. There were no other students present, and the two of them, in their undershirts, would go at it for long periods.

'We hung out together all that summer,' says Palmer, 'except when we had dates.' When Bruce's childhood sweetheart, Pak Yan, heard that he was in Hong Kong, she called him. In the five years he'd been away she had been featured in one picture after another. Now, she told him, she would soon begin work on a new film in which she was to play 'a bad girl'. She wanted to know if

Bruce would be able to help her prepare for the part. Over the next few weeks, he helped her prepare several times.

Whether or not his father knew about Pak Yan, a week before Bruce was due to return to Seattle, Lee Hoi Cheun decided that Bruce, at the age of twenty-two, should be circumcised. Even more astonishingly, Bruce agreed, returning to the apartment one day walking carefully. He quickly changed from the tight pants he normally wore into a pair of loose-fitting traditional ones borrowed from his father. Each morning the purple organ was inspected until it had taken on a more normal appearance. 'I remember him hobbling about,' chuckles Palmer. 'If he'd known how painful it was going to be, I think he would have had second thoughts.'

By the time Bruce Lee and Doug Palmer took off for the US, Bruce was able to walk normally again:

On the way back we stopped in Tokyo for a couple of days, then again in Hawaii. Through a friend, Bruce was asked to give a demonstration at a gung fu school in Honolulu; by then he had completely recovered from his operation. At that time, the gung fu schools in Hawaii, as elsewhere, were still strictly Chinese, so it was quite a surprise when I climbed on to the stage with Bruce to give a demonstration to fifty students and their teachers.

Afterwards a number of people gathered around to ask questions. One of them asked if Bruce was teaching me gung fu. From the way he asked and, since from the demonstration it was obvious that I'd had some training, his implication was clear: he considered it heresy that Bruce would be training a non-Chinese.

The same fellow, with a cigarette dangling from his mouth, now approached Bruce with questions about his technique. He asked Bruce how he would block a front kick and Bruce offered to demonstrate. The man kicked at groin level and Bruce blocked it with a slapping palm block, then resumed his explanation. The man kept his leg extended in the air, after the kick was blocked, and flicked his foot feebly after Bruce had with-drawn the block. 'See,' he said, 'you were open there.'

Although Bruce was smoldering, he had become adept at handling this type of person without hurting them. He con-tinued his explanation and offered to demonstrate a different block. The man obliged and threw a punch, but of course, this time Bruce did not withdraw after blocking it; he trapped it and followed with a counter of his own, just slow enough to allow the fellow to block it with his free hand. Bruce grabbed the second hand too, and tied up both of the man's arms. The force and speed of the second pull was so great that the man's cigarette went flying from his mouth as he jerked forward. The whole time, Bruce continued calmly explaining each move, his head turned to the growing audience, as he kept the man's arms pinned and demonstrated several alternative moves. Then, sat-isfied, he let the man go.

When Bruce returned to Seattle the US government had their own plans for him. As a prelude to possible service in Vietnam, he was called to take a physical exam for the US draft board. Surprisingly, he was considered physically unacceptable to the Army due to an undescended testicle. Had he joined the Army he would probably have been court-martialled within a week. Not only did he hate routine and regimentation, his temper was balanced on a hair-trigger. If Bruce Lee was unsuitable for work as a waiter, he was hardly cut out to be a soldier.

# 9

## *Linda*

In the summer of 1963, while Bruce and his friend Doug Palmer were in Hong Kong, Linda Emery graduated and took a vacation job. In September she started at the university while Bruce Lee began his junior year as a philosophy major. One Sunday, her friend Sue Ann Kay invited her along to her kung fu lesson. They went to the Chinatown basement where Bruce's class was held. Although it was a bare concrete room with a single lightbulb, the atmosphere was buoyant. Linda had expected to make this a single visit, but she surprised herself by enjoying the class and becoming one of the regulars.

Sunday afternoons were the social highlight of the week for the class. They were usually spent in Chinatown, where Bruce would crack jokes throughout lunch before they moved on to a movie theatre, often to see a samurai film. On the journey between the restaurant and the cinema Bruce would walk in front. Suddenly objects like an orange might come flying back at them, thrown by him. They learned to reach out and catch these without comment; it had to be instinctive. During the film Bruce would analyse the action, pointing out mistakes in the way it had been filmed. Later he would quiz everyone to see if they'd been paying attention, asking about minute details in the film or about people who'd been in the restaurant earlier or even about the weather. Bruce used everything as an opportunity to teach his students to become more aware and to make them realize that they could be a lot more aware.

Bruce asked the university for permission to use the men's gym to give demonstrations and these soon attracted more students. People began missing classes to spend time in the Student Union building where Bruce showed kung fu moves, explained the philosophy behind them and cracked jokes in between. At other times they would train outside on a grassy area lined with trees. During one afternoon session Bruce chased Linda Emery to one side and suggested dinner without the others. Unlike Amy Sanbo, Linda Emery turned out to be the perfect date: she listened attentively. As they sat in the Space Needle's revolving restaurant with the lights of Seattle turning slowly below, Bruce overflowed with his plans for the future.

Bruce was still living at Ruby Chow's and was feeling both stifled and restless. Taky suggested that they begin looking for bigger premises where they could all meet and train. The students would continue to pay so he could support himself and pay the rent. Bruce found a suitable place and in October 1963 he handed Ruby Chow his notice and moved the Jun Fan Gung Fu Institute to 4750 University Way, not far from the campus. The school occupied the entire ground floor of an apartment building, where showers were already installed. Bruce camped out in a windowless room at the back, sparsely furnished with things he'd brought back from his summer trip to Hong Kong. A school prospectus was printed, with Bruce offering a martial arts method that was fast, efficient and economical, though he warned that it could not be mastered overnight.

Every evening Bruce and Linda would run back to his window-less room at the back of the institute and fumble around in the dark for the light switch; then Bruce would turn on the TV so that they could watch *General Hospital*, the soap-opera they'd both become hooked on. Afterwards they would most likely eat in the Chinese restaurant across the street, where Bruce would eat beef in oyster sauce or, occasionally, shrimp in black bean sauce. Soon they were together constantly and Linda's school work began to suffer. Bruce would often do Linda's homework for her and could write an English essay with almost perfect grammar and spelling in no time at all. Unfortunately he wasn't as much help when it came to Linda's other pre-med subjects, chemistry and calculus, and she began falling behind on the 'points' she needed to graduate.

Keeping her new relationship secret from her mother and stepfather, Linda Emery spent most evenings with Bruce at the institute. Linda came from a white Protestant family, and while her mother could hardly object to her having Asian friends in a school where over half the student population was black or Asian, she did draw the line at dating. Linda's mother would certainly have had strong feelings about the affair, but what was now obvious to Linda was that her own feelings had become even stronger.

Towards the end of 1963, when Doug Palmer returned home to Seattle for the Christmas vacation, he accompanied Bruce Lee on one of his demonstrations, this time at Garfield High School, where Palmer had graduated one year ahead of Linda's class. Here Bruce gave the first demonstration of the 'one-inch' punch.

Palmer's diary recalls:

Garfield was a tough inner-city high school, over half black and Asian. The class that Bruce began speaking to had several football and basketball players in it who lounged in their seats never having heard of kung fu. Bruce started out by contrasting the karate-style punch with the wing chun punch. He then confided that there was a punch with even greater power which could be delivered from a distance of a single inch. Some of the students were stirred from their boredom to briefly register mild amusement at the idea. Bruce asked for a volunteer to demonstrate this one-inch punch on. While guys smirked at each other, Bruce singled out the biggest kid, sprawled out across his chair at the back of the class, and asked him to step forward.

The class perked up a little, giggling as Bruce stood dwarfed by his volunteer. Bruce placed his knuckles against the big guy's chest and steadied himself. 'Wait a minute,' said Bruce, suddenly. He then made a production out of finding a chair and placing it about five feet behind his stooge.

'OK,' said Bruce, as he resumed his position. 'Now we're ready.' This had the desired effect: the students were now watching in anticipation. The big guy glanced back over his shoulder at the chair five feet behind him. Up till then, he'd been laid back about it: now that it looked as if he were going to be laid out, he was damned if he was going to let a skinny little Chinese guy make a fool out of him. The big guy braced himself, one foot back. Bruce, the showman, kept up a constant patter, his arm extended and his fist touching the kid's chest. Suddenly, his arm shimmered, nothing more, and mouths fell open as the kid flew off his feet and into the waiting chair, knocking it over backwards as he sprawled ass over kettle onto the floor. Bruce now had the attention of the class.

Bruce had continued to keep in touch with James Lee, and in June 1964 they began making plans to open a branch of Bruce's Jun Fan Institute in Oakland. By now Bruce had lost interest in completing his philosophy doctorate at university, and at the end of the term he sold his 'police car' and shipped his furniture to Oakland. Linda drove Bruce to the airport, wondering how, or even if, she fitted in with his plans. Bruce told her he wanted to have some money behind him before even thinking about marriage or a family.

The air was thick and muggy in the Long Beach Sports Arena that July day in 1964. The air conditioning wasn't working and the crowd, who were there to watch the annual International Karate Tournament, was restless after sitting through hours of matches. Then Ed Parker, the sponsor of the event, went to the microphone to introduce Bruce Lee, who was going to put on a demonstration of the little-known Chinese martial art of kung fu.

Ed Parker recalls, 'He was very broad-minded about things,

very anti-classical kung fu; he felt that they were all robots. So I told him that if he were to come down to the tournament and demonstrate, people would have a better cross-section of the martial arts world.'

Wearing a simple black jing mo suit and slippers Bruce took to the floor. Just as he'd done with the students at Garfield, he drew the audience into his presentation, which climaxed with the one-inch punch as his victim flew back and gasped for breath. Although they were impressive, Bruce was against simply doing tricks like this if they had no real point to them. The real purpose of the one-inch punch was to show that there's a far more powerful way of striking someone than simply using the strength of the arm and shoulder muscles. The more relaxed the muscles are, the more energy can flow through the body; using muscular tensions to try to do the punch, or attempting to use brute force to knock someone over, only has the opposite effect.

Competing in the black belt division of Ed Parker's championships that day was a Filipino martial artist called Dan Inosanto. Apart from studying kenpo karate with Parker, Inosanto also trained in the Filipino arts of escrima and kali. After the match he went to meet Bruce at his hotel room to exchange ideas and techniques, but he was less than satisfied with the results of their short session.

Dan continues to teach at his Academy in Marina del Rey, California, still runs every day and looks as fit as he did twenty years ago. He recalls feeling completely flabbergasted: 'He controlled me like a baby; I couldn't do anything with him at all. He didn't really have to use much force either; he just sort of body-controlled me. I'd lost to other people before, but not in the way I lost to him; he dominated the action completely, calling all the shots like it was a game. I couldn't sleep that night. It seemed as though everything I'd done in the past was obsolete. He countered everything I knew without really trying. It was very frustrating.'

After Ed Parker's karate tournament Bruce Lee and Dan Inosanto spent a lot of time together, sometimes just walking and talking or exploring old bookstores. Inosanto took over Taky Kimura's role and helped Bruce give demonstrations in the San Francisco area. These shows followed a familiar format, including lightning-fast finger jabs, kicks, punches that stopped within a whisker of their target, Bruce testing his reflexes against a challenger, doing thumb push-ups or board-breaking.

Dan spent four days taking falls and punches for Bruce in demonstrations at the Sing Lee Theatre in Los Angeles, then in the evenings, at the Statler Hilton, Bruce taught him some of his fighting method, what Inosanto called 'a devastatingly improved version of wing chun'.

While Bruce was in Oakland he and Linda wrote to each other regularly, with Linda using a post office box so that her mother wouldn't find the letters. Soon Linda had a bit of news for Bruce that meant marriage was on the cards sooner rather than later. Facing a karate black belt was one thing, but facing Linda's mother was quite another and Bruce wondered just how he was going to deal with his future mother-in-law. In the end the formidable fighting machine suggested they get married first, make a tactical retreat to Oakland and then call Linda's mother with the news.

On 12 August 1964, Bruce returned to Seattle with a wedding ring lent to him by James Lee's wife, Katherine. Unfortunately, after applying for the licence at the County courthouse, the details of the forthcoming wedding were published in the local newspaper, as required by law, and when Linda's aunt saw the announcement she phoned Linda's mother to ask what had happened to her invitation. The immediate family was rallied in a show of strength designed to pressurize the couple into calling it off, but Bruce met them and, with economy and directness, told them, 'I want to marry your daughter. By the way, I'm Chinese.'

After the revelation that she was soon to become a grandmother, Linda's mother started making quick arrangements with the minister at the Seattle Congregational Church. Taky Kimura was the best man – 'the only person outside the family to be invited,' he recalls proudly – while Linda's mother and grand-mother gave her away (Linda's father had died when she was five years old). It was all so rushed that Bruce had to rent a suit for the ceremony, Linda didn't have a wedding dress and nobody thought to hire a photographer. 'He could at least have bought flowers,' sighed Linda's mother.

# 10

## The Oakland Years

When someone once asked Bruce what the secret of happiness was he replied, 'Get yourself a nondescript little place where you can work out with your buddies.' Although the years that Bruce Lee spent in Seattle and Oakland are often presented as little more than footnotes in his rise to stardom, they not only had a substantial impact on the man he would become, he later acknowledged that they were the happiest years of his life.

In the autumn of 1964, Bruce and Linda moved into James Lee's home at 3039 Monticello Avenue in the Maxwell Park area of Oakland. Soon after, James's wife Katherine finally succumbed to cancer, leaving him with a daughter, Karena, twelve, and son Greglon, eleven (who had been named after James's favourite actors: *Greg*ory Peck and Mar*lon* Brando). Soon Bruce, Linda, James, Greglon and Karena were living as one extended family, just as Bruce himself had done as a child in Hong Kong with various cousins and unofficially adopted siblings.

A dishevelled man with iron-hard hands, James Yimm Lee was twenty years older than Bruce and a former state weightlifting champion, amateur boxer and judo brown belt who now worked as a welder while teaching kung fu part time. He was also one of the few people in the US with any knowledge of the Chinese martial arts. He had trained for years in traditional kung fu but had become dissatisfied with its set patterns and lack of practical training, so had developed his own informal style. It was natural that James Lee realized what Bruce had to offer. Indeed, James said he learned more in the short period after they'd first met than he had in all his former training, because Bruce didn't teach obsolete routines, just the essence of self-defence in situations that weren't prearranged.

James and Bruce became partners and opened the second branch of the Jun Fan Gung Fu Institute on 4157 Broadway in Oakland. There were few students at first but Taky Kimura subsidized their income by insisting they receive all the takings from the school in Seattle. Neither of Bruce's schools was ever conceived as an out-and-out commercial venture. Bruce wasn't just trying to attract as many paying customers as possible; he wanted students who showed both ability and commitment. What he had to offer had to be taught on a one-to-one basis; it wasn't simply a matter of lining up students and rehearsing moves. Bruce needed to understand each student's particular physical make-up, temperament and attitude. Each student had to be developed in a different way. Dan Inosanto, for example, discovered that in order to progress further he first needed to free himself from mental tension.

For a while Bruce succeeded in his hope of avoiding the kind of conflict he'd had with the students of other martial arts schools in Hong Kong. Rule nine of the institute called for discretion when explaining the school's training methods to others, so as not to stir up ill feeling and rivalry with other schools. Ironically, the first trouble came early in 1965 from a Chinese martial arts instructor just across the Bay in San Francisco.

Wong Jak Man had recently arrived from Hong Kong, to teach kung fu. Seeking to make a name for himself he presented Bruce with a written challenge to fight, with the loser having to close his school. Behind the challenge lay the traditional martial arts community's objection to Bruce teaching their secrets to Westerners who, as they saw it, already had the natural advantage of size and strength. Wong and several colleagues turned up for the appointed fight with a long list of rules for the contest: no eye jabs, no groin kicks and so on. Bruce was incensed by this and became so eager to meet the challenge that Wong quickly suggested a more formal sparring match to decide the issue. But Bruce would have none of this and, unable to back down in front of his colleagues, Wong had no choice but to see it through.

According to reports from onlookers the fight was anything but smooth, fast or efficient. After a scrappy exchange, Wong turned to run, then his entourage tried to step in but were intercepted by James Lee. Bruce went after Wong, punching him on the back of the head, but was unable to land a finishing shot. In the end Bruce turned the delegation off the premises and they left without another word.

Bruce later told Dan Inosanto, 'I chased him and, like a fool, kept punching his head and back; my fists were already swelling from his hard head. Then I did something I'd never done before: I put my arm around his neck and knocked him on his ass. I kept whacking him as he lay on the floor until he gave up. I was so tired I could hardly punch him.'

Linda later found Bruce cooling off on the back porch, looking despondent and anything but satisfied with his victory. Bruce was deeply annoyed that what should have taken a few seconds had taken over three minutes, leaving him winded and facing the fact that he was in less than optimum condition. As a result, Bruce began to examine both his fighting and his training methods. Encouraged by James Lee, he also began an intensive programme of physical conditioning. He started every day with an early morning run of several miles, often with Bobo, the Great Dane he'd named after his childhood pet, the Alsatian Bobby. For Bruce, running was a kind of meditation, an opportunity to let things flow. Houses, cars and trees passed along just like his thoughts, feelings and sensations. After lunch, there was another run or an hour on the exercise bike.

Bruce's conditioning exercises centred mainly on the abdomen, using the tried-and-tested boxing method of having a heavy medicine ball thrown at his mid-section, along with sit-ups and leg raises. As his new approach took shape, he lost no time in criticizing the old guard: 'There are lots of guys around the world that are lazy. They have big fat guts. They talk about chi power things they can do, but don't believe it.'

James also started Bruce on weight training. At first he did reverse curls all day to develop his forearms but once he'd seen how it might add strength to his speed he bought a full set of weights and used them consistently.

William Cheung explains how Bruce was able to build his muscular strength through weight training, without sacrificing speed: 'Back in the 1950s, the Chinese martial artists were very conservative and knew that weight training would slow them down. But Bruce found a way to beat it. He would start his programme with heavy weights and low repetitions, then reduce the weight as he increased the repetitions. He continued to do this until the repetitions and the speed peaked.'

Dan Inosanto also describes Bruce shadow-boxing with small weights in his hands doing a hundred punches per series, using 1, 2, 3, 5, 7 and 10-pound weights and then reversing the series back to one. This also had the effect of building strength on the way up and developing speed on the way down. Ted Wong can recall Bruce using this heavy-light principle working up to 160-pound bench presses on his heavy days, then doing only the last three inches of the movement at a much lighter weight on his light days. In this way, Bruce was able to develop the ratio of power to speed and the momentum he needed, without sacrificing one at the expense of the other.

Bruce's workout schedule often listed the number of repetitions of exercises he'd set himself, and beside some was the note 'INF', meaning 'to infinity'. He would keep going until he could go no further, and then do some more.

Even out of the gym, Bruce never stopped training in one way or another. Back in the 1950s, every schoolboy had cut out a newspaper coupon to send away for details of a body-building method known as Dynamic Tension. Charles Atlas had built a mail-order empire by promising to help 100-pound weaklings get revenge against bullies who kicked sand in their faces. Dynamic Tension was in fact an exercise system known as isometrics, in which one group of muscles works against an opposing group. For example, by gripping the hands in front of the chest and trying to pull them apart without letting go, or by working against a dead weight. Bruce put this idea into practice whenever he could – for example, standing next to a wall in a casual conversation with someone, he would push against it with the back of his hand to 'flow the energy' in his triceps.

Bruce utilized whatever was to hand: he practised kicking by kicking trees until they were jarred by the force; he practised accuracy by kicking at pieces of litter that had been blown up by the breeze, and where no particular training equipment existed to meet his needs, he invented it, then called on James Lee's welding skills to construct it.

Go into any modern, well-equipped martial arts school and you will find a variety of practice apparatus. There will be a heavy bag for punching and kicking at full power, a top-and-bottom speed bag which springs back only if punched in a straight line, a selection of smaller bags (with various fillings) and padded mitts to practise punching with accuracy and power. You might also find air-filled kicking shields to practise depth of penetration and kicking on the move, and there will almost certainly be a loop and pulley device to stretch the legs. All of this equipment was first assembled in James Lee's garage.

Yet, even with the most comprehensive array of training equipment, Bruce still found ways of getting even more out of the apparatus, increasing both his own and James Lee's skills. The wing chun wooden dummy was also adapted, giving it a spring-loaded head, while bags were mounted on spring-loaded platforms so as to fly back unpredictably, or built oversize so that extra power was needed to make an impact.

Bruce also tried to get a little more out of the equipment by investing extra energy in his approach to it. The heavy bag wasn't punched passively: Bruce visualized it as an opponent who he needed to fight, ducking and sidestepping, moving in and out, while being aware of timing and relaxation. He felt that real sparring was most valuable against an untrained, uncoordinated fighter, because of his sheer unpredictability. By this combination of methods, the improved stamina, strength, flexibility and economy were gained by running, weight training, stretching and sparring. Bruce did everything he could to maintain these gains and also began experimenting with high-protein, weight-gain drinks, which he blended and supplemented with ginseng, royal jelly and massive doses of vitamins.

For Bruce Lee the spirit in which everything was carried out was as important as technique and this required harnessing mental and emotional force. The secret of this emotional content was a kind of purposefully directed anger. Once while Bruce was showing Taky a move, he wasn't satisfied with the way Taky did it and casually slapped him hard across the face. Taky's eyes narrowed and, forgetting it was Bruce, he moved in aggressively.

'Yes!' said Bruce, laughing. 'That's what I want!' Bruce tried anything in training that would add the anger and fear that are stirred up in real confrontation so that he could practise remaining centred under stress.

Before long Bruce had become so powerful and effective that he could only go all-out on the wooden dummy; it became too dangerous to do so on a person. Anyone holding an air shield for Bruce to kick would usually end up on his back; one unsuspecting visitor who held a punching mitt for him had his shoulder dislocated with the force of the blow. The power that he could channel wasn't merely the result of conditioning and training, it arose from regular periods of meditation, the wellspring of chi. Bruce was less inclined to talk about meditating than fighting but the first item of his daily to-do list was always 'Meditation and Mental Training'.

One evening, after a long day's training and teaching, Bruce and Linda went out for dinner to a restaurant in San Francisco. After being shown to their table Bruce thought he recognized one of the waiters on the other side of the room. Sensing Bruce's gaze on him, the man looked up and his eyes widened as the tea he was pouring for a customer spilled over the top of the cup and ran onto the table. The waiter was Wong Jak Man.

# 11

## Screen Test

Back when Bruce Lee did his kung fu demonstration at Ed Parker's karate tournament at Long Beach in July 1964, Jay Sebring was in the audience. Jay was the owner of a Beverly Hills hair salon and he'd trained with Parker. What he saw that afternoon impressed him as much as it did everyone else.

One of Sebring's clients was William Dozier, a TV producer whose credits included the *Gunsmoke* and *Perry Mason* series. Once, when Dozier was getting a haircut, he mentioned to Sebring that he was looking for someone to play the part of Charlie Chan's son in a new series about the Chinese detective. Sebring suggested he get in touch with Bruce Lee.

On 1 February 1965, at East Oakland Hospital, Linda gave birth to a son: Brandon Bruce Lee. Three days and as many sleepless nights later, Bruce found himself in front of the cameras at the studios of Twentieth Century Fox to take part in a screen test for a possible role in the *Charlie Chan* TV series.

On a chair in the centre of what looks like a smart suburban living room sits a young man wearing a neat black suit which looks a size too small, a white shirt and a black tie with a small tight knot; his hair is short and neatly brushed. He sits with his legs crossed and his hands clasped together as he smiles nervously – a quiet and unassuming man whose face might even be said to look slightly chubby. Suddenly he glances somewhere over to his left, where from the darkness a voice instructs:

'Now, Bruce, look into the camera lens and tell us your name, age and where you were born.'

'My name is Lee, Bruce Lee. I was born in San Francisco. I am twenty-four right now.'

'And you worked in motion pictures in Hong Kong?'

'Yes, since I was around six years old.'

'And when did you leave Hong Kong?'

'1959, when I was eighteen.'

'I see. Now look over to me, Bruce, as we talk,' continues the director. 'I understand you've just had a baby boy and you've lost a little sleep.'

'Yeah.' Bruce laughs. 'Three nights.' His voice flutters nervously and his facial expressions are a little exaggerated.

'You told me earlier today that karate and ju-jitsu are not the most powerful forms of oriental fighting. Which are the best?' asks the director.

'Well, I think kung fu is pretty good,' is the untypically modest reply. After further prompting, Bruce continues: 'Kung fu is a more complete system, and it's more fluid.'

Recalling the time that Yip Man sent him away from school to think things over, the day he had spent walking by the water, Bruce compares the principle of kung fu to the nature of water. 'You cannot punch it and hurt it; you cannot grasp hold of it. Every kung fu man is trying to do that, to be flexible, to adapt to the opponent.'

'What's the difference between a karate punch and a kung fu punch?' comes a further question.

'Well,' replied Bruce, 'a karate punch is like being hit by an iron bar – whack!' He pauses for a moment and smiles. 'A kung fu punch is like being hit by an iron ball swung on an iron chain – WHANG! – and it hurts inside.'

After a fresh reel of film is loaded Bruce acts out some of the characters from classical Chinese theatre, demonstrating the moves and gestures that represent the scholar and the warrior.

'Now show us some kung fu movements,' says the director.

'Well, it's hard to show it alone, but I'll do my best.'

To the delight of his sniggering colleagues a middle-aged man with silver hair and spectacles – a member of the studio staff – is 'volunteered' as Bruce's stooge.

Bruce catches the atmosphere and warms to the situation by joking, 'Accidents do happen!'

'There are various kinds of fights,' he begins. 'It depends on where you hit and what weapon you use. To the eyes, you will use the fingers.'

Bruce throws a lightning bil jee strike towards the man's eyes. The old man looks more than worried.

'Don't worry,' Bruce assures him and whips out another jab to his eyes. 'And to the face,' he says, as his punches make an audible rush of air, lashing within an inch of the man's nose as he explains that the power of the punches comes from the waist.

The director steps out in front of the camera for a moment to adjust Bruce's and the old man's positions in relation to the camera.

By now the subdued chuckles from the floor have become belly laughs and Bruce joins in the conspiracy with the studio technicians, trying to hide his laughter with his hand across his face. The director, sensing the hapless volunteer's rising desperation, asks Bruce to back off a little.

'You know, kung fu is very sneaky,' says Bruce, 'just like the Chinese.'

The old man is as jumpy as a rabbit. 'These are just natural reactions,' he pleads.

Bruce pats him on the shoulder to reassure him.

'Right!' smiles Bruce, who has spent years training to replace such human reactions with far more useful ones.

'Then there is the jab, the punch, the back fist . . . and then low!' he exclaims as he whips out three strikes that slice the air around the man's head, then drops low to strike at the groin the instant the man's hands have moved up to protect his face.

'Then there are the kicks, straight to the groin, then up!'

And, just as fast as the punches, there is a front kick to the groin, a roundhouse kick and a hook kick to the head.

'He looks kind of worried,' adds Bruce casually, now in complete command of the situation.

Everyone realizes the speed and accuracy of the movements they are witnessing. The technicians laugh openly, both at their colleague's predicament and in amazed disbelief at something none of them has ever seen before.

'He's got nothing to worry about,' says the director confidently. 'Now show us how a good kung fu man would coolly handle it and walk away.'

But before Bruce can demonstrate this slightly unfamiliar approach for him, the reel of film runs out.

Bruce might well have gone on to explain that martial arts' animal forms originated with Shaolin warrior priests' observation of various animals. The emphasis was not so much on the actual physical movements of the animal as on its vital energy. In the Shaolin tradition, imitating each animal developed a particular attribute. For example, the tiger strengthened bone; the dragon brought strength of spirit. Bruce Lee's first experience of the animal fighting styles was watching Master Kwan's films as a boy.

By now, a new reel of film has been loaded.

'Practising alone involves forms,' says Bruce as filming recommences, 'imitating for instance a crane, a monkey or a praying mantis.'

Despite the tight suit he's wearing, Bruce completes his screen test by demonstrating the crane form, stretching his arms and weaving them into fluid movements which suggest the neck, head and beak of a great bird and its flapping wings. Suddenly he stabs out a strike and then kicks high above his head, '*Biaah!*' an animal shriek is followed by another fierce jab, before he winds down the routine and looks over, almost bowing for a second, to the director.

'Show us one more and then we're all finished,' says the director.

As Bruce tries to pull his shirt sleeves and suit jacket back into shape, he continues, taking a forward stance with his hands extended and fingers curled into claws as he runs through the tiger form.

'Thank you very much.'

A week later, on 8 February, Bruce's father died in Hong Kong. With the new baby just arrived, Bruce decided to go alone to the funeral. In Hong Kong, he arrived at the mortuary where his father's remains lay and crawled from the front door to the coffin, wailing loudly for good measure. Chinese tradition requires penance from a son who was not present at the death of his father. Hopefully Bruce's noisy atonement brought some peace to Lee Hoi Cheun's soul.

While he was away Linda visited her mother, who still hadn't entirely accepted her daughter's marriage. When Linda arrived in Seattle with baby Brandon in her arms her mother greeted her with, 'How could you have done this?'

Two weeks later, when Bruce and Linda were back together in Oakland, William Dozier called to say that the *Charlie Chan* series had been shelved. He added that a good audience reaction to his new *Batman* series would allow him to follow it with an entirely new series, *The Green Hornet*, using the same formula of an adventure-strip hero and his partner. Bruce was signed to a one-year option to play the role of the Green Hornet's kung fu sidekick, Kato. In May 1965, with no filming yet scheduled, the Lees boarded a plane back to Hong Kong. In one of those little ironies that life sometimes arranges, their combined air fare came to $1,800 – the exact amount Bruce had been advanced by Dozier.

Life at Nathan Road was not smooth. Grace Lee was still grieving the death of her husband while Linda struggled with a baby who cried most of the night in the sweltering heat. Although Linda didn't encounter the same prejudice Bruce had endured from her family, she was unable to speak more than a few words of Cantonese and felt left out. Bruce tried to smooth things out by joking that the new member of the family was the only blond-haired Chinaman in the world, then added to Linda's problems by promising everyone that she would cook them a wonderful meal.

In the US, *Batman* was well received and *The Green Hornet* was set to follow it into production, but William Dozier still had no idea when. From Hong Kong Bruce made regular calls to the States about the series, but made no attempt to contact any of his friends and colleagues in the Hong Kong movie industry, even though most of them were still active in the business. It was obvious that it was in America that Bruce intended to make something of himself.

During the four months that Bruce and Linda spent in Hong Kong, he settled the details of his father's estate. He and Linda went on occasional outings, shopping trips or sightseeing. And Bruce took Brandon to visit Yip Man, to ask a favour of him. Hawkins Cheung was also back in Hong Kong at the time and the two of them happened upon each other in the street.

Hawkins recalls:

I was just about to say hello when Bruce stepped in quickly – I was surprised that his movement was so fast. His character hadn't changed at all; he still wanted to be top dog. Bruce told me, 'I have to train very hard to beat my opponents, so I've come back to learn more of the dummy techniques from the old man. I want to film him so I can show my students in America. I'm on my way to see him now.'

A few days later, Bruce gave a demonstration on a popular TV chat show. He didn't say anything about wing chun or Yip Man and I suspected that something had happened between them. I knew Bruce's character: if he wanted something, no one would stop him. If they did, then Bruce would go out on his own and come back and show you. I found out that the old man had refused to be filmed doing the wooden dummy form. His traditional thinking had come up against Bruce's Western thinking.

For the rest of his stay Bruce continued his intense training regime at a local gym. He alternated this activity with long periods of deep thought as he considered a complete break with tradition to forge his own martial arts way. At the same time, he was starting to feel concern about how he was going to earn enough to provide for his family. Maybe a return to acting would be the answer.

In September 1965, Bruce, Linda and baby Brandon returned to Seattle where they went to stay with Linda's family. Brandon was still not sleeping through the night, and his howling throughout most of the day was punctuated by remarks from Linda's mother, who was given to wondering out loud when Bruce was going to get himself a proper job. During these months of relative inactivity while waiting for the call to start work on *The Green Hornet*, Bruce began to suffer from severe backache. He tried to ignore it, because the need to push forward with his ambitions was even more intense.

Later that year, the Lee family hardly had time to settle back into James Lee's house in Oakland when the call came through from William Dozier that *The Green Hornet* was due to start shooting in three months' time. In March 1966, Bruce, Linda and baby Brandon moved to Los Angeles, to a small apartment at Wilshire and Gayley in Westwood, an upscale area in the west of the city. It was Bruce and Linda's first home of their own since they'd been married. Realizing he was going to be paid $400 for each episode of *The Green Hornet*, Bruce did what any man would: he went out and bought a new car, a modest blue Chevy Nova.

# 12

## The Green Hornet

*. . . Another challenge for the Green Hornet, his aid Kato and their rolling arsenal, the Black Beauty. On police records a wanted criminal, the Green Hornet is really Britt Reid, owner-publisher of the Daily Sentinel, his dual identity known only to his secretary and the district attorney. And now, to protect the rights and lives of decent citizens, rides the Green Hornet!*

*The Green Hornet* had been one of America's most popular radio serials of the 1930s. Created by writer George W. Trendle, the character of Britt Reid was the nephew of another one of Trendle's fictional characters, Dan Reid, better known as the Lone Ranger. At night, Britt Reid, played by Van Williams, changed his business suit for green clothes and a mask to become the scourge of criminals, while Bruce Lee was cast as the hero's chauffeur and sidekick, Kato. He wore a chauffeur's uniform and a mask and drove their own version of the Batmobile: the Black Beauty.

Thirty half-hour episodes were planned, and naturally Bruce was most concerned about how the action was to be staged. At first the fights were planned to be like the slugging matches seen in Westerns, but Bruce refused to take this approach, saying the essence of his kung fu was efficiency. To illustrate this, he suggested the fights be shown in slow motion, an idea used many times since. When it came to filming the fight scenes, Bruce was forced to slow down his movements because they only registered as a blur when filmed at normal speed. At the director's insistence,

Bruce agreed to some flashy flying kicks for visual impact, but not before he'd pointed out that, in a real fight, moves like that would get you into serious trouble.

Gene LeBell was a regular in stunt work and fight set-ups in literally hundreds of movies and became one of the few people Bruce Lee would openly accept lessons from. By the time Bruce and LeBell met on the set of *The Green Hornet*, LeBell had already won every major judo championship and a wrestling crown. In 1962, LeBell held the World Professional Wrestling Championship, even if it was only for twelve seconds. He would've held it longer had it not been for a ring fracas in which he 'accidentally' kicked the Texas wrestling commissioner in the head. Gene LeBell was as pre-eminent in the grappling world as Bruce Lee was to become in the world of Chinese martial arts. But while winning a dozen titles and having people say he was the toughest guy in the world was great, it still didn't add up to one car payment. LeBell realized that his money was going to have to be made some other way, even if it meant getting beaten up by every wimp in Hollywood.

Gene first met Bruce on the set of *The Green Hornet* after Benny Dobbins, the stunt coordinator for the show, called LeBell and told him me he was needed to take some falls from a guy called Bruce Lee, who was unbelievably athletic and was stealing all the scenes. He added that he kicked like a jumping bean. At the time, no one, including LeBell, had ever seen anything like Bruce's fighting style.

When LeBell got to the set, Benny pointed out Bruce and told him to go and put Bruce in a headlock or something. The wrestler grabbed Bruce and put him in a fireman's lift over his shoulder, then ran the length of the set and back again.

'Put me down!' shouted Bruce. 'Put me down or I'll kill you!' But LeBell just carried on running, with Bruce still shouting, 'Put me down!'

LeBell replied, 'I can't put you down, or you'll kill me!' In the end they both had a good laugh about it.

'We ended up becoming great friends,' LeBell says. 'We would work out together and exchange techniques. Bruce loved to learn grappling, but said that people would never go for it in movies or TV because most of the good stuff was hidden. He said they wanted to see fancy kicking, acrobatics and weapons. One time he kicked me really hard and I remember thinking it was a good thing he only wore a size six shoe instead of a fourteen like me, otherwise that kick would've sent me all the way to China.'

*The Green Hornet* premiered on 9 September 1966. A dramatic voice intoned the introduction over a jazzy version of 'The Flight of the Bumble Bee' blended in with a buzz created on a Theremin. The narrator was the same as the one who opened the *Batman* shows, the producer himself, William Dozier.

The first episode introduced the American television audience to kung fu. In the opening scene of act two, the Hornet and Kato are surprised by three hoods. Kato kicks a wooden box into their midst, distracting them for the instant he needs to act. The fight is short and sweet, a few fast kicks and powerful punches. In the following fight scene Kato overcomes gun-toting criminals by flinging poison darts at them, while the Hornet carries a gun that shoots a powerful but non-lethal sleep-inducing gas. The Hornet's 'sting' was a collapsible device which fired an ultrasonic beam powerful enough to shatter metal. Kato mainly used his fists and feet, though in one episode he introduced a Chinese weapon, the nunchakas, two short sticks linked by a chain.

The duo's car, the Black Beauty, was a matt-black 1966 Chrysler Imperial, adapted by Hollywood automobile customizer Dean Jeffries at a cost of $50,000. The car was armed with rockets and other deadly devices, with green headlights that allowed the heroes to see four miles ahead at night with the aid of a built-in camera. It was stored underground in Britt Reid's garage, suspended upside-down on a rotating platform ready to replace his convertible when he set out as the Green Hornet. Access to the

Hornet's stronghold was through a hole in a Candy Mints poster (an early bit of product placement).

In a review of the first episode, one critic commented, 'Those who watch him would bet on Lee to render Cassius Clay [later to change his name to Muhammad Ali] senseless, if they were put into a room and told that anything goes.' We can speculate for ever about what might've happened in such a situation. But not long after this review Bruce Lee was at a dinner where one of the other guests was Senator John Tunney, the son of the former heavyweight champion Gene Tunney. Bruce amazed the senator by being able to describe all his father's fights in detail and added that he had books and films about him in his library. Senator Tunney then asked Bruce if he thought he could have beaten his father. Bruce replied, 'If I stood still and your father hit me, then forget it! The question is: Could he have got close to me?' Bruce said that while the boxer had only two hands, he had his hands and feet, elbow, knees and fingers.

The series marked the first time that kung fu had been seen in the West outside the movie theatres of the Chinatown districts, and younger viewers were astonished by what they saw. The real star of *The Green Hornet* was Kato, and Bruce was soon making personal appearances in character across the country, sometimes making several stops in one day as he did the usual round of local radio guest spots and TV shows, opened supermarkets and appeared at fairs, in public parks or at martial arts tournaments.

Although Bruce was a natural showman and even an outright show-off, he put limits on how far he was prepared to exploit his skills, even at the then handsome fee of $1,000 or more per appearance. He exclaimed again and again that he had no time for tricks like breaking boards, adding, 'Boards don't hit back'. Although he was mobbed by enthusiastic fans on these public appearances, he was hardly getting his face known by appearing as Kato and wearing a mask.

Surprisingly, nearly half of Bruce's fan mail was from young girls. In reply to one of these letters, from a girl called Vicki, he explained that as Kato he practiced gung fu and *not* karate as she had presumably assumed. He also advised her rather sternly to work on her technique. Mastering that should be her goal rather than aiming to break boards or bricks – a practice he dismissed as a stunt. 'If you want to break something, use a hammer,' he wrote.

Younger audiences loved the show, but because it was played straight, adults weren't as enthusiastic, preferring the more camp *Batman*. As 'real' characters, Kato and the Green Hornet were simply unbelievable, which was particularly ironic given that this was probably the first time any authentic fighting skills had been seen on TV outside the boxing ring. In the end *The Green Hornet* closed on 14 July 1967 after twenty-six weekly episodes finishing with an additional two-part show in which the Green Hornet and Kato teamed up with Batman and Robin in a crossover episode to launch the second *Batman* series.

In this episode the Green Hornet and Kato battle Batman and Robin, who somehow manages to match the skills of the world's pre-eminent martial artist. The director, not wanting to upset fans of either series, had Batman and Robin fight the Hornet and Kato to a draw, and eventually all four combine their resources to defeat the villainous stamp thief, Colonel Gumm. As he read the script for this final episode a wicked grin spread across Bruce Lee's face.

On the day of the filming, Bruce maintained an icy silence but his eyes burned through the holes in the mask he wore. Once or twice actor Burt Ward, who played Robin, cracked a feeble joke. When the cameras began rolling for the fight scene, Bruce began to stalk his opponent menacingly. Ward backed away spluttering that it was only a TV show, but Bruce ignored him and closed in. Off-stage someone squawked like a chicken and Bruce exploded into laughter, unable to keep up the act any longer. 'Lucky it *is* a TV show,' he added with a wry smile.

The Hornet and Kato made two further TV appearances. Bruce Lee and Van Williams made a personal appearance as themselves on a rock 'n' roll variety show, *Where the Action Is*, on 1 September 1966. This show toured throughout the US and featured popular music acts of the day, such as the Mamas and

Papas and the Knickerbockers, playing games and interviewing celebrities. On *The Milton Berle Show* during the autumn of the 1966–67 season, the Hornet and Kato appeared in character in a comedy skit in which Berle was cast as a stuntman supposedly working on an episode of their show.

Ironically, it was Bert Kwouk's parody of the Kato character that went on to greater mainstream success in the series of *Pink Panther* comedies starring Peter Sellers as the hapless Inspector Clouseau. Kato was Clouseau's valet and had standing instructions to keep his master's martial art skills honed by launching attacks on him without warning, resulting in the response, 'Not now Kato, you little yellow fool!' As you can see, there was still some way to go before the Chinese stereotype was laid to rest.

With the cancellation of *The Green Hornet* series, the Lees were soon on the move once more. Although the large twenty-third-floor apartment in nearby Barrington Plaza was one they could afford even less, Bruce arranged to give martial arts lessons to the landlord in return for a rent reduction. The landlord, as it turned out, had similar arrangements with many of the tenants and soon both he and the Lee family were uprooted.

Despite the fact that Bruce had generated almost all of the fan mail for *The Green Hornet*, further roles did not materialize and Bruce felt as though he'd taken a big step back. While continuing to make occasional appearances as Kato, he again directed his energy into what he knew best, teaching kung fu. As a teacher, Bruce's role was to expose his students' vulnerability, but privately he was being forced to deal with his own. Introspection and inactivity had been followed by success and then disappointment. As he would have to do several times throughout his life, Bruce was forced to strike an increasingly fragile balance between his ambitions and his art.

# 13

## Jeet Kune Do

When they were working together at the Statler Hilton, Bruce Lee and Dan Inosanto had talked about swordsmanship. Bruce said that the most efficient way of countering in fencing is the 'stop-hit', where you parry and counter in one move so that when the opponent attacks, you intercept the move with a thrust of your own. The idea is to score a hit in the middle of your attacker's action, making it the most economical of all counters.

Bruce then said, 'We should call our method the stop-hitting fist style, or the intercepting fist style.'

'What would that be in Chinese?' asked Inosanto.

'That would be jeet kune do,' said Bruce.

Bruce Lee came to regret coining the phrase 'jeet kune do'. When he proposed it, he had no intention of creating a new martial arts style. 'It's just a name, don't fuss over it,' he would often say later. 'There's no such thing as a style if you understand the roots of combat.'

He would describe how a student learning a martial art passes through three stages. In the first stage, he or she understands very little about the art of combat. In a fight, all of their blocks or strikes would be uncontrolled and inaccurate. Like the person who is attacked by surprise in a dark street, the untrained angry or fearful reaction is to withdraw defensively or lash out wildly, to freeze or flail, rather than to fight efficiently.

In the second phase, the student finds that he or she must move and breathe in a completely new way, which means thoughts and feelings will also change. In fighting or sparring, there will be moments of 'psychic stoppage', where he freezes for a moment to analyse what's happening and calculate a response. For the time being, the student loses the ability to fight without thinking. This phase involves a long period of training in which the student learns various techniques of striking, kicking and blocking. Here a long period of repetition to open up the neurological circuits and commit the moves to 'muscle memory' is essential – remember, 'kung fu' means 'time spent' or 'effort put in'. As Bruce Lee put it, 'I have no fear of a man who practises ten thousand kicks once, but I do fear a man who has practised one kick ten thousand times.'

The final stage, when the right moves happen automatically, involves the combination of factors that Bruce Lee was aiming to instil in his students: the physical, emotional and mental coordination that allows the spontaneous and spirited flow of appropriate action in combat. Bruce once showed Dan Inosanto what he meant by flinging an object at him without warning. As Dan caught it, Bruce pointed out that Dan had simply acted directly and naturally, without adopting any special stance or needing to wear a special uniform.

At this level, technique and strategy mean simply fitting into the opponent's movements and intentions, neither opposing an attacking force head-on with too much resistance or over aggression, nor giving way completely. Pliable as a spring, the fighter becomes the complement of the opponent's energy. Sensing and understanding the interplay of energy involved, the fighter no longer feels himself as separate from either his opponent or the fight. He no longer opposes or struggles but simply completes his own half of a single whole. The fighter and the fight take on an ego-less impartial quality in which the conflict resolves itself naturally. This is a level of ability that can never be reached by learning more and more techniques, but only by moving to an entirely new level of sensory perception. At this level of ability, the martial artist is beyond mastering techniques: everything just flows, simply and directly, according to the training that has been embodied. As Bruce put it: '*It* hits.'

Dan Inosanto likened the process of learning a martial art to learning to read. 'Eventually you learn to read groups of words. Where a student will see three motions, the experienced man will see one, because he sees the overall energy path.'

In a letter to Dan Inosanto, Bruce wrote, 'Use your common sense to see what is the real thing and what are merely lessons in routine dancing. Gung fu is simply the direct expression of one's feelings with the minimum lines and energy.'

To summarize: the objective of martial art training is to replace wrong or inappropriate reflexes with more useful ones. At first the student will fight any old way. Then he or she practises for a long time, repeatedly and conscientiously, to discover a new way. Eventually this new way becomes instinctive. Bruce Lee firmly rejected the idea that this learning process is one of accumulation. Mastery is approached, he said, not through acquiring more and more knowledge, but through stripping away the non-essentials. A stone sculptor, rather than building in clay, chisels away everything he doesn't need to reveal the underlying form hidden inside the material. Continuing this analogy, Bruce often referred to his kicks and punches as tools.

Bruce Lee found it both difficult and frustrating to try and teach people right from the beginning. Jeet kune do was a conceptual approach, and as such it was of no use to people at the first stage of a martial art, only to those experienced martial artists who had reached the third stage and who were willing to search further.

# 14

## *Student-Master*

After improvising for several months in various temporary Chinatown locations, such as Wayne Chan's pharmacy, Bruce Lee opened his third school in February 1967 at 628 College Street, just a few blocks from the Los Angeles Dodger Stadium. The institute, like those in Seattle and Oakland, was in an anonymous building. On Bruce's orders no visitors from outside were allowed into the school, and to ensure complete privacy the windows were painted over with red enamel paint. Dan Inosanto was appointed Bruce's assistant, and membership was strictly limited to martial artists who showed talent. If Bruce found a martial artist who already had some grounding or someone who could use what he had to offer, he was often prepared to teach them for free.

An early student Jerry Poteet recalls, 'I was short of money and unable to pay for training, but Bruce wrote me a letter saying, "Come on in. Forget about paying until you can. You're sincere and that's what counts."'

Bruce encouraged his students to train in their street clothes, saying that this was what they would most likely be wearing if they were involved in a fight. But while he liked to keep things relaxed and friendly, he could be strict when the situation demanded it. He once addressed the whole class: 'I know that a lot of us are friends and that outside of the school I'm Bruce, but in here you call me Sifu. Because of the informality, there has to be some discipline. If this school was in China, there would be a lot of people here now missing their front teeth.'

Classical martial arts training traditionally combines the development of strength with testing a student's patience and sincerity by having him spend considerable time standing in the deep, wide horse stances. Bruce saw this practice as divorced from the reality of fighting and as pointless as 'learning to swim on dry land', but even so, during the first few months of training his students endured a similar probation period. Each week included several gruelling sessions of physical conditioning when quite a few people fell by the wayside. Serious teaching began only for those who remained. Dan Lee – now a tai chi instructor in Pasadena, California – was an electrical engineer and language instructor when he became the Los Angeles school's first pupil in 1967.

'Part of the high standards Bruce maintained involved giving everyone a personal fitness programme,' Dan explains. 'He looked at you and saw what area you needed to work on most. He really meant business and worked very hard. He was the one person I respected most. He was a straightforward person, intense, but most of all honest. He didn't hold back any punches.'

Dan Lee's last remark has a double edge to it. While Bruce insisted on discipline in his classes, he sometimes struggled to control his own volatile nature. One night after class, Dan Inosanto, Dan Lee and Bruce Lee were in Bruce's kitchen at home. Bruce got out some boxing gloves and challenged Dan Lee to a knockabout. While they were jabbing at each other, Dan got through with 'a lucky punch', which caused Bruce to go after him for real.

Dan Inosanto recalls, 'Bruce broke his jaw as he followed him, hitting him with short punches all the way down to the ground. He must have hit him fifteen or twenty times, or at least it looked that way. It was all incredibly fast, but he did control the blows.'

'Yes, it happened,' confirms Dan Lee. 'It was a long time ago. I was very privileged to work with Bruce Lee.'

'If Bruce had one drawback,' adds Dan Inosanto, 'it was his

temper. He once told me that it was because he was in a rush to educate people and wanted fast results.'

Bruce didn't have years to spend building the foundation he'd received in Hong Kong. He simply couldn't spend the time needed on one-to-one sticking hands practice to induce the required reflexes and awareness. So instead he'd work at the highest level from the moment students walked through the door. Anyone with no previous experience of these methods would have been left overwhelmed and bewildered.

Bruce also had a generous spirit, Dan Inosanto recalls: 'I was in a sporting goods store with Bruce when I saw a set of weights I wanted to buy, but then I realized I only had twelve dollars on me. Bruce said that, while we were there, he should probably buy a set of weights for Brandon. I thought, He's starting Brandon a bit early; he's far too young for weight training. Later that day, when we arrived at my house, Bruce turned to me and said, "I really bought these weights for you, so you'd better start using them." I almost cried because of his generosity.'

Shortly after the Los Angeles school opened there was a confrontation, as had happened in Oakland, this time with two local martial artists who turned up at the institute wanting to fight. Bruce explained that they were in the middle of a class and, if they wanted to fight him, they would have to wait until the class was over. He quickly rearranged the class so that Dan Lee, one of his best students, was working out in front of the two challengers. During a break in the class, Bruce sauntered over to the spectators and said that if they still wanted to fight he'd be more than happy to let them spar with his students. The pair politely turned down the invitation and left. Bruce had used what was, for him, a new kind of strategy: 'The art of winning, without fighting,' says Dan Lee.

Because Bruce could teach only small classes, he decided to boost his income by taking on private students who paid a $50-per-hour rate instead of paying the regular monthly fee. The celebrity hairdresser Jay Sebring, whose clients included James Coburn,

Roman Polanski and Sharon Tate, put Bruce in contact with Steve McQueen and the movie star became one of Bruce's first celebrity pupils. Sebring acted as something of a go-between for Bruce and others, putting entertainment industry movers and shakers in touch with each other. In addition, Bruce's growing reputation meant he attracted many professional fighters, including several karate champions, for personal training.

Karate was first introduced to America by former Second World War servicemen who had learned the art while stationed in Okinawa. The first karate school in the United States was opened by Robert Trias in 1946, and a decade later karate was popularized by Ed Parker, the man who organized the 1964 Long Beach Tournament where Bruce was discovered. At that time Western teachers were still at great pains to adhere to the Asian tradition they were passing on, but in abandoning tradition, Bruce Lee both anticipated and set the stage for a new breed of martial artist. Traditionally, the mixing of martial arts was frowned upon, but things changed when Chuck Norris mixed Korean and Japanese arts to his own advantage, out-kicking the Japanese stylists and out-punching the Korean.

Joe Lewis first met Bruce Lee briefly at Washington's Mayflower Hotel, where both were guests at the 1967 National Karate Championships. Lewis was the defending champion, while Bruce was appearing as Kato! But it wasn't until they were back in California that they had a chance to speak, when they met again in a parking lot outside the offices of a martial arts magazine.

Joe Lewis recalls:

As I left the building to get into my car, Bruce Lee called me over and gave me this pitch about becoming my instructor and showed me various moves. Here was this little kung fu guy trying to tell me something about fighting, and I'm saying to myself, 'I'm an international karate champion and this guy's going to tell me about fighting?' What he was saying just went in one ear and out the other. He spent a long time trying to convince me about some of the things he was doing, but I just had a blank screen up.

Anyway, I was in partnership with Bob Wall and Mike Stone [also karate champions] and one day, some time after this meeting, Mike started telling us about this guy Bruce Lee who was phenomenal with all the different techniques he was doing. For him to compliment somebody unknown like Bruce Lee was strange, because I couldn't remember hearing Mike Stone ever compliment anyone. Mike Stone sold me on Bruce's theories which came from utilizing fencing footwork and wing chun to make it applicable to kickboxing, which is what I was into.

Bruce set it up so that Mike Stone, Chuck Norris and I would visit his house once or twice a week. He showed me a lot of fighting principles and emphasized footwork and the importance of using distance and mobility against an opponent. Bruce had hundreds of books on all the fighting arts as well as hundreds of boxing manuals and dozens of films. We used to sit and analyze boxing and wrestling films. We studied the way Ali punched, and the way he could control people even while backing up. Bruce said that he wanted to train Ali how to kick. He said that if he could do that then Ali would be like someone from another planet.

The 1951 championship fight between Willie Pep and Sandy Saddler was a particular favourite of Bruce's. In this fight Pep uses interesting footwork borrowed from judo. During the course of the fight, which Pep was losing, he wasn't averse to using an open hand so he could jab Saddler's eyes with his thumb. Once or twice, on the blind side of the referee, he used a judo leg trip to unbalance his opponent, along with many other non-boxing techniques.

Joe Lewis continues:

We would study the strategies on film and go to tournaments and watch guys fight. Then I would go out in a tournament and prove whether it worked or not. You can't have a better set-up than that. I thought it was the greatest life that ever existed, and I don't think there was ever anything like it before, or ever will be again.

In person, Bruce had a charm that didn't come across on the screen. I guess you could use the word 'magic'. What does the word magic mean? There's a spark of enthusiasm in everybody's mind. Bruce used to ignite that spark. He could explode that sense of imagination in you. You'd say, 'Wow! That's what martial arts is all about! Yeah, Bruce, you're right on the money!' It had that kind of flavour. He could just inspire you to love martial arts. The word ought to be 'inspiration'. He was an incredibly encouraging, inspiring spark of energy.

It should be noted that Bruce Lee's karate star students were already formidable fighters before they met him. In Okinawa, where Joe Lewis was stationed with the Marine Corps prior to serving in Vietnam, he became a black belt in an unprecedented seven months, then won his first national tournament in 1966. Bruce Lee would claim that even great champions recognized his genius, and perhaps he was right, but Bruce was also shrewd enough to realize that he had as much to gain from them too.

Joe Lewis says:

Bruce wanted people who would go out and represent what he stood for. He figured he'd get the biggest names at that time and build up his credibility as an instructor. The masters on the Chinese kung fu circuit looked down at him, and Bruce resented it, because he felt that most, if not all, of these kung fu masters couldn't fight. I think he wanted the prestige of being able to say that he was a master and that his students were champions. He didn't get any respect from the kung fu masters at that time and felt very misunderstood by people around him.

He needed attention and a sense of people looking at him and feeling he was significant. He didn't just want to be looked on as a kung fu expert. That was the label he had and it was hard to shake off. He'd come to me and say, 'Joe, I'm not a master. I'm a student-master, meaning that I have the knowledge of a master and the expertise of a master, but I'm still learning, so I'm a student-master.' That was the term he used to my face.

Dan Inosanto commented that Bruce never really believed in the word master. Bruce had told him that the master was only a word that could be used when they closed the casket. Inosanto says that Bruce avoided a term he thought could only be used posthumously.

An account of Joe Lewis's win at the 1968 International Karate Tournament, which followed a period of intensive training with Bruce, described Lewis as 'a fighter reborn'. His often surly disposition was put to one side and he displayed a new-found mobility that had never been seen before. When he was awarded the crown, Lewis humbly thanked his teacher, something he'd never done before. Within a year of beginning training with Bruce, Joe Lewis became unbeatable in tournament competition; he was even dubbed the 'Muhammad Ali of karate' as he went on to win an unprecedented ten titles.

Bruce Lee had now been training in kung fu for over half his life and had reached such a level of 'student-mastery' that there were only a handful of people around who could give him a serious workout. Yet many of the traditional martial arts fraternity saw Bruce as an upstart whose methods were little more than glorified street fighting. Bruce himself had no misgivings about his abilities and he took great delight in pointing out the shortcomings of the more traditional approaches to the fighting arts. He even had a mock grave complete with tombstone installed in the school. The inscription on it read: 'In memory of the once fluid man, crammed and distorted by the classical mess'.

From the outset, Bruce stressed that training had to relate as much as possible to actual combat and to situations that might be encountered on the streets, using only the simplest and most effective moves. Bruce said the best way to develop the power to punch and kick was simply to keep punching and kicking. Likewise the best training for fighting was to fight, or at least to practise the nearest thing, which was to pad up and spar all out. There was nothing sophisticated about it, and there were certainly no rules. When he was dismissed as a brawler by many of the traditional martial arts fraternity, Bruce would explain that not adhering to set methods didn't mean he was unskilled or without form. It meant that he was not limited to what he'd practised but could improvise and adapt.

Bruce's attitude to fighting brings to mind a scene from the film *Butch Cassidy and the Sundance Kid*. Cassidy, played by Paul Newman, is about to fight a rival for the leadership of an outlaw gang. Just as they're squaring up, Newman asks innocently, 'Just a minute, what rules are we having?' His tough opponent replies indignantly, 'No rules!' The words have hardly left his lips when Cassidy's boot hits him in the groin. As he buckles in pain and drops to the floor, we can see him trying desperately to say that he hadn't meant it like that, coupled with the awful realization that he'd just been outwitted. Bruce Lee would certainly have enjoyed that scene.

Bruce Lee practised and taught what was necessary to win simply and scientifically. The difference between the classical martial arts and Bruce Lee's evolving fighting method had become as radical as the difference between eighteenth-century soldiers fighting in rank-and-file formation and the methods of modern guerrilla warfare.

Throughout the 1960s Bruce assimilated as much knowledge and experience as he could about every aspect of fighting he could use. He amassed an extensive library, paying as much as $400 for a rare book. As long as a book had something to do with fighting, he bought it. Bruce placed great value on his books; he didn't regard them merely as possessions but as treasuries of knowledge.

He would study a new book intently, analysing its fighting techniques to find the weaknesses by acting them out. Although he never practised karate, he knew the names of all the techniques in Japanese and could demonstrate them. Not only did Bruce have books on every type of hand-to-hand fighting art, but also on archery, ballet and fencing. His books on philosophy concerned not only the insights of Chinese sages like Confucius and Lao Tzu, there were also works by Krishnamurti, Spinoza and Kahlil Gibran, along with popular psychology books on self-help and positive thinking by writers like Norman Vincent Peale and Napoleon Hill.

Bruce also collected films of Joe Louis, Rocky Marciano, Max Baer, Gene Tunney, Jack Dempsey, Muhammad Ali and other great boxers. Bruce used to watch Ali's films over and over to analyse and imitate his movements. As an orthodox boxer, Ali led with his left hand. Since Bruce was experimenting with a right lead stance, he set up a mirror so he could watch Ali's movements and practise them the appropriate way.

The first time Bruce put on boxing gloves, as a teenager, he became an inter-schools champion, beating the three-year title holder. He had fenced with his brother Peter, a Commonwealth Games champion, and done some tai chi with his father. He had trained intensively in wing chun while being involved in almost daily street fights in Hong Kong. Before coming to America he learned forms from other styles of kung fu, such as choy li fut, eagle claw and hung gar. Soon after arriving in the US he had visited his father in New York and trained with the praying-mantis master Gin Foon Mark. Bruce had met with Wally Jay, a judo and ju-jitsu exponent who was responsible for many innovations in that field, and he had become close friends with karate and kung fu pioneer James Yimm Lee. He'd practised judo with Taky Kimura, Fred Sato and Jesse Glover. He had trained in Filipino martial arts with Dan Inosanto and travelled to meet with instructors in other styles. The champion wrestler Gene LeBell played Bruce's patsy in many episodes of *The Green Hornet* and the two had become close friends and traded

# 15

## The Warrior

Along with his partner Tom Kuhn, Fred Weintraub runs an independent production company in Century City, Los Angeles. In 1968, Weintraub was head of Warner Brothers' film division and Kuhn was in charge of television.

Weintraub remembers, 'At that time I used to spend time looking at Chinese movies. They were four hours long and boring as shit, but in the last thirty minutes a guy in white came in and defeated all the bad guys. Because of that interest, friends introduced me to Bruce Lee and we became friends. I hired two young writers [Ed Spielman and Howard Friedlander] and tried to put a feature together for Bruce, but I could never get anything off the ground.'

Bruce Lee himself had already spent some time working on an idea concerning the adventures of a Shaolin warrior priest who used kung fu skills against the outlaws of the old West. Eventually his idea found its way over to Tom Kuhn, who suggested a TV movie as a pilot for a possible series, with the working title *The Warrior*.

By now, Bruce had attracted several more celebrity students, including the actor James Coburn and screenwriters Stirling Silliphant and Joe Hyams. Silliphant was one of the most highly regarded and successful writer/producers in Hollywood. He had written the cult TV series *Route 66*, and his credits eventually included *The Towering Inferno*, *The Poseidon Adventure*, and an Oscar for *In the Heat of the Night*. Despite the fact that he hired lots of actors, Silliphant had great difficulty getting to Bruce, and to become his pupil he had to go through what was, in effect, an audition.

Bruce Lee first came to Silliphant's attention through a story that was making the rounds in Hollywood. The story went that Bruce had met the singer Vic Damone in his Las Vegas hotel suite after one of the singer's performances. Damone had an interest in the martial arts, but the singer insisted that a tough Italian street brawler would always beat a slightly built Oriental. Damone had two huge bodyguards who also had a low opinion of the martial arts and they were enlisted to prove the point.

Bruce agreed to be tested and asked that one guard be placed behind the door to the suite, with the second man about five feet behind him, smoking a cigarette. Bruce explained that when he came through the door, the first man was to try and stop him. The cigarette was there to represent a holstered gun. Bruce told Damone that before the singer could count to five, he would be through the door and knock the cigarette from the second guy's mouth. Bruce had given them a further advantage by telling them exactly what he was going to do, forfeiting the element of surprise.

'If I succeed,' said Bruce, 'will you take this as an acceptable example of the effectiveness of the martial arts?'

'Sure,' came the disdainful reply.

Bruce left the room and the singer told his guards to go easy on the little Chinese guy. 'Just knock him on his ass with one good shot.'

Suddenly there was a loud wrench as the door flew clear off its hinges, taking the first guard with it, then Bruce followed through by kicking the cigarette out of the second guard's mouth while he was frozen in place.

The singer only managed the comment, 'Holy shit.'

After three months of searching, Silliphant succeeded in finding Bruce, via the *Green Hornet* producer William Dozier. In an

August 1980 article for *Kick Illustrated*, Stirling Silliphant wrote
in detail about their meeting and the events that followed:

Bruce had a school in the Chinese center of Los Angeles. It
was very low profile, with no exterior signs. You had to know
its location in advance and you had to be invited; you couldn't
just walk in off the street. So first I had to track Bruce down.
Eventually, I called Bill Dozier, the producer of *The Green
Hornet*, which by that time had already gone off the air. He put
me in touch with someone who knew where he was.

I called him and said, 'I've been looking for you for three
months; I want to study with you.'

Bruce said, 'Well, I don't really teach; I only have one or
two private students.'

Aside from Steve McQueen and maybe one or two others,
Bruce wasn't into teaching privately. In order to discourage
Hollywood dilettantes he charged $250 an hour. He wanted to
make the cost of lessons prohibitive so that whoever took one
would damn well concentrate on the business in hand. He
didn't charge these prices just for the sake of charging, but to
place value on his instruction. It was an Asian attitude, a way of
showing that the lesson has worth and the fee is merely the
token of this, not the point of it.

I recall the moment of my first meeting with Bruce above all
others. He arrived at my office at Columbia Pictures on Gower
Street like the winds around the outside of a hurricane. At the
time I was about fifty, but not flabby; I was in pretty good
shape but nothing like the condition I was later to achieve after
three years training with him. Bruce asked how old I was.
When I told him he was appalled, even though he added,
grudgingly, that I didn't look that old. He said he didn't know
if he wanted to teach anyone that old, it seemed pointless. But
then he added that it wasn't unusual for people in China to
begin training in martial arts at the age of sixty and said that it
would depend on my speed and reflexes.

So he brought out a catcher's mitt.

He said, 'I'm going to hold this out. Hit it as hard as you can.'

So I did. I used all my boxing knowledge, torqued my hips and gave it my best shot.

'Man, that sure wouldn't hurt anyone, would it?' was his response.

So I tried again.

'I will say that you've got speed and your reflexes are good,' he conceded. 'But I have to tell you, you could hit someone and they wouldn't even know it. I can tell we've got a lot of work to do with you.'

Even so, he agreed to start instructing me, but I think it was because of my enthusiasm more than anything else.

The first time I went to Bruce's house in Culver City there were some people from his downtown studio; they were nearly all young Chinese. The entire practice session was devoted to timing. Bruce wanted to determine how long it would take for each of us, from a given instant, to close the gap to a heavy bag and land what he considered an effective kick. He wanted to see what we would have done in a real situation. The difference in timing among us all was amazing. I found, to my ego's delight, that of everyone there, even though I was twenty or thirty years older than those downtown dudes, I had the fastest time.

I often went to his house in Culver City; at this point we were working out three or four times a week. No matter how hard I worked, how much I exercised, how much I sparred, or how much I ran, I never stopped aching. I mean, there were times when I woke up in the morning and wished I was dead, so overwhelming and total was the pain from every aching muscle. I remember arriving at Bruce's house one day and being unable to get out of my car. When I started to move my leg to get out, the pain exploded through my whole body. That's how wracked-up I was from these work-outs.

Bruce finally came out and said, 'What are you sitting there for?'

I said, 'I can't move, I ache too much.'

He pulled the car door open and said, 'Get out!'

Well, when you're dealing with a master you get out fast, because you know that if you don't he's going to pull you out and it's going to hurt even more. So, painfully, I pulled myself out of the car.

Bruce then said, 'You know, in ten minutes you're going to feel great. What you're doing is like diving into a cold ocean with a wet suit on. There's that first shock of cold, then everything warms up. The first minute you test all of your muscles, they're going to hurt. After that you'll feel better.'

He was right, of course.

I found his training methods fascinating. His methods changed with every lesson he taught. They weren't structured, always spontaneous and improvisational. The first thing he did with me was concentrate on body movement and 'bridging the gap', the relationship between you and your opponent. Then we started on the hand movements. He wanted to introduce me to the historic background on the use of hands, wrists and arms. Bruce always said that the leg is the more powerful weapon, but the one who can punch best will win.

He taught me the wing chun sticking hands technique and we did that blindfold. Joe Hyams and I found it fascinating that when we were blindfolded and followed Bruce's instructions, we felt the power of this defense. It was almost impossible for anyone to force his way through to the target, into your face or body. The more he forced, the more you reached him. The sticking hands help a weaker person to nullify an attack by a stronger person. If you are really good at it, it's almost impenetrable, extremely difficult for an opponent to land a blow above the waist, which in turn might force the opponent into a low-line attack, for which you're prepared.

Bruce taught me to dissect time into infinite degrees. It's what he called playing between the keys of the piano. It's the understanding that you actually have worlds of time within seconds to do something unanticipated while your opponent is already committed to his announced [telegraphed] action. Almost to the point where the fist is at the tip of your nose, there's still time to react. The only thing that can defeat you is lack of understanding and appropriate movement based on this principle. You must do a helluva lot of work to arrive at this stage of cool thinking. But if you can attain it, you won't be defeated just because an opponent is bigger, stronger or meaner, only if he thinks in the way you do.

Bruce and I were working out in his garage one day. He had a few friends from Hong Kong there who were exponents of sticking hands. Bruce wanted to see what I could do with these guys. So we put on soft gloves, because he wanted us to spar full contact, and he disallowed any kicking. So we went at it. By that time I had been with Bruce for nearly two years and I found it embarrassingly easy to hit these guys, to the point where I did so at will. I was hitting each opponent continually in the face, and I wasn't being hit myself. Bruce told me later that both of his friends had been disgraced, but he was so proud of having taught me. I won because of the spontaneous reaction [contact reflex] that he'd instilled in me – instinctive, spontaneous reaction without conscious thought.

Once when Bruce was accompanying Stirling Silliphant on a three-mile run, towards the end Bruce said that they should do a couple of extra miles. The writer protested that he was older and couldn't do it, and after an extra five minutes' running, Silliphant's head was pounding.

'If I run any more, I'll have a heart attack and die,' he gasped.

'Then die!' said Bruce.

This made Silliphant so mad that he went the extra miles.

Later, in the showers, Bruce explained. 'If you always put limits on yourself and what you can do, physical or otherwise, you might as well be dead. It will spread over into your work, your morality, your entire being. There are no limits, only plateaux.

But you must not stay there, you must go beyond them. If it kills you, it kills you.'

During 1968 and 1969, Stirling Silliphant succeeded in getting Bruce some bit-part acting work. He made minor appearances in TV episodes of the detective series *Ironside*, in which he played a martial arts teacher, and the sitcom *Blondie*. In *Here Come the Brides* Bruce had a non-fighting cameo role, and he was also the technical advisor for the Matt Helm detective thriller *The Wrecking Crew*, which starred Dean Martin and Roman Polanski's wife, Sharon Tate.

Despite Silliphant and others being willing to help him, there weren't that many opportunities. There were very few parts in Hollywood that called for Chinese actors outside of the usual stereotypes. Silliphant realized that Bruce would need something to be written especially for him, then they would have to overcome the problem of getting a studio to back the idea with hard cash.

Silliphant was just completing a script for *A Walk in the Spring Rain* for Columbia, in which Anthony Quinn and Ingrid Bergman were set to star. Although it was a love story, Silliphant contrived to include a fight sequence, the problem being that the story was set in the mountains of Tennessee, where there aren't that many Chinese martial artists! In the end he managed to get Bruce involved by having him choreograph the fight. This wasn't simply for Bruce's benefit, though, it was also so that Silliphant could continue his training schedule.

Just as happened with Vic Damone's bodyguards, Bruce's ability was openly doubted by the two rough rednecks whose fight Bruce was due to supervise. Silliphant elected to clear a few things up straightaway and organize a demonstration, which resulted in the two stuntmen being side-kicked, in turn, almost clear across a swimming pool.

Eventually Silliphant did manage to write an acting part for Bruce, that of Winslow Wong in the 1969 detective feature *Marlowe*, and although Bruce was only in a couple of scenes, it marked his debut appearance in a full-length Hollywood picture. The film starred James Garner as the hard-boiled private detective Philip Marlowe, in a script based on Raymond Chandler's novel *The Little Sister*. In the story, Bruce works as a heavy for the villain of the piece, and one scene was specifically written to show off Bruce's athleticism. He comes in to smash up Garner's office, culminating in a stunning kick high above his head to shatter a light fixture. After that, Marlowe's handling of Bruce Lee's character is quite unrealistic and unconvincing. Standing on the edge of a balcony he taunts Wong by casting doubts on his manhood, then simply steps aside to avoid the flying kick that sends Wong sailing off the edge of the roof to his death.

Aside from the acting jobs cooked up by Stirling Silliphant, Bruce's only income was from his teaching and a trickle of royalties from *The Green Hornet*, yet despite money problems and with Linda pregnant again, Bruce decided it was time to buy a new house. At first he set the budget at $30,000, but soon realized that it fell far short of what he had in mind. Bruce felt the need to provide a good life for his growing family, and it was difficult for him to admit that he couldn't afford it. He also felt that he belonged with his successful friends in the movie business, so reasoning that it was only a matter of time before he joined them, he went to look over a bungalow just off Mulholland Drive in the upmarket Bel Air district.

Mulholland Drive winds and dips for twenty miles along the crest of a ridge that runs from Hollywood to the Pacific Coast at Malibu through some of the most desirable real estate in Los Angeles. To the north, there are views across the San Fernando Valley, while to the south lie the canyons and spectacular vistas of the city and ocean. The Bel Air estate is entered through gates on Sunset Boulevard or Mulholland Drive. Roscomare Road is lined with detached bungalows, with gardens of cypress, bougainvillea and hibiscus. There are no sidewalks, because no one walks in Bel Air. The air is warm and still and there's a feeling of space and calm. There can't be many better places to live in any city.

Although it needed work done, Bruce bought the bungalow at 2551 Roscomare Road and hung his training bags under the eaves at the back, but at $47,000 he was in way over his head and was soon struggling to meet the mortgage repayments. On top of this, the running costs were much higher than he was used to, so he didn't have any money left to furnish it properly. To add to his problems, the Internal Revenue Service was knocking on the front door . . . which had yet to be repainted. Yet when Bruce received a windfall of $8,000 from the sale of one of his father's properties in Hong Kong, instead of buying furniture or paying the bills, he bought a red Porsche and went racing along Mulholland Drive with Steve McQueen.

In a long letter dated 6 January 1969, Bruce Lee wrote to William Cheung, who was now living in Australia. He updated his friend on his activities over the previous ten years, discussing his career as a martial artist and his more recent forays into acting. He described his achievements in the field of martial arts as 'the most satisfying' to him, and he was justifiably proud that the importance of Chinese martial arts was now recognized thanks to the fact that all three American karate champions were studying under him. He went on to admit that he had lost faith in the traditional forms of Chinese martial arts, even wing chun, because 'basically, all styles are a form of land swimming'. Instead he was teaching a form that was closer to 'efficient street fighting with everything goes, wearing head gear, gloves, chest guard, shin and knee guards, etc.' Telling William he was calling this style jeet kune do, he wrote that the creation of this new style was 'a major event in my life'.

He went on to say, 'I've been doing good too in the field of acting' and told William about *The Green Hornet* as well as his most recent role in MGM's *Little Sister*, which was due to be released later that year. He informed his friend that he was setting up a production company 'with a few important backers here in the States' which would focus on producing martial art films and television series. Describing his home in Bel Air, which was perched on top of a hill, he joked that while he might be enjoying plenty of fresh air, running up and down the hillside was 'tough on the calves'.

Despite the upbeat tone of his letter, Bruce was only too aware that he had more to do than simply convince his old friends that he was now a great success. Although he had always taken a fiercely positive attitude to life, whether he called it faith, confidence, determination, ambition or a vision that things would work out, no longer mattered. Bruce Lee had spent sixteen long years developing his skills and perfecting an art that, so far, no more than a handful of people had benefited from, and he had just spent $47,000 on a new home. Now, things just *had* to work out.

# 16

## The Silent Flute

In the habit of making predictions about his future, Bruce Lee said that he would make kung fu known throughout the world, but he also knew beyond any doubt that the only way he could do this was by making films. Though he had allies, the fact that they agreed that he had all the qualities needed but could find no outlet for them only made things worse. In addition, Bruce also had the same directness in the film world that he had with the martial arts fraternity: he always said exactly what he thought. Sadly this didn't win him many new friends in an industry whose wheels run smoother when oiled by bullshit. Nobody knew quite what to do with him, and more to the point, nobody was willing to risk money on an unknown actor who also happened to be Chinese. More than once it must have made Bruce question why he'd fought against his own countrymen for the right to teach kung fu to Westerners.

If an opportunity wasn't going to arise naturally, then just as his motivation had created his abilities, so it would also create the opportunities to use them. In short, he would go to Hollywood with a film. Bruce realized that a starring role was out of the question, but reasoned that a stronger supporting role than the one he'd had in *Marlowe* would reveal enough of his talents to open the door further. He already had an idea for a film which he had quite literally dreamed up.

For some years, Bruce had been having a recurring dream about 'a seeker', a character who he'd come to realize was himself, and these dreams had left enough of an impression for him to have made a few notes about them. Bruce wanted to use these notes as the basis of a screenplay, which he now asked Stirling Silliphant to write.

*The Silent Flute* would tell the story of a martial artist called Cord who seeks a book which is said to contain the ultimate truths about fighting. Every five years a competition is held to pass it on to another person. When Cord finally obtains it, he has no need to look inside: the journey itself has been his enlightenment. Along the way he has to fight battles with a number of characters, all of whom represent his different weaknesses, and all of these characters were to be played by Bruce Lee.

Rhythm Man is a skilled martial artist who travels with several musicians, and his greatest asset is the broken rhythm of his movements, which he uses to confuse opponents. Monkey Man is a fighter who is known to gouge out eyeballs; the fight with him is brutal and it serves to unite Cord with his animal instincts. A fierce growl signifies the entrance into the story of Panther Man, who represents the fear of death. Ah Sahm, a blind flute player and martial artist, meets with Cord at different points until it's revealed that he is not an enemy but a projection of Cord's enlightened self, drawing him forward. One disturbing scene involves Ah Sahm killing a child, who he says would have grown up to be a tyrant.

After Cord has proved himself, he meets with the book's current holder, Yamaguchi. Various other seekers attempt to defeat him, but it is not until Cord engages him that he discovers the secret. Cord and Yamaguchi engage eye contact and stare at each other until Yamaguchi concedes that Cord's spirit is the stronger, telling him that the highest form of fighting is no fighting at all, as Cord is presented with the book. Although the lead role would be played by a star name, it was already clear that Bruce was going to dominate the action.

Bruce wanted Steve McQueen to play the starring role of

Cord, so he and Silliphant went to talk to the actor. McQueen, who had never really stuck to the discipline of training with Bruce, made the excuse that he was too busy, but as Bruce became more enthusiastic and pressed him to get involved, the real reason emerged.

'Be honest,' said McQueen, 'this is a film to make Bruce Lee into a star. I like you, but I'm not here to make you a star. I'm not going to carry you on my back.'

McQueen's words burned so deeply they would never be forgotten, though Bruce said nothing and he and Silliphant left soon after.

Outside, he turned to Silliphant and said, 'I'm going to be bigger than he is.' Then, more quietly, he repeated the same vow to himself.

The two went back to James Coburn and told him the situation. Coburn said he was with them and offered to play the lead role himself, but now it was Silliphant's turn to get cold feet and try to pull back from the project, saying he was already up to his ears with writing commitments.

*The Silent Flute* began as an idea to make a definitive martial arts film which would give Bruce the exposure he needed, but now other pressures were mounting and there was more at stake. Not only was Bruce becoming increasingly concerned about getting his break in pictures, his income from teaching and bit parts didn't cover his huge mortgage. Bruce needed to make some money soon or he'd be in danger of losing the house. *The Silent Flute* went from being a good idea to a necessity to an obsession. When it began to look as if the whole project would have to be abandoned, Bruce became distraught. He was about to lose both his chance of stardom and his ability to provide for his family. He always tried to picture the best possible outcome of any situation and not dwell on the more fearful possibilities, but his concerns became more acute with the birth of his daughter Shannon on 19 April 1969.

In an attempt to solve everybody's problems it was agreed that he should hire a scriptwriter to develop his ideas with Silliphant and Coburn, putting up the $12,000 fee. The new writer, however, managed to lose most of Bruce's plot by turning it into a jumble of science fiction and sex. He was fired and Silliphant's nephew had a try. Again, none of the three was happy with the outcome. As Silliphant saw Bruce becoming increasingly desperate he finally gave in and proposed a regular writing session three nights a week to dictate their ideas to his secretary. No excuses for absence would be accepted. Although this work was purely speculative, they met without fail at the appointed times, and before long a story began to come alive.

Despite the financial crisis looming, things were moving along well. Then one morning, as Bruce began his morning workout, he felt a stab of pain in his lower back and the barbell across his shoulders went crashing to the floor. Over the following days, heat and massage treatment brought no relief and the pain grew steadily worse until a doctor's examination was necessary. The final diagnosis wasn't good: Bruce had damaged a sacral nerve and was experiencing a severe muscle spasm. He asked the obvious question: how long would it be before he could start training again? The doctor advised complete rest.

Bruce found himself flat on his back, unable even to support himself upright, let alone support a family in a house he couldn't pay for. Meanwhile the bills began piling up. It wasn't simply that Bruce could no longer train or practise as a martial artist: he felt he had no future. To anyone, let alone someone with Bruce's energy and ambition, such a situation would be a nightmare. Only a few months earlier, it was Hollywood that had no idea what to do with Bruce Lee, now Bruce Lee had no idea what to do with himself. For perhaps the first time in his life, Bruce was truly frightened.

As he tried to acknowledge and go with his injury rather than resist it, he felt both his autonomy and self-esteem being eroded. At times he was close to exploding with frustration. For several weeks, he lived between the bed and the chair at his desk, fighting depression by drawing plans for a bed that would help him rest his injury better. He also began to write down the precepts by which he lived and worked, collating his notes, which were written in succinct paragraphs derived both from his own experiences and from the books where he found vital information or inspiration.

Unable to fight physically, just like the hero of *The Silent Flute*, Bruce had to battle his fears and doubts using his strength of will and mastery of his emotions. He thought that only through his self-belief would things work out, so he battled every negative thought as it arose by visualizing it written on a piece of paper, which he then mentally crushed into a ball and burned to a crisp. Every inner voice that said 'I can't' was replaced with one that said 'I can.' Every image of failure was replaced with one of success. Bruce once told Joe Hyams that he considered the mind a fertile garden in which anything that's planted – flowers or weeds – will grow. One of the most well-thumbed books in Bruce's library was Napoleon Hill's *The Law of Success*, and lesson six of this book counsels the positive use of the imagination and affirmation by creating a 'definite chief aim'.

In one of his darkest hours, Bruce sat down and wrote out the following:

### MY DEFINITE CHIEF AIM

I, Bruce Lee, will be the first highest-paid Oriental superstar in the United States. In return I will give the most exciting performances and render the best of quality in the capacity of an actor. Starting 1970, I will achieve world fame and from then onwards till the end of 1980 I will have in my possession $10,000,000. I will live the way I please and achieve inner harmony and happiness.

*Bruce Lee, 1969*

Having done that Bruce simply got up and began to train and teach again. While everyone assumed that he'd recovered, he was still in agonizing pain, he was just willing himself to carry on as if everything was all right.

At the invitation of his friend, tae kwon do pioneer Jhoon Rhee – who wanted to help get Bruce back on track – in early 1970 they made a brief promotional visit to the Dominican Republic. Bruce enjoyed the unpretentious character of the Dominicans but was exhausted by the constant attention of the children, who swarmed around him everywhere they went, after the success *The Green Hornet* had enjoyed there. Bruce took advantage of this by swiftly setting up an exhausting round of exhibitions, interviews and promotional appearances.

In one TV interview he responded to a question about his acting career:

> In terms of films, I've been in *Marlowe* and *The Green Hornet* TV series, as well as appearing as a guest in several others. Presently we have plans to make a movie with James Coburn, the star of *Our Man Flint*, and it will be the first martial arts picture ever filmed in the United States of America. The entire movie will be about martial arts, and I will supervise the script.

But during Bruce's dark times, Stirling Silliphant had quietly completed the script for *The Silent Flute* and presented it to Warner Brothers. The studio was willing to give it a shot, but only so long as the film was made in India, in order to free up money that previous Warners pictures had earned there but which the Indian government would not allow them to take out of the country. As Bruce began planning the trip Coburn and Silliphant shot each other a sidelong glance.

Almost a year after the idea for the film was first dreamed up, Bruce Lee, James Coburn and Stirling Silliphant flew to India to scout for locations. They landed in Bombay, flew on to New Delhi, then hired a car and driver to take them north, over dirt roads and through searing heat. From the moment they started looking, they knew that enormous changes would need to be

To save Bruce's pride further, it was agreed that no one else would find out about the arrangement. With neither qualifications nor experience, Linda could only get a minimum wage job. After a day parenting and managing the household, she worked from late afternoon to midnight, and soon her health began to suffer. Once Bruce had put Brandon and baby Shannon to bed, he spent the long evening hours alone reading, writing or in enforced contemplation, his back still racked with pain. It was not the best of times.

# 17

## *Longstreet*

Despite the failed trip to India, Stirling Silliphant again tried to help lift Bruce's career by writing a part for him in the pilot show for a new TV series called *Longstreet*. Silliphant had begun work on the script before they left for India, when Bruce was still frustrated by the delays with *The Warrior*, and the episode was even titled 'Way of the Intercepting Fist'. Written with help from Bruce, the story portrayed him as a martial arts instructor who teaches a blind detective how to defend himself. Silliphant then approached the head of Paramount TV, Tom Tannenbaum, who was in charge of developing the series and who trained in karate with Ed Parker, so had seen the Bruce Lee demonstration at the 1966 Long Beach International Karate Tournament.

Tannenbaum recalls:

I was very impressed with him and wanted to meet him. The kung fu or jeet kune do – whatever he was doing back then – I'd never seen before. Someone else in the industry had seen him perform at an earlier tournament and had tested him for the role in *The Green Hornet*. I got hold of a copy of that screen test and again was very impressed. He had an intensity in his eyes and he was extremely confident.

I called him up and told him I'd like to take lessons. Bruce said, 'Come on down to my school in Chinatown at nine o'clock on Sunday morning. Knock twice on the door.' So I did. There was a little spy panel on the door, which slid open and Bruce let me in. There was a small class going on, and as I waited I saw a notice on his desk which read, 'Show me a classical karateist and I'll show you a dead man.'

Then he came over and said, 'I'm going to hold this catcher's mitt; you hit it.' I weighed about 200 pounds and Bruce, at that time, weighed about 132. I hit it, and I hit it hard. Bruce said, 'Now you hold it.' Without even pulling his striking hand back, just using the torque of his body, he literally knocked me across the room. In fact, I hit the wall so hard a picture fell down. It was embarrassing, because all the students in the class looked at me. I was fascinated: I'd never met a man who weighed almost seventy pounds less than me but could knock me across the room.

Bruce said, 'That's the power. Now I'll show you the speed.' He put a nickel in my palm and said, 'Close your fingers before I grab it out of your hand.' He moved like lightning and I quickly clenched my fingers. When I opened my hand, the nickel was gone and in its place was a dime. That's all I had to see. I said, 'That's fine, I'm yours.' So I started taking lessons from Bruce.

In Silliphant's script, Mike Longstreet, played by James Franciscus, is present during a murder; but he's blind and can't make a positive identification on the evidence of his hearing alone. He tracks down the killer, a tough longshoreman, and plans to unmask him. Bruce plays an antiques dealer named Li who saves the blind detective from being forced off the dock by a gang. Longstreet wants to know how Li managed to do it and wants to learn how to fight like him and go after the killer. Li refuses, saying he has the wrong motives, but as the story develops, Li begins to teach Longstreet, working both on his attitude to life and on a fighting method, in preparation for the coming confrontation. Now Bruce only had to wait, yet again, for filming to begin.

In the meantime, Bruce took Brandon with him to Hong Kong to arrange for his mother to come and live in the US. But when he arrived in Hong Kong, he was astonished at the welcome he received. Twentieth Century Fox, anxious to turn a profit from what had been a relatively unsuccessful TV series in the States, had recently marketed *The Green Hornet* in Hong Kong and throughout Southeast Asia, three years after it had first been aired in America. When dubbed in Mandarin, the show broke ratings figures in Singapore and the Philippines, and it was Kato, not the Hornet, who was its acknowledged star. Much to Bruce's surprise, when he stepped off the plane he was surrounded by TV and newspaper reporters ready to boast of the local boy made good.

Hong Kong newspapers, radio and TV stations clamoured for interviews, and Bruce, along with Brandon, appeared on talk shows on Hong Kong's two TV stations. One show host, Joseph Lau, persuaded Bruce to overcome his aversion to doing tricks and Bruce leapt, kicked and broke four one-inch boards dangling in the air. Then five-year-old Brandon managed to break one almost as big as himself. After a year of inactivity, dreading that it might all be going wrong, Bruce's charm, wit and star quality were suddenly on tap again.

Seizing the moment, Bruce sent his boyhood friend Unicorn to probe his employers, the Shaw Brothers film studios, about a possible film offer. Bruce gave Unicorn information about his schools and copies of magazine articles to take to Shaw Brothers, but all the information was in English, so Unicorn first had to set about translating it.

To Westerners at the time, Chinese films veered between being too understated and too over-the-top, but when watching them one must remember that they are not acted realistically as Western films are. Film-making in the East stems from a long theatrical tradition, and the plots, set designs, costumes, gestures and expressions are rooted in the mime traditions of theatres like the Cantonese Opera Company, for whom Bruce's father used to act.

If a comparison can be made, similar elements are seen in the silent movies of Hollywood.

The Hong Kong film industry made these films the way Detroit made cars: on an assembly line, wrapping up a normal production in three days while a big-budget extravaganza might require a week. The Shaw Brothers – Runjy, Runme and Run Run – had almost singlehandedly set up the Hong Kong film industry and were the biggest studio outside of Hollywood and Europe, accounting for two thirds of the Chinese films produced in the world. Shaw Brothers Studios were a mixture of purpose-built sets and sound stages, where everything from pagodas to concentration camps was perched on a windy hillside overlooking Clearwater Bay. An average of seven features were permanently in production and the sound-dubbing rooms were shared on a tight schedule of three daily shifts.

The secret of Shaw Studios' success was a hard-nosed policy geared towards speed and economy. Films were shot without sound and, like Italian-made spaghetti Westerns, were later dubbed into whatever language was required. The films were often shot without a written script, being more or less made up by the crew as they went along and edited directly on camera with few retakes. Stories were lifted straight from Western films with little or no adaptation, in what the Cantonese called 'warming up yesterday's cold rice'. The emphasis was on 'fist and pillow' – violence and sex – and a director was lucky if he'd earned half the budget set aside to pay for the fake blood required for the more violent scenes.

Like the directors, writers and production crew, actors and actresses were also overworked and underpaid. Even so, local prospects were so poor that there was a waiting list to join Shaw Brothers' contract players. For a reasonable fee, Run Run Shaw would enrol them in the Southern Dramatic School – his own acting academy – where actors were expected to provide their own lunch and transport to and from locations. Furthermore, contracts were ironclad and could only be broken by leaving the profession or the country. With an air of benevolent paternalism, Run Run Shaw told one interviewer that a number of actors' suicides and breakdowns over the years had been caused by the sudden pressures of fame, adding that he was always available to assist if it looked as if anything like that was about to happen to one of their stars.

Shaw Brothers films were guaranteed good distribution as the studio also owned 140 movie theatres throughout Hong Kong, Singapore, Indonesia, Malaysia, Taiwan and parts of Vietnam and Burma – known as the Mandarin circuit. They also booked for an additional 500 theatres, including those in the Chinatowns of San Francisco, Los Angeles and New York. The Shaw dynasty embraced companies throughout Southeast Asia, with interests in real estate, banking, insurance, breweries and amusement parks. In fact, their only serious filmmaking rival was the Singapore-based Cathay organization, which looked ready to give them a run for their money until a plane crash over Taiwan claimed the lives of several of Cathay's top executives.

A slight, dapper, bespectacled man, Run Run Shaw was as sleek as he was slick. He ran his empire from a padded chair behind a desk that dwarfed him, in an elegantly austere office decorated with modern Chinese art. In the late 1960s, when one newspaper interviewer questioned Shaw about accusations of low wages and bad conditions, he brushed the questions aside with an elegant hand. He was more willing to explain his approach to filmmaking, though: 'If audiences want violence, we give them violence. If they want sex, we give them sex. Whatever the audience wants, we'll give them.'

Unhappily, it would appear that Run Run could not apply the same simple credo to his family's requirements. He told the same interviewer how he regretted that he could not spend more time with his grandchildren because he was compelled to spend so much time with some of his young actresses out of a strong sense of duty to the company. Lavish parties were thrown in a house surrounded by lush gardens on a quiet corner of the huge studio lot. Shaw owned several houses and country villas, so naturally he required a fleet of Rolls Royces, Cadillacs and Lincoln Continentals to travel between them. However Run Run did note, with great wisdom, that he could only travel in one of them at a time.

With Bruce Lee's translated publicity material in hand, Unicorn approached one of Shaw's senior executives, Mona Fong. She hadn't heard of Bruce Lee and neither had a director who was present in her office at the time, so Unicorn went directly to Run Run himself, with Bruce's proposal to do one picture for the studio for a fee of $10,000. In addition, Bruce insisted on the right to make script changes where necessary and to be solely responsible for arranging any fight action in the proposed film. The bemused mogul didn't know what to make of such a strongly worded proposal; it was so far outside his experience. Ironically, Hollywood thought Bruce was too different from everyone else, while the Hong Kong studio thought he was just the same as all the other actors in the Mandarin martial arts films that were their stock in trade.

By the time Shaw responded to his proposal, Bruce had already returned to the US, where he received a counter-proposal from Shaw in which he graciously noted Bruce's 'modest' success in the US and offered a seven-year contract for $2,000 a film – in other words, their standard junior actor's contract. Bruce politely declined.

Back in the US, Bruce began work on the episode of *Longstreet* in which he virtually plays himself. Entire sequences of the script amount to what is a lesson in his fighting method and philosophy, which makes it one of his most important works on screen.

> Mike Longstreet is getting a lesson in how to sidekick. Lee asks Longstreet to hold the air bag so that he can feel the depth of the kick. One of Longstreet's colleagues arrives just in time to see the detective sailing backwards through the air to land in a flower bed.
>
> 'Now what exactly is ... this thing you do?' says the colleague.

'In Cantonese,' replies Li, 'jeet kune do, the way of the intercepting fist.'

'Intercepting fist?'

'Or foot,' adds Li. 'Come on, touch me anywhere you can.'

As his opponent steps forward to throw a punch, Lee snaps out a low side kick to his kneecap.

'You see,' explains Li, 'to reach me, you must move to me. Your attack offers me an opportunity to intercept you. In this case I'm using my longest weapon, my side kick, against the nearest target, your kneecap. It can be compared to your left jab in boxing, except it's much more damaging.'

'I see,' says the friend nonchalantly. 'Well, speaking of a left jab—'

But Li blocks the sudden punch, having already been told the intention before the punch was even thrown. 'You see, from your thought to your fist, how much time was lost.'

Bruce used to explain to his students that a lot of martial arts are taught in the block-hit, one-two manner when it's more efficient to break the rhythm and perform a simultaneous block and hit. At an even more efficient level, awareness is so attuned that as soon as the opponent moves he can be intercepted and struck. At an even more refined level, even the intention of being attacked can be felt and neutralized before it is begun.

In the story, Bruce also teaches Longstreet to listen to what is going on around him, not just to move for the sake of moving but to relate it to what is going on. Li asks Longstreet if he can hear the bird that has been singing quietly in the background throughout their conversation. Because Longstreet is blind, Li cannot get him to become more aware of his peripheral sight, but he can get him to expand his overall awareness through listening more attentively. In writing *Longstreet*, Silliphant based the blind detective's lessons with Li on his own experiences, explaining, 'The first thing Bruce did with me was to concentrate on body movement and understanding the relationship between you and your opponent. At first, Bruce blindfolded me and made me move

improved Shaw's offer just enough to make Bruce bite. It was a simple deal: two pictures for a straight fee of $15,000, and Chow also included a generous one-way ticket to the location as part of the deal. Coburn and Silliphant advised Bruce against accepting the offer, saying that he should hold out for more, but Bruce was tired of waiting. After seeing previous opportunities slip away, he was determined not to lose this one and so signed the deal.

Bruce did his homework and viewed Golden Harvest's current batch of releases, then called Raymond Chow and asked him if that was the best he could do. This was one of Bruce's favourite tactics: putting a person of some authority on the back foot, and it meant that Chow had to explain and justify himself to Bruce rather than the other way round. In the end, though, the two found enough common ground for a workable relationship.

Once Run Run Shaw heard about Bruce's decision to work for Golden Harvest he countered with an improved offer, but Bruce had already signed and intended to honour the contract. Even so, a worried Chow tried to insist that Bruce fly directly to the Thai film location rather than risk temptation by going via Hong Kong.

Bruce asserted his autonomy by breaking his journey with an overnight stop in London – the only time he ever set foot on British soil. Feeling upbeat, and perhaps compensating for the inferior room he'd had in Bombay, he booked himself into a room at the Dorchester Hotel on Park Lane, though he decided not to eat there, electing instead to stroll down Piccadilly and into Chinatown to eat in one of the restaurants in Gerrard Street.

On arrival in Bangkok, Bruce was driven north to a film set in the remote village of Pak Chong. In the middle of the hot season, the small hotel was a hell-hole with no air-conditioning to alleviate the soaring heat and humidity. Even the water was polluted and there was no fresh food or mail service to speak of. Pak Chong was a place that only insect lovers might enthuse about, yet Bruce didn't complain. He was there to make a film called *The Big Boss*, and that was good enough for him.

# 18

## The Big Boss

*The Big Boss*'s budget was less than $100,000 which, at the time, wouldn't have paid for a sixty-second TV commercial in the US. Initially the star of the film was intended to be James Tien, then a major star in Hong Kong, but Bruce Lee's strong performance soon relegated Tien to second billing.

The simple plot of *The Big Boss* concerns the struggle of the Chinese community in Bangkok, who live in fear of Thai gangsters run by a Japanese boss. Bruce Lee plays Cheng Chao An, who has left behind a troubled life in China to start afresh in Thailand. In turning over a new leaf, Cheng has vowed to his mother that he will not get into any more fights and wears her locket to remind him of his promise. He is met in Thailand by his cousin, played by James Tien, and gets a job in the local ice factory, where his other cousins work. The factory turns out to be a cover for a drug smuggling operation, and workers who discover the truth, including two of Cheng's cousins, are murdered. Discovering Cheng's fighting skills, the 'big boss' of the title attempts to lure him into his web with a promotion and prostitutes, but eventually a showdown ensues between Cheng and the boss.

In the first week of filming, Bruce found it harder and harder to keep his frustration in check. The equipment used for filming was old and in bad repair and the 'script' consisted of a few basic ideas scribbled on scraps of paper. The director, Wu Chai Wsaing, had a violent temper and screamed and ranted at the entire cast and crew until the production manager – the same Mrs Lo Wei who had signed Bruce to the Golden Harvest contract – could take no more. Mrs Lo Wei called Raymond Chow and demanded the director be replaced, and by a happy coincidence, one of Chow's other directors, a certain *Mr* Lo Wei, had just finished a film in Taiwan and was duly dispatched to Thailand.

The new director proved to be no better than the first. A compulsive gambler, Lo Wei was far more concerned with what was going on at the racetrack than what was happening on the film set. Because sound wasn't recorded at the same time as the action was filmed, Lo Wei arranged to have horse race commentary booming across the set while the actors attempted to play a scene. Unsurprisingly, Bruce became incensed by Lo Wei's lack of commitment to the picture.

After Bruce twisted his ankle landing awkwardly from a jump, he was only able to drag his injured leg, so in several scenes he had to be filmed in close-up. A recent cut in his hand had still not healed and he needed rest and injections for back pain after every scene. In addition to this discomfort, he was racked with aches and fever and had difficulty keeping food down. Lo Wei responded by calling Bruce a hypochondriac and filming continued.

During filming, Bruce kept trying to improve the poor script. Although Han Yin Chieh, the actor who plays the boss, was the official fight coordinator of the film, Bruce also took control of his own fight scenes, and whenever there was a dispute, he would disrupt the situation by some little strategy, such as 'losing' one of his contact lenses while filming in an ice-cutting factory where there were thousands of tiny ice chips on the floor.

Other scenes were filmed in a local brothel which was both dirty and smelly. With the exception of Thai actress Malalene, who plays Wu Mang, the prostitutes in the film were real prostitutes who were used to being paid less than a dollar a trick.

\*

While Bruce was isolated deep in Thailand, *Longstreet* opened the autumn TV season in the US to good reviews. At last, Bruce Lee and Stirling Silliphant had realized a small part of what they had been hoping to achieve together for many years.

Bruce's episode generated more fan mail than the rest of the entire series, proving that Stirling Silliphant was right when he claimed it was Bruce's first good film and one of the best martial arts shows ever seen on TV. Tom Tannenbaum immediately tried to track down Bruce to get him to agree to appear in further episodes of *Longstreet*, but no one could get a message to him as he was filming hours away from the nearest city. In the end, the situation worked to Bruce's advantage, since the telegrams meant that Golden Harvest executives weren't slow to notice that US producers were chasing their new actor.

On his return to Hong Kong, as he ploughed through the pile of telegrams waiting for him, Bruce found offers to appear in three further episodes of *Longstreet* for $1,000 a show. Knowing that a second picture for Golden Harvest was already in the bag, Bruce asked Paramount to double their offer and they agreed. Linda could now quit her job, but they were still not out of trouble over the house repayments.

When Bruce returned to Los Angeles, it turned out that the three *Longstreet* episodes in question had long been written and, in view of Bruce's surprise success in the first episode, Paramount had quickly tried to work him into further stories. Bruce found himself making brief, hastily written appearances that were little more than walk-on parts, but despite this, there was a feeling that his luck was about to 'turn'. Paramount made a new option offer for an as yet unspecified television project and, having more or less excluded him from their earlier plans, Warners briefly reconsidered taking the risk of making him the lead role in *The Warrior* TV series.

More than once Bruce mulled over everything that was happening. What was the best course for him to take at such a critical point? How were audiences going to react to *The Big Boss*? Should he keep his options open? There were more questions than these to be considered, yet Bruce felt increasingly certain about one thing: his time had come.

Although Bruce was met only by a local Boy Scout band when he returned to Hong Kong, there was a big enough crowd of journalists to indicate that even before *The Big Boss* had opened, his star was rising. On 3 October 1971, together with Raymond Chow and his partner Leonard Ho, Bruce and Linda sat and waited for the midnight premiere of the film. They joked a little, trying to ease the apprehension they all felt. Hong Kong audiences would openly jeer at a film they didn't like and were even known to attack their seats with knives if it was really poor. When the film ended, a stunned silence lasting a few seconds was followed by an outburst of euphoria and complete uproar. Bruce was mobbed as he tried to leave the theatre and the next day's press was equally ecstatic.

It's obvious from the opening credits that *The Big Boss* was made on a shoestring budget, since the credits are drawn by a rather shaky hand and there are enough wobbly camera shots to suggest that most of it was shot without any retakes. In addition to this, canned cocktail-jazz muzak adds a bizarre note to the death scenes, but *The Big Boss* is still better acted and plotted than any comparable film of the time and a half-credible story line strings the action sequences together.

To Western eyes *The Big Boss* may have seemed like one more in a long line of cheap exploitation films streaming out of Asia, but in the context of the Hong Kong film industry whose staple fare was windmilling fist fights and buckets of blood, the film was a breakthrough. Bruce used his American experience to give his and the other characters some human touches, and what to the West might appear overstated, clumsy or even camp was the closest anyone had come to realism in the Asian film world. More importantly, the Mandarin audiences had a genuine star. Bruce Lee wasn't a jobbing actor who'd been put through his paces at Shaw's drama academy, he had natural charisma. The fight scenes alone would have been enough to make him a star in the East, and to prove they weren't merely the result of camera trickery or slick editing, Bruce insisted on long takes in which the camera runs for up to half a minute on a single shot. Though the exaggerated feats of the old-style Mandarin films are not absent, Bruce managed to include the kind of action that had never been seen on film before.

From the audience reaction at the premiere, Bruce knew the film would do well, but he hadn't anticipated a runaway hit, and neither, of course, had Run Run Shaw, who was left to bemoan his fate. 'Bruce Lee was just another actor,' he sighed heavily. 'How could I know?'

Within three weeks of its release, *The Big Boss* smashed all box office records, earning over $HK3 million. The film then played 875 performances in Hong Kong before going on to break records throughout the Mandarin circuit.

While Bruce prepared to make his second film, Golden Harvest provided a small furnished apartment at 2 Man Wan Road, in the Waterloo Hill area of Kowloon. The elevators in the building rarely worked, but rather than have everyone trudge up and down the stairs, Bruce turned it into a game in which they ran up the thirteen flights. Wu Ngan, Bruce's 'adopted' brother, lodged with the family and soon became Bruce's steward, then later, when Wu Ngan married, his wife joined them too. Two-year-old Shannon started attending a local nursery school, while six-year-old Brandon went to La Salle, the school from which Bruce had been expelled some years earlier.

# 19

## *Fist of Fury*

In 1971, before the premiere of *The Big Boss*, Bruce Lee had already started work on his second film, *Fist of Fury*. The film was a hymn of revenge that played on the deep animosities between the Chinese and Japanese, which are similar to those between the Greeks and the Turks, or the Catholics and Protestants in Ireland. As with *The Big Boss*, this second picture went into production with the story little more than an outline of how the action might develop. Even so, *Fist of Fury* was completed in six weeks, again with a budget of $100,000, and with many of the same faces that were seen in *The Big Boss*.

The story begins with a real historical event, the death of a Chinese martial arts teacher Ho Yuan Chia in Shanghai in 1908, where the Japanese had established a strong political presence. Ho was a stevedore of extraordinary strength and ability who once routed an entire troop of Japanese challengers. Bruce Lee plays Chen Zhen, a former student of the old master, who arrives back at his old school to pay his respects to his teacher, only to find that he has just died. At the funeral a distraught Chen flings himself into the grave and tries to claw open the coffin, wailing, 'How can a healthy man die?'

The master's memory is insulted when Wu, a reptilian Chinese who works as a translator for the Japanese martial arts association, presents the students with a tablet inscribed: 'To the Sick Nation of Eastern Asia'. He tries to goad Chen into retaliating with one of the worst unintentional dubbing puns ever heard in a film: 'What's the matter? Are you yellow or something?' Chen is so enraged that despite his teacher's code, he goes to the Japanese club and single-handedly wipes out the entire membership, smashing the insulting tablet. The Japanese association's president demands Chen's arrest, so Chen goes into hiding. Lo Wei, who was also directing this film, played the role of the detective on Chen's trail.

Chen discovers that two Japanese infiltrators played a part in poisoning his teacher, but what's not immediately obvious to Western audiences is how Chen achieves this: by noticing the difference between Chinese and Japanese-style underwear. Chen kills them and hangs their bodies from a lamppost outside the house of the Japanese consul, but in retaliation, the Japanese wreck the Chinese school, showing no mercy to the women students and desecrating the shrine to the master's memory.

Meanwhile, the Japanese school holds a welcoming party for a Russian wrestler who has left his country. Leering at belly dancers and guzzling sake, the Japanese insult their Chinese collaborator, Wu, who crawls away drunk. Outside, he staggers to a rickshaw, which happens to be driven by Chen, who's now in one of his many disguises. Chen picks up the whole rickshaw and holds it and its passenger several feet in the air to make him confess that it was Suzuki, the head of the Japanese school, who ordered the murder of his teacher – stunts and impossible feats like this were all included at Lo Wei's insistence. As Chen kills Wu, more badly translated dialogue has Wu whining, 'Why is everyone always picking on me?' before he too is hung from a lamppost.

Disguised as a Japanese telephone repairman, Chen gains entry to the Japanese school – Bruce posing as a Japanese was something that sent the Chinese fans wild with delight. Once inside the school, Chen fights his way past a swordsman and the Russian wrestler to the inner sanctum, where he avenges his teacher by killing Suzuki in combat. Chen returns to his own school and sees that a massacre has taken place, but when the police arrive, threatening to close the school down under pressure from the Japanese authorities, Chen emerges from his hiding place and surrenders to the Shanghai police, with the assurance that his fellow students will be spared and his school's honour will remain intact. At the school gates, a row of armed police level their rifles at him. Bare-chested and defiant, Chen runs headlong at them, launching himself in a glorious death leap into a hail of bullets – an image lifted straight from the final scene of *Butch Cassidy and the Sundance Kid.*

From the start of filming the already strained relationship between Bruce Lee and Lo Wei went from bad to worse. Bruce was furious with Lo Wei's continuing lack of attention – patient forbearance wasn't Bruce's strongest quality and there were several clashes as the film progressed. In Thailand this hadn't been too damaging, but now that Bruce was a local hero and filming was taking place in the heart of Hong Kong, the press was quick to make the feud public knowledge. Lo Wei had started in the film industry as an actor in 1948, before becoming a director in 1957. He had made over eighty low-budget feature films, mostly for Shaw Brothers before Raymond Chow brought him to Golden Harvest, and he was not about to be told his business by a young upstart who was only making his second film. It wasn't long before the two couldn't agree on anything.

Much of the film's budget was spent creating the two Japanese buildings and gardens, complete with bridges and pools. One week was spent on location at a nearby park, and there Lo Wei had to contend with local street gangs, whose leaders demanded payment for using 'their bit' of road. This 'protection money' was usually paid, much to the annoyance of Bruce, who had to be restrained from seeing off the hustlers.

The production values of *Fist of Fury* were higher than those of *The Big Boss*. Spaghetti Western-style soundtrack music was added, but far more evocative were the noises made by Bruce – strangely beautiful cries that sound like a wild cat or screeching bird and which only enhanced his animal grace. In the English language version, some of the effect is lost to the inappropriate voice used to dub the speaking parts, but at least the animal cries are Bruce's. In addition to the power of his fighting action and cries, some of Bruce's facial expressions have an almost elemental power to them. At times his face registers an extraordinary blend of emotions – shock at taking a life, the ecstasy of revenge, regret that it has to be this way – as well as the strange gaze that enters his eyes as he kills an opponent in scenes where the fist of the title appears almost to have a will of its own. Yet all of this was overshadowed by his introduction of the weapon that will forever be associated with him: the nunchakas. Although the nunchakas had made a brief appearance in *The Green Hornet* series, *Fist of Fury* marks their first real use.

The nunchakas are two short hardwood sticks connected by a flexible chain or cord. When one of the clubs is grasped, the other can be swung to strike with up to 1,600 pounds of force at the point of impact. The shock of this impact is not transferred to the club held in the striker's hand which is isolated by the short connecting cord.

The 'chucks' that Bruce Lee uses on screen are lighter than the heavy wooden weapons normally used for combat, and these lighter versions could be spun and switched even faster, adding to the excitement. When the swooping noises of rushing air were overdubbed later, the scenes became even more impressive. Although Bruce was still not the film's official fight coordinator, his influence is overwhelming, and nowhere more than in the nunchaka scenes, although these were edited out in many countries and the weapon itself was banned in many states, including Bruce's home state of California.

The nunchakas didn't start life as a weapon but as a tool, used by farmers on the island of Okinawa for flailing rice to separate the grain from the husk. When the Japanese invaded Okinawa they confiscated all the weapons on the island. The islanders, a melting-pot community at the heart of several trading routes, had over the centuries merged fighting skills from China with those of other Asian cultures, and resourcefully they developed a system of fighting by employing their farming tools as weapons. Also on the island were many Chinese families, including several Shaolin monks who had set up home there, and the Okinawan rebels persuaded these monks to teach them the secrets of Chinese hand-to-hand combat.

Eventually the Japanese discovered this method and absorbed the fighting techniques into their own culture, and this new style was called karate, a literal translation of 'Chinese hand'. The fact that karate, barely forty years old, was far better known in America than kung fu, which was many centuries old, was due to karate being brought back by US servicemen after the war. The fact that karate originated with Shaolin monks, who had taught their skills to the Okinawans in order to help them repel the Japanese invaders, was not wasted on Bruce Lee.

The opening scenes of *Fist of Fury* dug deep into Chinese popular feelings. The Chinese had been plundered and exploited for centuries by stronger foreign powers. For hundreds of years the relationship between the Chinese and Japanese was one of open hostility, punctuated by regular periods of war. Japan was responsible for the territorial division of China at the turn of the century and went on to humiliate China, Hong Kong and the rest of the Far East during the Second World War. It was during this war – only thirty years before the film was made – that the Japanese performed atrocious medical 'experiments' such as cutting their living Chinese prisoners in half.

Feelings of resentment for tourists were often hidden behind smiling faces, but real hatred was reserved for the Japanese. Despite his years in the United States, Bruce was well aware of national feelings and played on them freely, taking great satisfaction from portraying a lone kung fu artist wiping out an entire school of karate practitioners. When Bruce Lee cast his gaze over his Japanese opponents and declared, 'Now you listen to me, and

I'll only say it once: we are not sick men,' audiences went wild, leaping to their feet or on to the seats to howl their approval and delight.

A similar standing ovation occurred when Chen shattered the 'No Dogs and Chinese Allowed' sign at the entrance to the park; elderly members of the audience who had actually lived in Shanghai during that oppressive era openly cried and embraced each other in joy. Strictly speaking, the existence of the infamous sign is probably a myth, although rules to that effect were certainly in place and would have been evident to park visitors.

En route to the film's climax, Bruce dispatches the samurai who killed his master and finishes off the Russian fighter. By the end of the film, Bruce had advanced from being a screen fighter who was as good as he appeared to much more. He had done something dreamed of by every politician: he was a household name and a national hero.

In the weeks following the release of *Fist of Fury*, the atmosphere on the streets of Hong Kong was akin to that in England after the English football team beat Germany in the 1966 World Cup Final. It wasn't simply a matter of winning a game of football, just as what was happening on the streets of Hong Kong in 1971 was more than simply popular reaction to an exciting new movie. It was a matter of national pride and triumph over a bitter rival. In that sense, *Fist of Fury* was no different from the great rash of war films that came out in the 1950s, in which the Germans and Japanese are always villainous caricatures. Bruce Lee had struck a nerve that ran right into the heart of his countrymen, and through his films he replaced a sense of self doubt and inferiority with one of dignity, identity and victory. To their astonishment, the new hero of the Hong Kong Chinese was Chinese!

In its first four-week run *Fist of Fury* broke the records set by *The Big Boss* and took over $HK4 million at the box office. Outside the theatres, tickets changed hands for up to $50. In Singapore, the film had to be withdrawn for a week while traffic police found a way of dealing with the numbers of people clamouring to see the film. In the Philippines, the government withdrew the film in order to give some of their own movies a chance to earn some money.

Though hardly a soul in the West was aware of it, Bruce Lee had become the fastest rising star in the world and the film industry's hottest property. Suddenly he was unable to walk down a street or eat in a restaurant without drawing a crowd. While young men everywhere in Southeast Asia wanted to be Bruce Lee, it seemed that every young girl wanted to marry him. And it wasn't only young people who were aware of him. A middle-aged Englishman in a neat business suit who was interviewed as he left a theatre showing the film said, 'He's in a league of his own. It's a question of body movement and choreography; the timing, the overcoming of human limitations.'

But there were troublesome aspects to Bruce's instant celebrity, including a rapid increase in the number of challenges to fight he received from every street punk wanting a moment of glory. Photos of Bruce appeared daily in the Chinese newspapers, alongside articles linking him to every local starlet, or revealing the latest twists in his running battle with Lo Wei.

The director had taken to calling himself Hong Kong's first 'millionaire director', while claiming all credit for the success of Bruce's films. But Lo Wei destroyed any credibility he might have had by claiming to have taught Bruce to fight on the set of *The Big Boss*, saying that while Bruce was a good street fighter he'd found it necessary to teach him how to fight on film.

The truth of the matter was that Bruce Lee had not only propelled Lo Wei to his ten minutes of glory, he'd single-handedly saved Golden Harvest and Raymond Chow from obscurity. Now that Bruce had fulfilled his two-picture contract for Chow, he was free to negotiate a new one, and producers across Southeast Asia were desperate to secure his name on a contract. People would stop Bruce in the street and hand him cheques for large sums, which he immediately tore up, knowing that if he cashed any of them he would have found himself committed to one project or another. Some producers were offering a reward of $10,000 to anyone who could get Bruce's signature on a contract. Run Run Shaw, who only a year previously had thought that $10,000 was too much to pay Bruce, now proposed the biggest pay rise in history by offering him twenty times that sum. When Bruce refused, a blank cheque followed.

More than one of Bruce's distant relatives was suddenly inspired to seek out their long-lost cousin, but all this served only to make Bruce wary. He no longer knew who to trust or who was trying to take advantage of him.

One thing was certain: Bruce Lee would no longer work like a hired hand for wages. He went to see Raymond Chow and suggested they become partners. Chow, realizing that Run Run Shaw was waiting for Bruce just down the road, rightly figured that half the profits from an association with Bruce was a lot better than none. The two men formed Concord Productions, with Bruce supposedly making the creative decisions while Chow was in charge of day-to-day business matters.

Unfortunately, Chow's first move was to ask Lo Wei to direct a new film with Bruce called *Yellow-Faced Tiger*, which was set to start filming in Japan in January 1972. Once again there was no script for the film and Bruce refused to commit to the film until there was one. Although they went through the charade of several abortive planning sessions, in truth, Bruce had no intention of letting Lo Wei anywhere near another of his pictures and had already said as much in public. Bruce declared that he wanted to write his own scripts and direct his own films, and he wanted a share of the profits too, because it was his appearance in the films that drew the crowds. No Hong Kong film actor had ever done this before, but Bruce had no respect for hack directors and believed his enthusiasm would result in a far better film than anything from Lo Wei's conveyor belt.

As Bruce began work on a film called *Way of the Dragon*, ripples spread throughout the Hong Kong film industry. Before Bruce decided to write and direct, actors had just taken their wages and done what they were told. And no matter how well a film did, only the producers saw any profit; everyone else took a salary, usually not a very good one. Now that Bruce had opened the door, other leading actors pressed for better pay and conditions, and the effect filtered all the way down the line as far as technicians and film crews. Not only did Bruce think it was fairer that key people got a share of the profits, he reasoned that it would increase everyone's enthusiasm and involvement in a project, which would in turn raise the standards of the films being made. That Bruce Lee's films captured international attention and resulted in Hong Kong films being more competently made was in no small part due to his revitalizing effect on an industry whose methods had become tired and routine. One Hong Kong newspaper commented, 'Bruce Li [sic] is clearly an asset amid a local film industry bankrupt in everything but quantity.'

It was during this period that Bruce gave interviews and wrote articles for the Far Eastern press. Taken together, they reveal both his ambitions and his dilemmas. Bruce found himself answering charges of glorifying violence for scenes like the one in *The Big Boss* where he splits a man's head in half with a saw. Bruce claimed that the way he portrayed it was simply action bordering on fantasy. The real violence, he said, was the slaughter happening in Vietnam. For Bruce, the problem was that all his audiences wanted from him was action; they saw him as a superhero. Bruce complained to the *Hong Kong Standard* that if he really expressed what he wanted to in his films, his audiences wouldn't understand him most of the time. His real ambition, he said, was to make films that were serious, philosophical and entertaining, and to take some responsibility for educating his audience.

Bruce saw the root problems of the Hong Kong film industry as its lack of quality, commitment and basic professionalism. He thought Mandarin films were overplayed with poor scripts, and he told *New Nation* – an English-language newspaper in Singapore – that he was often the only one who turned up to work on time, with other crew members drifing in up to an hour later. He declared he was as willing to invest as much energy in filmmaking as he had in martial arts, and he viewed his twelve years in the US as a period of preparation and growth. To those who said he was simply lucky, he replied that it was odd, but the harder he worked the luckier he was.

As Bruce basked in the attention, continuing to clarify his intentions and share his ambitions with the press, who now called him The King of Hong Kong, he was forced early in 1972 to sell the Bel Air home that had drained his money faster than it could be earned. It was sold at a small profit, still in need of some repair.

# 20

# Way of the Dragon

Bruce Lee had made two successful films in the East, but his ambitions still lay in the West. Even as he planned his third film, he anxiously awaited a decision from Warners and the ABC network about *The Warrior*. He wanted the part desperately and had set his mind on it so much that he told both his friends and the local press that matters were virtually settled. However, towards the end of 1971, an interview he did for Canadian TV indicated that things weren't going his way at all. The Canadian news reporter Pierre Berton, who was one of the first in the West to realize the new phenomenon that was Bruce Lee, flew to Hong Kong to interview Bruce.

**Berton**: Are you going to stay in Hong Kong and be famous, or are you going to the United States to be famous?

**Bruce**: I'm gonna do both. Because I have already made up my mind that in the United States, I think something of the Oriental, I mean the true Oriental, should be shown.

**Berton**: Hollywood sure as heck hasn't.

**Bruce**: You better believe it man. I mean it's always the pigtail and the bouncing around, chop-chop, you know, with the eyes slanted and all that.

**Berton**: Let me ask you about the problems that you face as a Chinese hero in an American series. Have people come up to you in the industry and said, 'Well, we don't know how the audience is going to take a non-American'?

**Bruce**: Well, the question has been raised. In fact, it is being discussed, and that is why *The Warrior* is probably not going to be on . . . They think, businesswise, it's a risk. And I don't blame them . . . If I were the man with the money I would probably have my own worry whether or not the acceptance would be there.

**Berton**: How about the other side of the coin: is it possible that you are – well, you're fairly hip and fairly Americanized – are you too Western for Oriental audiences?

**Bruce**: I have been criticized for that.

On 7 December 1971, Bruce received a telegram from Warners saying that 'due to pressures from the network regarding casting' he had been dropped from *The Warrior* TV series, which had by now been renamed *Kung Fu*.

In his 1993 book *The Kung Fu Book of Caine: The Complete Guide to TV's First Mystical Eastern Western*, Herbie Pilato writes about the casting history for the series:

Before the filming of the *Kung Fu* TV movie began, there was some discussion as to whether or not an Asian actor should play Kwai Chang Caine. Bruce Lee's name was put forward for the role. But in 1971, Bruce Lee wasn't the cult film hero he later became for his roles in *Fists of Fury* and *Enter the Dragon*. At that point he was best known as Kato on TV's *Green Hornet*.

'In my eyes and in the eyes of Jerry Thorpe [director],' said Harvey Frand [production supervisor], 'David Carradine was always our first choice to play Caine. But there was some disagreement because the network was interested in a more muscular actor and the studio was interested in getting Bruce Lee.' Frand says Lee wouldn't have really been appropriate for the series, despite the fact that he went on to considerable success in the martial arts film world. The *Kung Fu* show needed a serene person, and Carradine was more appropriate for the role.

Ed Spielman [scriptwriter] agrees: 'I liked David in the part. One of Japan's foremost karate champions used to say that the only qualification that was needed to be trained in the martial arts was that you had to know how to dance. And on top of being an accomplished athlete and actor, David could dance . . . The character was half-Asian and half-Caucasian, so either an Asian or a Caucasian would have been a reasonable choice; a Eurasian would have been the most natural choice.

Many of these later comments by those involved have more than a hint of retrospective justification. For the record, Bruce Lee's mother was half-German and he was the 1957 Cha-Cha Champion of Hong Kong, making him in fact a Eurasian dancer – although hardly a 'serene' one! But as one senior TV executive at Warners later admitted, although they knew he wanted the role, Bruce Lee was never seriously considered.

Before taking the role of Caine, David Carradine openly admitted he had only heard the expression 'kung fu' twice and had certainly never practised the art. Yet he confidently asserted that 'No one on the planet was more prepared on as many levels to play the role of Caine as I was.' In fact, most of the early action from the series features judo moves allied to Jewish Torah philosophy, because the technical advisor, David Chow, also knew little about kung fu, and its writers knew little about Taoism. Eventually a new technical director, Kam Yuen, was brought in.

On 22 February 1972, ABC TV's Movie of the Week was the pilot for the *Kung Fu* series. The accompanying press release explained the theme: 'Kwai Chang Caine, a Chinese-American fugitive from a murder charge in Imperial China, becomes a superhero to the coolies building the transcontinental railroad through his mastery of an ancient science-religion.'

On 8 August 1972, due to public demand the *Kung Fu* pilot was repeated following thousands of letters flooding into the production office. It became a weekly series in January 1973 and quickly became the number-one TV show in the US.

Joe Lewis, the karate champion who trained with Bruce Lee, recalls Bruce's own idea for the opening of what became the *Kung Fu* series: a Chinese-looking stagecoach with lots of ornamentation pulls into a dusty main street. As all the local cowboys amble up to look it over, the doors fly open, and out jumps a man in a kung fu suit. Lewis says that when Warners gave the part to David Carradine, Bruce decided he would concentrate on Hong Kong to begin his climb to success, just as Clint Eastwood and Charles Bronson had gone to Europe to become stars first. Lewis adds, 'It hurt Bruce when he failed to get the *Kung Fu* series. He experienced a lot of rejection.'

Bruce Lee had been thinking about writing and directing long before he went to Hong Kong to make his first film for Golden Harvest. Joe Lewis says that during the time he and Chuck Norris were training with Bruce, he would often mention ideas for films. Although Joe and Bruce worked together when Bruce choreographed the fights for *The Wrecking Crew*, Lewis declined to get involved in Bruce's new venture. He felt that in this film, Bruce was aiming to show that the Asian martial artist was superior to the Caucasian.

Lewis claims that Bruce wanted to cast him as 'a big, strong, muscular, blue-eyed, blond-haired, all-American punch bag'. But Bruce countered that the problem was finding Western martial artists – who almost always had a bigger physique – who were fast enough to fight him convincingly. Bruce said that he asked Chuck Norris to appear in *Way of the Dragon* because Norris was one of the few Western martial artists who was fast enough. Bruce commented that he'd worked on his own speed because a smaller man who can swing faster hits as hard as a heavier man who swings slowly. 'And besides,' he added, 'you can't keep fighting midgets.'

Joe Lewis obviously felt that the power of the stronger, heavier Western martial artist would ultimately prevail over the speed of the faster, lighter Asian martial artist and that's why he declined to act to the contrary. Lewis continues, 'Bruce knew that he was asking me to get involved in a movie where I got my butt beat by a little 128-pound Chinese guy who'd never been in the ring.'

A succinct comment from Bruce's mother shows that Joe wasn't far off the mark. Grace Lee recalls, 'Bruce told me: "Mom, I'm an Oriental person, therefore I have to defeat all the whites in the film." I don't believe he ever mentioned this to Chuck Norris.'

However, Bruce *had* mentioned this to Chuck Norris, who recalls:

In 1972, Bruce was directing *Way of the Dragon* and wanted me to be in it. 'I want you to be my opponent,' Bruce said with excitement. 'We'll have a fight in the Coliseum in Rome – two gladiators in a fight to the death. Best of all, we can choreograph it ourselves. I promise you the fight will be the highlight of the film.'

'Great,' I said, 'who wins?'

'I do,' Bruce said with a laugh, 'I'm the star!'

'Oh? You're going to beat up the current world karate champion?'

'No,' said Bruce, 'I'm going to *kill* the current world karate champion!' I laughed and agreed to do the movie after gaining twenty pounds, at his request, because he wanted me to look more formidable as his opponent.

In early 1972, in preparation for filming *Way of the Dragon*, Bruce Lee bought and read a dozen books dealing with all aspects of filmmaking. Placing incredible demands on his energy, he intended virtually to make the entire picture himself: to write, produce, direct and star in it; to scout the locations, cast it, choose the wardrobe and choreograph the fight scenes. In the process he lost several pounds of hard-won weight.

For the storyline, Bruce drew on his memories of leaving Hong Kong for San Francisco in 1958, and on his experiences as a waiter at Ruby Chow's restaurant. When he'd first arrived in the

US, Bruce had bought a Chinese-English dictionary; but he now found himself referring to it to find the appropriate Chinese words, rather than English ones, so that he could express his ideas when planning meetings with his assistants.

*Way of the Dragon* was the first Hong Kong-based picture to be shot in Europe. At $130,000, the budget was slightly higher than his previous films, but production costs were already covered by pre-sales to Taiwan. On 4 May 1972, the first team arrived in Rome. It consisted of Bruce, Raymond Chow and Nishimoto Tadashi, a Japanese cameraman Bruce hired because he considered the Japanese to have more technical expertise. Leading actress Nora Miao, along with other members of cast and crew, arrived three days later, after spending nineteen hours on a plane routed via Thailand, India and Israel.

Bruce let the crew rest for a couple of days, but when shooting started on 10 May, he proved to be a demanding director who expected the same level of commitment from everyone else as he was prepared to invest himself. In the following days they buzzed around Rome, pausing to film illegally at the Colosseum. At the Trevi fountain, they stayed long enough for Bruce to throw a coin in the water and make a wish. It's not hard to imagine what it was.

Having shot the location set-ups, Bruce could now turn his attention to more important matters: the fight scenes. Knowing how it would look on camera, Bruce spent a lot of time teaching his co-actors how to react convincingly. In contrast to the speed at which he'd hounded everyone around Rome, shooting over sixty scenes in one day alone, he then spent over forty-five hours on his fight scene with Chuck Norris. Bruce's choreographed directions for this scene took up nearly a quarter of the script. As with all the fight scenes, Bruce watched the daily rushes, and if he saw any unconvincing moment of action, the whole scene would have to be re-shot. By the time the film wrapped, Bruce had been involved in yet another aspect of filmmaking: he played percussion on the music for the soundtrack.

In the film Bruce plays a country bumpkin named Tang Lung (China Dragon) who leaves Hong Kong and goes to Rome. While waiting to be met at the airport he goes into a restaurant where, due to problems with the language, he finds he has mistakenly ordered four plates of soup. Tang is later met by his cousin, played by Nora Miao, and as they drive to her apartment, she explains that she has inherited a restaurant on some property wanted by the mob. In the scene itself the story is more concerned with Tang's need to find a toilet, something that had them rolling in the aisles in Hong Kong.

*Way of the Dragon* is played as a comedy, with pauses to accommodate audience laughter and a soundtrack punctuated with comic 'wah-wah' sounds and 'boings' from the timpani. Yet, for all that, it features some outstanding fight scenes and one or two excellent kung fu lessons.

All the waiters in the restaurant are learning karate in order to repel the thugs who are harassing them and driving away the restaurant's customers. Tang attends a training session at the back of the premises, where one of the waiters – Bruce's old friend Unicorn – is drilling the others – including Bruce's adopted brother, Wu Ngan. An argument starts about the merits of the various fighting systems. 'It doesn't matter where it comes from,' says Tang, 'you can learn to use it.' Later, when the thugs return to intimidate the customers, Tang does battle with them outside. The waiters are so impressed with what they see that they vow to give up karate and learn Chinese fighting.

A further confrontation between Bruce and the thugs is played for laughs, but it contains some superb fight sequences, especially those featuring Bruce using the nunchakas. The weapon's potential for being more dangerous to an inept user than to his opponent is a comic possibility seized on by Bruce. One of the Italian hoods manages to grab a pair and having seen Tang wielding them with nonchalant grace, he believes he too is imbued with the supernatural power of an Excalibur, but as he goes to strike Tang, he knocks himself out.

No matter how skilled a martial artist is, however, he can't beat a bullet, which is why kung fu movies were more credible in the East than in the US and Europe, because the martial arts tradition in places like Hong Kong and Singapore was intertwined with the British custom – at the time – of having mainly unarmed police. Likewise, most of the population were similarly unarmed, because there was no access to guns and most people couldn't afford them. Men fought with their bodies, hand-to-hand, or used traditional and makeshift weapons.

In *Way of the Dragon* Bruce had the gangsters carry guns and attempted to confront the problem by having Tang carve poison darts, which he fires with unerring accuracy into the gangsters' gun hands, just as Kato had done in the first episode of *The Green Hornet*. These sequences do no more to overcome the major drawback of the martial arts genre than any other attempt and are the most unlikely scenes of the film, though the action that follows more than compensates.

Once Tang has dispatched the local heavies, the Godfather has to import hired fighters played by Wong In Sik, a Korean hapkido exponent, and karate stars Bob Wall and Chuck Norris. In the Western version of the film, Norris's character is named Colt. By offering a truce, the gang lures Tang into a trap. The first two opponents are dealt with, then in a sudden shift of scene from the countryside to the centre of Rome, the final scene is fought out under the arches of the Colosseum. Tang and his ultimate Anglo-Saxon enemy, Colt, face each other with all the dignity and formality of two samurai warriors; their only spectator a tiny kitten. Again there are comic moments, such as when Tang rips a handful of hair from Colt's chest, but this fight scene is the best that Bruce Lee ever committed to film. In it Bruce was anxious not to make the fight a completely one-sided affair, but there was never any doubt as to what the outcome would be.

In the first half of the screen fight, it is Colt who has the upper hand, knocking Tang to the floor a couple of times and bloodying his mouth. The turning point comes when Tang bounces back, dancing and moving like Muhammad Ali, bewildering Colt. As Tang speeds up the cadence of his footwork Colt follows him, not realizing that Tang has regained the initiative and is now dictating the pace.

In one sequence Bruce Lee overwhelms Chuck Norris with a cluster of punches that are almost too quick to count. It's a sequence taken directly from Muhammad Ali's fight with Cleveland Williams, which Bruce studied over and over again on his home movie projector. It's even shot from exactly the same camera angles. In the ensuing action, Tang delivers a devastatingly fast combination of strikes as he begins to overwhelm Colt, who sustains a broken arm and leg but struggles to his feet to continue the fight. Tang glances down at Colt's broken leg and shakes his head, as if to say, 'Look, you've got nothing to prove. Stop this while you can.' But Colt's warrior code leaves him only two options: victory or death. Colt almost smiles in acceptance of his fate, then attacks with one last flurry of blows until in the final exchange Tang breaks Colt's neck. At this moment a strange expression of remorse spreads over Tang's face, then he lowers Colt's body to the ground and respectfully places Colt's jacket and black belt over his body.

In beating Norris in the Western world's greatest historical arena, Bruce Lee was once again giving his audience what they wanted to see, but he was also aware of the sentiments he was stirring and sought to include other lessons. The way he honours the opponent he has just killed is also in accordance with one of the tenets of the warrior's code: that a worthy opponent be treated with respect.

Bruce Lee told his friends that *Way of the Dragon* would be a hit on the Mandarin circuit but that he had no plans to release it in the West. The humour, which had Eastern audiences convulsed with laughter, would be missed in the West. The 'soup scene' was a big hit in the East because Campbell's had recently begun importing their soups there and indigestion from this unfamiliar food was common. Bruce's script was based on a real understanding of the Chinese psyche. Bruce's character in the film has a much softer persona, with his hair brushed down and pointed sideburns that gives him an almost elfin look, but he slowly strips this character of his superficial naivety to reveal the capable hero at heart.

To a chorus of disbelief from the Hong Kong press, Bruce predicted that the picture would earn $HK5 million. Shaking their heads in amazement, journalists also showed some irritation. They were no longer interested in celebrating the success of Bruce Lee, they were looking for flaws, so while dutifully reporting the new milestone in Bruce's career, the press began speculating about who he might be sleeping with.

In August 1972, Miss Pang Cheng Lian, a reporter on *New Nation*, the English newspaper in Singapore, went to Hong Kong for a week to write four daily features based on interviews with Bruce Lee. She spent time with him at the Golden Harvest studios where he was dubbing *Way of the Dragon* and there they had lunch together, after which Bruce made his customary call home. When he returned, Miss Pang brought up the subject of female martial artists. Bruce told her that a woman could never match a man for strength, so her best bet was to use her powers of seduction and persuasion to gain an opportunity to jab her assailant in the eyes or kick his groin before running like hell. With talk of seduction and vital parts, the questions turned to Bruce's relationship with a certain actress. His response was that the people of Hong Kong had too much time to invent stories that would upset the girl in question, Betty Ting Pei.

In 1967 Tang Mei Li changed her name to Betty Ting Pei and signed up as one of Run Run Shaw's jobbing actresses. The 'sultry Taiwanese sex bomb' – as her publicity described her – had acted in around thirty films – dramas, comedies, musicals and martial arts films – though most often she played roles that ended up in the bedroom. The twenty-five-year-old rising starlet had yet to break through into leading roles when she and Bruce were introduced on the film set by Raymond Chow, and within days, Bruce told his friends, 'She brightens up an otherwise dull film set. She quite makes my day.'

The Lee family now moved from the small apartment on Man Wan Road into one of the few two-storey detached houses in Hong Kong, at 41 Cumberland Road in the Kowloon Tong area.

Although the large eleven-room house might have been considered average in Beverly Hills, in Hong Kong it was a palace. It had wrought-iron gates and an eight-foot stone wall enclosing a large Japanese garden where a stream wound through the trees to a goldfish pond spanned by an ornamental bridge, all of which could be viewed from the balcony of the main room, where Bruce had set up his new hi-fi system. Best of all, the house had enough space for a study to house his thousands of books and a fully equipped gymnasium.

Bruce replaced the red Porsche he'd given up in Los Angeles with a new red Mercedes 350 SL, most likely the same one seen in the closing shots of *Way of the Dragon*. And in response to Bruce's taste for silk suits and even a fur coat, the press duly voted him 'Worst-Dressed Actor of the Year'.

The move to their new house happened just in time, and it became Bruce's sanctuary and the only place he could enjoy some peace and privacy. A few years before he had put on impromptu displays of kung fu at dances, doing one-finger push-ups to attract an audience. Now he couldn't visit a restaurant without having to sit at a corner table with his back to everyone, hoping not to be noticed. But once the waiters began to hover, there would soon be a queue of people demanding autographs and asking familiar questions, and by the time Bruce left the restaurant, he would be faced with a jostling crowd of paparazzi. What's more, if he reacted badly to any of this, the next day's headlines would report his arrogance and ill manners.

Bruce's fame was a double-edged sword, and he said he now understood why stars like Steve McQueen avoided public places and regretted that they could no longer lead a normal life. Yet, in recalling his earlier vow to be a bigger star than McQueen, Bruce couldn't resist revelling in his celebrity.

The pressure of sudden stardom may be an entertainment business cliché, but it is real enough. While it drives some to become recluses or surround themselves with bodyguards, in Bruce's case another contradiction emerged. On the one hand he fed off the public's response and the recognition he'd been trying for years to achieve, on the other he could no longer pursue his art in the way that had made all this possible. The paradox revealed itself at a party once where a guest failed to recognize him. With a healthy dose of self-mockery he extended his hand and announced, 'Bruce Lee, movie star.'

The old money problems had eased, but new problems arose to take their place. Producers extended big offers, usually with maximum fanfare and minimum resources to back them up, simply as a way of increasing their own prestige and getting some free publicity. *The China Star*, a down-market Hong Kong daily, ran a series 'written' by Yip Chun, the son of Yip Man, who at one time had trained alongside Bruce. The article quoted Yip Chun as saying that he had seen Bruce knocked down by an opponent during training. While no one could expect Bruce to have been invincible from the age of thirteen, the tone of the article upset him enough for him to track down Yip Chun and ask if he'd really said what had been printed. Yip Chun denied it, claiming it was an extravagance on the part of the article's ghostwriter, *The Star*'s boss, a hard-bitten Australian named Graham Jenkins, who duly reported that Bruce had threatened his paper's contributor. Bruce began a legal action against the paper, only to find himself being followed everywhere by photographers and reporters wanting to hype up a sensation on the slightest pretext.

What the media didn't report were Bruce's simple acts of consideration for others. Bob Wall offers an example:

> Both Bruce and I wore contact lenses and when we were fighting in the dust, in the Roman countryside, we kept getting choked up. Bruce had some really good eye lotion and we were able to get through our fight scenes by using it. Later, as I was about to board the plane back to the US, I saw a commotion outside the airport departure lounge where a crowd of people had gathered. Then I saw Bruce's red Mercedes and a few moments later he appeared in the lounge. He'd driven out to the airport to give me a whole case of this eye lotion as a gift.

*B*ruce in a scene from one of his childhood films.

*T*he 'teenage tearaway' with his parents.

*B*ruce began to find his feet as a philosophy student at Seattle's University of Washington.

*K*ato in action.

*M*editating at Hermosa Beach.

*T*he results of years of
intensive training.

With James Garner in a scene from *Marlowe*.

Linda, Brandon and Bruce.

*B*ruce succumbs to the charms of Malalene in *The Big Boss* . . . and Betty Ting Pei on the set of *Way of the Dragon*.

*F*rom the *Longstreet* episode 'The Way of the Intercepting Fist'.

*T*he Big Boss gets his comeuppance.

*T*he climax of *Fist of Fury* – a scene lifted straight
out of *Butch Cassidy and the Sundance Kid*.

*A*nother shot from *Fist of Fury*.

*E*nter ... the Dragon!

*B*ruce with nunchakas in *Way of the Dragon*.

*B*ruce in his extensive library on the fighting and philosophical arts. Note the nunchakas hanging from the centre of the bookcase.

*T*he house on Kowloon Tong.

*T*he bungalow in Bel Air.

*B*ruce rehearsed this kick on Kareem Abdul Jabbar over 300 times.

*A* scene from *Enter the Dragon* –
Bruce's peripheral awareness almost
comes off the page.

*I*n period costume for a screen test
for Shaw Brothers Studio – a coded
message to Raymond Chow.

*S*trength of spirit … just weeks before his death.

Even with all the demands on his time, he'd taken the trouble to do that.

Bruce Lee had never been motivated purely by matters of wealth or status. Bombarded with invitations both to present and accept various awards and trophies, he elected instead to spend the time studying or training. Neither fame nor money was an end in itself, they were simply the by-products of him doing his work well. The biggest advantage of money was that it allowed him the autonomy to set his own standards. As a martial arts teacher, Bruce had maintained standards that prevented him from over-commercializing his art by opening a chain of 'gung fu' institutes that would have been connected to him in name only, and he sought to apply the same values to his films. It's doubtful whether the producers who now hounded him would have understood the principles by which he tried to operate; they just wanted to lure him to their sets with promises of huge sums of money. Just as fame was a side-effect of being the best, so wealth would be the natural outcome of work done with commitment and attention. For Bruce, what remained important was the quality of one's work, so a good studio carpenter could earn his respect more easily than a hack director like Lo Wei.

In the slipstream of three successful films Bruce Lee now planned a new film, which would feature some of the world's foremost martial artists, because he wanted to involve his friends and show his appreciation to them, both as teachers and students. *Game of Death* would be a crowning achievement.

# 21

## Game of Death

In 1967, when Bruce was given the opportunity to meet the basketball giant Big Lew Alcindor, he jumped at it. He *had* to – Big Lew was over seven feet tall, and Bruce was intrigued as to how he might fight a man of that height. Big Lew became one of Bruce's celebrity pupils, and when he later converted to Islam he took the name Kareem Abdul Jabbar. As the ace centre for the Milwaukee Bucks, and later the Los Angeles Lakers, he became one of the top players in the game.

With *Way of the Dragon* completed, an exhausted Bruce planned to take a short rest, but in the spring of 1972 – after *Fist of Fury* was released – when Bruce heard that Jabbar was in Hong Kong, he swiftly arranged some action scenes to be filmed for *Game of Death*. There was no script for *Game of Death* as yet, but Bruce had enough of an idea of the story to be able to take advantage of Jabbar's visit, and the two of them spent a week sparring and acting out fight scenes in front of the cameras. To make sure the action was convincing, Bruce rehearsed one particular kick nearly 300 times. The result is some intriguing and strangely elegant footage of Bruce fighting a man who towers above him.

In Bruce's mind the opening shot of the film was also clear; his notes read:

As the film opens we see a wide expanse of snow. Then the camera closes in on a clump of trees while the sounds of a strong gale fill the screen. There is a huge tree in the centre of the screen, covered in thick snow. Suddenly there is a loud snap and the branch of the tree falls to the ground. It cannot yield to the force of the snow, so it breaks. Then the camera moves to a willow tree, which is bending with the wind. Because it adapts to the environment, it survives. What I want to say is that a man has to be flexible and adaptable, otherwise he will be destroyed.

The rest of the story had been evolving in Bruce's imagination ever since he'd stood on the northern border of India and looked out on the pagodas of Nepal. A national treasure is stolen and placed on the top floor of a pagoda on an island off the coast of Korea. As the hero, Bruce Lee has to recover the treasure. Outside, the pagoda is defended by a band of fighters, led by a hulk of a man, while inside each floor is defended by a master of a particular martial art. The pagoda is a training school for martial artists of different traditions, where each floor is given over to students of different forms of combat. The climax of the film occurs on the uppermost floor where Lee, the master of 'anything that works', fights Jabbar, the master of 'no style', a giant who fights unpredictably. Here all the rule books are thrown out as each man relies entirely on his wits and natural native fighting skills. This, the final scene, entitled 'The Temple of the Unknown', was now in the can.

Bruce Lee was determined that expertise and quality would be the hallmark of this film. He intended to assemble the most talented array of fighters available and had already called on Dan Inosanto to be the guardian of one of the floors. Dan practised escrima, together with its variants kali and arnis, the ancient Filipino art of stick fighting. The art was named by the Spanish conquerors – *escrima* is Spanish for 'skirmish' – who soon realized its effectiveness and banned it. In the northern Philippines, the movements were kept alive by practitioners who disguised it as a dance, while in the south, where the native Muslims expelled the Europeans, the art continued to flourish.

Bruce forwarded a China Airlines ticket to Inosanto, who flew out as soon as he could make a break in his schedule. Linda met him at Kai Tak airport because Bruce couldn't have gone there without being mobbed. Within a couple of days they were working out their moves, using a video machine to check the action after each take, a technique Bruce pioneered in his *Green Hornet* days. Over several days, they worked out the basis of their episode, which was entitled 'The Temple of the Tiger'.

Three weapons are used during this confrontation. First, Inosanto uses the double sticks while Bruce uses a Chinese bako, a thin whip-like bamboo. As the two face off, Inosanto taps out a traditional challenge with his stick. Bruce's mocking response is the 'rat-tat-ta-tat-tat' knock of the postman. After Bruce disarms Inosanto, they pick up nunchakas for a duel to the death. Inosanto had originally introduced Bruce to the weapon; but the resulting footage of this scene shows that Bruce had mastered it better than his teacher.

Inosanto recalls that shortly after he met Bruce in 1964, he showed him a few basic escrima techniques. At the time Bruce hadn't been much impressed and Inosanto had thought no more of it. On this visit to Hong Kong, eight years later, when the subject came up, Bruce told Dan what he liked and didn't like about what he'd seen of escrima.

'I was flabbergasted when he grabbed the sticks and said, "OK, now I'll show you what I would do,"' says Inosanto. 'I watched him closely, and with no previous background or training he ad-libbed a style of escrima he could never have known existed. Shocked, I yelled out, "Hey, that's larga mano!" Bruce said, "I don't know what you call it, but this is my method."'

Inosanto adds that *Game of Death* was intended to illustrate the same point: 'Bruce wanted to show imagination rising above tradition.' So while Inosanto was dressed in the traditional Muslim costume and headband, Bruce wore a modern yellow and black catsuit.

Bruce had revelled in the free hand he had in making *Way of the Dragon*. Now, in *Game of Death*, he continued to improvise as he went along, taking advantage of the fact that the sound would be dubbed on later. Like a silent film director of old, he even shouted directions to his actors as the cameras were rolling.

Bruce forgot all about resting as he enthusiastically planned further duels. A third combat scene was filmed with Chi Hon Joi, a seventh-degree black belt in the Korean art of hapkido, which relies on high kicks. While filming their scene, the Korean had a rigorous enough time of it to comment that he didn't want to act in any more movies with Bruce Lee. Bruce's pointed response was that he was considering re-shooting the scene, this time with a female martial artist called Angela Mao.

Bruce's disparaging comment to Chi Hon Joi related to an earlier incident. When Bruce had been finishing scenes for *Way of the Dragon* in Hong Kong, another film *Hapkido*, aka *Lady Kung Fu*, was being made there with some up-and-coming martial artists called Carter Wong, Jackie Chan and Sammo Hung. The female lead in the film was Angela Mao, who was being taught hapkido by the film's star, Wong In Sik, who said he wanted to 'give her an edge' over Chinese martial arts actresses. Wong In Sik had apparently been hitting his Chinese stuntmen without any holding back, saying he wanted to show that the Korean art was by far the most powerful and effective. Word of this had got to Bruce, who arranged to bring in the Korean for *Way of the Dragon*. Bruce then gave him a robust demonstration of the Chinese arts that left him in no doubt of the error of his ways. In doing the same to Chi Hon Joi, Bruce had been making doubly sure his point had not been missed.

For *Game of Death*, at a later stage Bruce was planning to include Betty Ting Pei and the Australian actor George Lazenby, but neither they nor Bruce had any idea what their roles would be. Lazenby, like Bruce Lee, had shot to fame overnight – in Lazenby's case, from doing chocolate bar commercials to replacing Sean Connery as James Bond in *On Her Majesty's Secret Service*

– but Lazenby hadn't been a great success as Bond and his career was in the doldrums. Fortunately the film had only just opened in Hong Kong and Lazenby had chosen exactly the right time to go knocking on Raymond Chow's door.

Taky Kimura, who was also asked to play a role in *Game of Death* but declined, says, 'He sent me a plane ticket to go to Hong Kong but I said, "I've got three left feet and you know it. You don't need me. Do me a favour, I'm not looking for fame and fortune, I'm happy to see you doing well." He said, "I'm the director and producer; everyone looks good in my films." I said, "I guess I can't refuse." I recognized the feeling behind what he was doing. But in October the import business I had started was just about to go and I wasn't able to go to Hong Kong. Then Linda called me and said don't bother, something else was breaking and *Game of Death* was being put on the back burner.'

At the time, Taky Kimura was also going through a severe personal crisis which left him emotionally devastated and haunted by the idea of suicide: 'I lost two brothers a month apart and then my wife left me,' he explains. 'Bruce said, "Taky, I haven't met your wife, but I've counselled you before. You must do everything in your power to solve the thing but, at some point in time, you may just have to walk on." I'd lost everything. When people tell you things like that, there's not always a lot of pith in it, but coming from him . . .'

From wherever he happened to be in the world, Bruce would call to give support to his friend, saying, 'Walk on, Taky. Just walk on.'

When Bruce's old friend Doug Palmer arrived on a visit to Hong Kong with his wife, he managed to track Bruce down via Golden Harvest, who passed on a message.

Palmer's notes recall:

Five minutes later the phone in our hotel room rang. 'You son of a gun,' Bruce yelled when I answered. 'What are you doing in Hong Kong?' He and Linda came and picked us up and took us back to the huge house he was having work done on in an exclusive part of town called Kowloon Tong. The lot had a high wall around it with broken glass and spikes set in the top. He had made it, but fame had a price. His kids had to be escorted to and from school so they would not be kidnapped. My wife, Noriko, had to use the toilet; Bruce produced a bunch of keys to unlock the bathroom – apparently he had to keep every room in the house locked to guard against theft by the workmen.

While we were at his house, Bruce was looking through his mail and he read a letter from his old friend, James Lee, in Oakland. I could see Bruce frowning as he read, then I heard him whisper to Linda to send James five hundred dollars. Bruce told me later that James was dying of cancer.

Later we went out to dinner. When we stopped at a light, people on the street or in adjacent cars would gawk in at him. The restaurant was full and we had no reservation, but they soon produced a table. I'm not sure if anyone else in the place got their dinner because every waiter was hovering near our table.

The next day we visited the movie studio where Bruce was filming *Game of Death*. He had recently brought Kareem Abdul Jabbar over to Hong Kong to shoot a fight scene, which had a very powerful David and Goliath quality about it. Bruce was very happy about the way the scene had turned out, in contrast to a more recent one where he had flown in a martial artist from Korea and was very disappointed with the calibre of the man's performance.

Bruce also had a few stories to tell about Kareem Abdul Jabbar. When he arrived in Hong Kong, Kareem let it be known that he was very interested in having 'a date'. Bruce tried to arrange something for him. When the girl showed up and was introduced to Kareem, she flat refused. No one had told her how big Kareem was. Kareem became very angry. 'He's very sensitive about his height, you know,' said Bruce, chuckling.

\*

In May 1972, Bruce Lee's boyhood friend Unicorn met with Tang Di, a representative of the Sing Hoi Film Company, at the Peninsular Hotel. With the sudden popularity of martial arts films, the company decided it wanted to get in on the act. As Tang discreetly put it to Unicorn, 'Frankly speaking, your name, of course, won't sell; but if you have "another" who can help you, the film will not only sell, it will earn a lot of money.'

In short, Bruce Lee's involvement in the picture was the condition that would secure the starring role for Unicorn. Bruce gave Unicorn the role of the head waiter in *Way of the Dragon*, but when Unicorn had presented the idea to Bruce, suggesting that he might do the fight choreography, he didn't expect him to go for it. After all, the budget for the film was so low it was close to the earth's core. Bruce replied that, although he realized he was being manipulated, he would do what he could to help, but when Bruce attended a publicity bash for the film at the Miramar Hotel in Kowloon, he got all the attention and had to ask the press photographers not to ignore Unicorn.

As filming started in August 1972, it soon became obvious that Unicorn was out of his depth as a leading actor and again Bruce had to step in. As well as supervising the action, Bruce came up with several script ideas, spending a day at the set while the cameras rolled.

When the film – imaginatively titled *Fist of Unicorn* – was released soon afterwards, Bruce Lee was not only credited as the martial arts advisor but was given star billing. Footage of Bruce arriving on the set and of him rehearsing the actors had been contrived to fit a new storyline. Bruce could only issue a legal letter condemning the sorry project, and although Bruce's friendship with Unicorn continued, the incident increased his wariness of others.

As for Unicorn, one reviewer wrote, 'One only has to witness his stolid approach to every scene, his constipated countenance, resplendent as it is with a neck that is evidently part of his chin, and eyebrows modelled on Roger Moore at their tugging fishhook best.'

Bruce Lee's superstar status made him vulnerable to all kinds of exploitation. His name was used to endorse products he'd never heard of, much less used, while quotes attributed to him were used to hype films he'd never seen. Producers advertised offers to him in the pages of the Hong Kong press, while seeking only to generate publicity for themselves and increase their prestige by some kind of association, however tenuous. The situation in which he now found himself had changed so quickly that a normal life was no longer possible. As the press became ever more ridiculous in its excesses, Bruce used to wake up to find parts of a previous evening's conversation in a restaurant splashed across the newspapers, and headlines like BRUCE LEE LINKED TO MASS MURDER because his friend Kareem Abdul Jabbar had rented a house in the US whose occupants had recently been killed.

In the 1960s, audiences had tired of Shaw's musical epics and begun flocking to see samurai movies. Without missing a beat, Run Run Shaw switched production from the sentimental to the bloody, but soon samurai movies came to a messy end, quickened by a series of speeches made by Chinese leader Chou En Lai attacking Japanese imperialism. With no gunfighting or sword-fighting tradition to base his films on, Shaw set out to revive kung fu films, starting with *The Chinese Boxer*, a film whose appeal was a combination of national feeling, secret societies and action. This was quickly followed by *King Boxer*, *The Killer* and *The New One-Armed Swordsman*, starring Wang Yu, who became kung fu's top star by beating Shaw's contract system and hiring himself out on a film-by-film basis whereby he was able to command a fee of $20,000 per film. These movies broke out of the Oriental market to find success around the world, and the Hong Kong press started calling Shaw 'Mr Kung Fu'.

But audiences were quick to realize that there was a new kid on the block who was the genre's natural star. Ironically, Shaw had opened the door for his most bitter rival to better him. When *Newsweek* wrote about the emerging phenomenon, the story was headlined: BRUCE LEE: THE BRIGHT STAR RISING IN THE EAST. The *LA Times* columnist Robert Elegant also wrote an article heralding Bruce, and Raymond Chow lost no time in setting up US distribution.

In his office at Golden Harvest, Bruce Lee was besieged with offers that continued to arrive daily. The only reminder of his past struggles was a pair of broken spectacles, which he kept to remind him of the time he couldn't afford to have them fixed. They were the same spectacles he'd worn when he'd disguised himself as a telephone repairman in *Fist of Fury*. Now he was in an almost unprecedented position for any movie actor, let alone a Chinese one. He was potentially the highest-paid actor in the world, and could work in Europe, the US or the Orient, plus he was a partner in his own production company.

Some years after Bruce Lee first came to Fred Weintraub's attention, the Warners executive was still trying to secure him a starring role.

Weintraub says, 'When I kept failing to get a feature going for Bruce, I told him to go to Hong Kong and make a film I could show people. He eventually sent me a print of *The Big Boss* and I went to Richard Ma [Warners head of Asian distribution] with it because he was the only one who understood the genre. I also arranged a private showing for Ted Ashley and he said, "Try and get something going."'

When Bruce completed *Fist of Fury*, Weintraub was again sent a print. Now, along with box-office figures from the Mandarin circuit, Warners realized that Fred Weintraub might be on to something, though he adds, 'There still wasn't a lot of enthusiasm for it. Nobody believed it would ever get done.'

At the time of Nixon's high-profile visit to China, awareness of Asian culture was stirring in America, and Richard Ma thought it might be just the time to expose kung fu films to a wider audience. Rather than give money to Run Run Shaw by taking his films, Ma suggested an original project, saying he knew a guy by the name of Bruce Lee. Ma had a hard time trying to convince his senior executives that this was a good idea, even though the budget for the proposed film was roughly equal to what they'd spend on a TV pilot episode. Fortunately, Warners president Ted Ashley was convinced, so Fred Weintraub and Paul Heller were appointed co-producers and a subsidiary company, Sequoia, was set up to manage the project.

Scriptwriter Michael Allin was hired to write a martial arts film to be called *Blood and Steel* and Weintraub set off for Hong Kong to do a deal whereby Sequoia and Concord, the production company Bruce set up with Raymond Chow, would co-produce the picture. This proved not to be the simple formality Weintraub had hoped for, and after two weeks in Hong Kong, he still didn't have Chow's signature on a contract. Although Weintraub found Bruce to be in favour of the project, he could never seem to get the two Concord partners together in the same room at the same time. Raymond Chow seemed to be dragging his heels, sensing that he was losing control.

Weintraub was about to call it a day, return home and ditch the project, but the evening before he was due to return to the US he decided to give it one last shot.

That evening he managed to get Bruce and Raymond to go to a restaurant, and after dinner Weintraub told Bruce that Raymond Chow was right to protect him and that the attempt to go international wasn't worth risking the successful career he had built up in Hong Kong. Weintraub said that it was all academic anyway as he couldn't make a deal. Bruce looked over at Chow and said, 'Make the deal,' so Chow could only smile and add that he thought it was a wonderful idea.

In October 1972, Bruce Lee and Raymond Chow flew to the US to finalize the details and meet with the actors and director with whom Bruce was to work. In his room at the Beverly Wilshire hotel Bruce had hardly unpacked his suitcase before he called Steve McQueen to tell him that he was to star in his own US-made film. Bruce wasn't about to take a chance that McQueen might have missed the many interviews in which he'd reminded McQueen that he was just as famous now.

Bruce Lee then called Stirling Silliphant. Part of a deal Silliphant had just done with 20th Century Fox included the script of *The Silent Flute*. The writer thought Bruce would be delighted, but Bruce hadn't forgotten about India, and far from giving his blessing to the film being made, he told the writer he was now worth a million dollars and that they couldn't afford him any more, even though Coburn and Silliphant had done more than most to help Bruce when he'd been struggling. Bruce then suggested that if *The Silent Flute* were ever made, James Coburn would have to accept second billing. Using the very same words that had stung him so many years ago, he added, 'And why should I carry him on my shoulders?'

All of Bruce Lee's closest friends belonged to the period of his life when he was first and foremost a martial artist. Now, because of his success, he was experiencing a shift in his relationship with many of them, like Unicorn. He realized that these old friendships were changing or fading away, but in enjoying his success, even at the cost of alienating the few people who had genuinely helped him, he was now *driving* some of them away.

Perhaps Bruce's behaviour was partly due to the blow he'd taken when he realized that one of his greatest friends, James Lee, was dying of black lung, an occupational disease of the welding trade. James had been given only weeks to live when Bruce invited him to Hong Kong for the premier of *Way of the Dragon*, hoping that James would at least see the city and that Bruce would see his old friend before he died. Sadly James wasn't able to share in Bruce's success as he was far too unwell to travel, and he died on 28 December 1972, leaving Bruce emotionally devastated.

Two days later, as Bruce grieved, *Way of the Dragon* opened and, almost unnoticed, surpassed his prediction that it would make $HK5 million by earning $HK5.5 million in the first three weeks of its opening run. Bruce knew that a good deal of his success was due to his friend's help and encouragement with his conditioning and training. At times, James Lee had been more like a father to him than his own father.

# 22

## Enter the Dragon

By the time pre-production on the new film began, Bruce had managed to persuade the studio to change the title, so *Blood and Steel* became *Enter the Dragon*. The proposed $500,000 budget would hardly have covered one episode of a Hollywood TV show, but by Hong Kong standards it was sufficient for an epic.

Although Robert Clouse had only made two features, he got a call from Fred Weintraub, inviting him to meet Bruce Lee and Raymond Chow at the Warners offices in Burbank, with a view to directing the picture. According to Clouse, he was hired for *Enter the Dragon* because Bruce had been impressed by a fight scene in one of his films, but according to Fred Weintraub, 'Nobody else wanted to direct the picture.' To be fair to Clouse, who began his career as a stills photographer at CBS TV, two short films he composed from sequences of stills both received Academy nominations in that category.

In early February 1973, just after Chinese New Year, the American party followed Bruce Lee and Raymond Chow to Hong Kong. Clouse and Weintraub had by now been joined by leading lady Ahna Capri, Bob Wall – one of the featured martial artists – and scriptwriter Michael Allin, whose trip to Hong Kong was a perk to compensate for his low fee. Nobody's fee for the picture was generous, and it was for that reason that the world never came to hear of Rockne Tarkington, an actor who quit over his low pay three days before they were due to set off for Hong Kong. He was quickly replaced by karate champion Jim Kelly.

Robert Clouse wasn't the first person whose introduction to Bruce Lee was a lightning-fast kick that skimmed the end of his nose. On the director's first night in Hong Kong, Bruce insisted they go together to a theatre and watch one his films. Bruce told Clouse that he wanted him to experience the atmosphere, but the real reason was that when they'd first met, the director hadn't been aware of Bruce's reputation, and Bruce wanted him to know just who he was working with. Although this outing was to impress Clouse, it was also for Bruce's benefit, to psych himself up for the production that was about to get underway.

*Enter the Dragon* follows three international martial artists who enter a tournament on an island beyond international jurisdiction. The island is owned by arch-criminal Han who, conveniently for the martial arts plot, forbids firearms on his island. Lee (Bruce Lee) Roper (John Saxon) and Williams (Jim Kelly) – each has his own reason for being at the tournament, though they all find themselves at odds with their host, played by Shih Kien.

An intelligence agent called Braithwaite has recruited Lee to investigate Han's criminal operations using his participation in the tournament as cover, but Lee also has personal reasons for dealing with Han, who was expelled from the Shaolin temple in disgrace and whose students were responsible for the death of Lee's sister. Roper and Williams are former army buddies who have both had to leave the US in a hurry. Gambler Roper is wanted by the mob and is hoping to win prize money to pay off his debts, while black-activist Williams is wanted for beating up a couple of redneck cops who've been harassing him. In the course of the tournament, they discover that Han uses his untouchable island and the tournament as a front to recruit new talent for his drug-running and prostitution operations, but the three martial artists form an alliance to put an end to this.

Bruce Lee was genuinely concerned about the character he was to portray in *Enter the Dragon*. After the rejection he'd experienced with the *Kung Fu* TV series, he wondered if mainstream audiences in the West were ready for a Chinese hero and, at the same time, whether the Chinese audiences would accept his new Western approach. He couldn't be seen to favour the Western element at the expense of his own people, nor act in a way that would make him appear foolish to his countrymen. While his earlier films also showed him battling against gangsters involved in drugs and prostitution, these films all involved factory-floor-level crime – the sweatshop or the restaurant – which the overworked and underpaid workers of Hong Kong could identify with. Now Bruce was no longer simply playing the naïve country boy for his fellow Chinese; he had to look and act like a man of the world, an Asian Bond at home in both East and West.

Scriptwriter Michael Allin made flippant remarks that Bruce needn't worry himself about such things, claiming that the only reason the film was getting made was that it was cheap and Bruce Lee's name would guarantee enough of a success for the studio to at least recoup its costs. Allin added that the film wasn't being made because it was a work of art, and although Bruce tried to brush his comments aside, he found Allin's smart-ass routine hard to bear. There are stories that Allin made script alterations, knowing that Bruce, like many Asians, found the letter 'r' difficult to pronounce.

'The walls of the dressing rooms were paper-thin,' Bob Wall recalls, 'and Bruce overheard Bob Clouse talking about him, saying that it was ridiculous making a film with an actor who couldn't even speak properly. It was Clouse himself who asked Michael Allin to change the name of the British agent in the script to fuck Bruce up. Clouse changed the character's name to Braithwaite because he knew Bruce would have trouble with "Yes, Mr Bwaithwaite; no, Mr Bwaithwaite." It made him sound like Donald Duck.'

In the end Bruce demanded a new script and the producer suggested Allin lie low for a few days. But a few days later, when Bruce was out in public disguised in a beard and dark glasses, he happened to get on the same ferry as Allin. Of all the millions of people in Hong Kong, they had to meet. Having been under the impression that the writer had been sent home, Bruce was angry at the deception.

From the first day of filming little went right, and major difficulties arose from using both American and Chinese crew. There was a shortage of translators and often no adequate Chinese words for some of the English jargon and technical terms, and vice versa. Even the simplest instruction went along a torturous route of misinterpretation, which was further complicated when people who made mistakes went absent from the set rather than lose face.

Hong Kong's methods were not Hollywood's. There were no power tools for set construction and some of the sets were built from nothing more than chicken wire and mud. The 'steel bars' of prison cells were made by shaving down pieces of scrap wood because the hours of manual labour came cheaper than round lengths of wood, so 500 Chinese workmen built everything from scratch.

After an argument with Raymond Chow, Bruce walked off the set almost as soon as he'd arrived. Bruce felt that Chow was trying to assert himself as mastermind of the project, a situation he found intolerable knowing that it was his own creative efforts and abilities that would make or break the film, and his own career and reputation on the line. There were daily arguments between the two because Bruce felt he wasn't being kept informed of everything that was going on in their partnership, but Chow thought that business was his domain and that he didn't have to consult Bruce about every decision. He told Bruce to get on with the acting.

The whole project was coming closer and closer to being cancelled and there was a growing anxiety that Bruce was about to withdraw from the film. As the days passed, he continued to be absent from the set. Warners kept sending telegrams pleading 'WHERE'S BRUCE?' along with new versions of the script, the latest of which brought Fred Weintraub's comment that it was 'a piece of shit; all philosophy and no action'.

On 28 February, as another 'WHERE'S BRUCE?' telegram arrived Bruce was in fact back at his old school, St Francis Xavier, as guest of honour to present the sports-day prizes. On the platform he stripped to the waist to flex his muscles for his young admirers, laughing and joking for an hour or two and happy to be away from all the problems.

Meanwhile actor John Saxon arrived in Hong Kong, believing and acting as if he was the real star of the picture, saying that he'd been hired to give the film some class. But there was never any argument about who was the real star of *Enter the Dragon*. That week, Bruce Lee's face was on the cover of no less than twenty-seven different magazines, adding to the many pressures and tensions he was feeling. During the years that he managed Neil Diamond and Bill Cosby, Fred Weintraub had seen how, as their ambitions were realized, they changed – indeed, they *had* to change. 'But Bruce had got so big, so fast,' adds Weintraub, 'it scared him.'

Bruce Lee was only too aware that *Enter the Dragon* was the big chance he'd worked his whole life for, but he had yet to prove that he could pull it off, not only to himself but to people like James Coburn and Steve McQueen. Bruce kept telling the producer that he would only be happy if *Enter the Dragon* out-grossed the film McQueen was currently making.

In just two furious years, Bruce had made three hit action movies and interrupted work on a fourth to begin a fifth. Despite the deep inroads he'd made into writing, acting and directing, it was as if all his incredible energy, self-belief and motivation were suddenly deserting him. He even began to talk about what should be done 'if anything happened' to him. Despite his new-found fame and massive potential wealth, Bruce was painfully aware that his family's future depended more than anything on his supreme physical fitness and special abilities. But suddenly everything had become very fragile.

Eventually filming started without Bruce as Linda continually assured everyone that he would eventually show up. Even then the simplest of things would not go smoothly. A brief scene was attempted in which seven praying mantises, specially flown in from Hawaii, were to fight to the death, but they too refused to perform. Meanwhile on the set, real fights broke out between stuntmen and extras hired from rival Triad families, the Chinese crime syndicate that had a finger in any pie with money in it, including many aspects of the Hong Kong movie business.

Run Run Shaw had informants at every level of the production team of *Enter the Dragon* and was well aware of what was happening in the rival camp. While he said publicly that the film would never be made, privately he might well have hoped that it would ruin Raymond Chow. Perhaps seizing an opportunity to make mischief, Shaw invited Robert Clouse and Fred Weintraub to dinner at his opulent house in his studio grounds, where they were met at high gates and escorted up the long sweeping drive by his armed, uniformed guards. At the long dinner table, Shaw sat next to his associate, the wily Mona Fong. Other guests included actor William Holden – there to pitch a film version of the book *Tai Pan* – and a British film censor who moralized pompously, saying that he would remove any nunchaka scenes from the British version of *Enter the Dragon*. While they dined on snake soup Shaw praised Bruce Lee, showed his concern for the picture and asked questions to which his spies had already told him the answers.

Nearly two weeks into the shooting schedule, there was still nothing of Bruce Lee on film. Fred Weintraub continued to assure Warners that everything was going well, but in reality he began asking Linda what on earth they could do.

'There was a lot of tension,' Weintraub comments. 'Bruce was so nervous – he'd wanted this so much – that his tension was the tension of the film. He argued with everyone and played everyone off against each other. Sometimes I kept out of the way and sometimes I stepped in to help. But any time I had a real problem I would go to Linda; she was the only one who had the sensibilities to deal with Bruce. *Enter the Dragon* would not have been made without Linda's help.'

Linda made one last attempt to calm Bruce and restore his confidence, then called Weintraub and told him that things were going to be all right. But right away there was a new problem. In the first scene that Bruce filmed, where he is talking to the female agent played by Betty Chung, his face developed a nervous twitch that was obvious in close-ups. Nothing was said about it, as long shots and various angles were improvised. The ploy worked and after lunch the twitching nerve had settled down, never to reappear.

On top of the tremendous psychological stress Bruce Lee was under, enormous demands were made on his physical energy. In just one take he might have to fight ten or twelve attackers in rapid-fire succession, leaping to the side, to the front, twisting behind, spinning, striking, kicking, blocking with inch-perfect accuracy and split-second timing, all with the right expressions and reactions, and all in a way that was totally convincing. He couldn't even use a stand-in to rehearse the other stuntmen because, as the choreographer, he had worked out and timed all the moves and he needed to fine-tune them himself. And besides, who could match his abilities? Bruce was the only person in the world who could do what he did. If only one man missed his cue or miscalculated, the whole sequence would have to be run again, meaning that some fight scenes required fifteen or twenty takes.

The intense demands on Bruce Lee's physical and nervous energies, the heat and humidity and the draining ever-present back pain, all dug deeper and deeper into his internal resources, so that he suffered from dehydration and weight loss at an alarming rate. At night he couldn't sleep and so spent most of the night working out fight scenes and drawing complex diagrams of the action. People who'd known Bruce for years said his skin tone changed completely and that he didn't look well. Even so, on set Bruce declined the privilege of special meals, electing to eat with the rest of the crew. 'No director could ask more from a performer,' wrote Robert Clouse in his book *The Making of Enter the Dragon*.

Bob Wall remembers it differently, though: 'How Bruce kept

from punching out Robert Clouse, I'll never know. Bruce wasn't greatly secure in his acting ability, but he knew how to direct action – something Clouse had no idea about. While Clouse got at Bruce through Michael Allin, Bruce insisted Clouse be barred from the set during fight scenes. Bruce said that if he couldn't direct the action then he wouldn't go on. *That's* why Bruce spent so many days not showing up: he refused to show up until Clouse was off the set.'

Along with the challenges in front of the camera, Bruce also had to face challenges off-camera, when he should have been able to snatch a moment's respite and a cup of his favourite chrysan-themum tea. Bruce got on well with the stuntmen; they had become a team and Bruce had earned their respect just as they'd earned his. They too were taking risks; unlike the way stunts were arranged in Hollywood, there were no air bags or mattresses out of shot to break their falls, no fake glass bottles or balsa-wood chairs. At any given time one or two of the stuntmen would be injured, and Bruce did what he could to help, lending them money or arranging a bonus.

Along with the professional stuntmen, there were also hundreds of extras – sometimes between three and four hundred – most of them street kids. Every so often one of these kids would walk up to Bruce and openly question the genuineness of his abilities. The usual way was to tap one's foot three times in front of him, a reference to the nickname Bruce had been given by the stuntmen, who called him Bruce Three Legs or Three-Kicks Bruce because he could deliver consecutive kicks so rapidly.

For the most part, Bruce would ignore it, but as he knew only too well, most of these kids had little to look forward to and had seen the opportunity for a moment of glory. They might even get in a lucky punch, then who knew what opportunities might follow for 'the man who beat Bruce Lee'? Bruce himself would never actually initiate a fight, but if the challenger kept insisting or insulting him, he might ask what his challenger knew about fighting, anticipating the reply, 'As much as I need to.'

It was in these brief confrontations that one could witness the vast difference between Bruce Lee's movie fighting style and his real fighting method. The movie style used a lot of visually spectacular, spinning and flying kicks from Northern Shaolin kung fu, whose original purpose was to unseat people attacking on horseback. But when Bruce Lee fought for real, there were no fancy moves and no wild noises, only simple, direct, efficient strikes, with no facial expression except for the look in his eyes – a fierce, unflinching gaze of what he himself called 'controlled cruelty'. He did just as much as he needed to let the kid know the game was over.

There were even newspaper ads in the Hong Kong press offering rewards in the form of movie contracts to any challenger who could topple Bruce Lee. One aspiring hero succeeded in getting over the wall and into the compound of Lee's home on Cumberland Road, where he confronted Bruce with, 'So just how good are you?' The trespasser soon found out as he was side-kicked in the ribs and thrown off the property. Bruce later admitted he'd kicked him harder than he'd ever kicked anyone in his life. 'I gave it all to him,' he said.

When cameraman Gil Hubbs first arrived at Golden Harvest studios he'd found most of the camera equipment in a bad state of disrepair and none of the lenses he wanted to use. Hubbs took the initiative of hiring the equipment he needed from another supplier, upsetting both the producers and Golden Harvest, who were presented with additional costs. Even so, the entire picture was shot using just two cameras and three lenses. The second cameraman, Charles Lowe, was presented with similar problems in the lighting department, where equipment was so badly rusted it was, he said, good only for one last stand in India. To add to difficulties there were voltage fluctuations in the electricity supply. On top of all this the Golden Harvest studios were originally a textile mill and the daily rushes were usually covered in tiny white specks.

Contrary to usual production methods, sound was recorded while filming, but it was impossible to keep the hundreds of extras and crew quiet during shooting. A feast scene was scheduled, but there was no food. Someone misinterpreted an order and instead of doves, frogs arrived. Props that had been there the day before weren't there the next. Lighting set-ups were changed overnight, meaning that scenes had to be shot all over again. Extras who arrived for an exciting day in the movie business found themselves sitting around for hours, so would fail to show up the next day.

As the sumo wrestlers ate their way through tons of food, there was the occasional flutter of feathers as an exotic bird tumbled from its perch, roasted by the heat of an arc lamp. Each morning the sound stages had to be cleared of dogs and squatters who had spent the night sleeping on the couches or floor. The hundreds of extras needed to play the derelict prisoners were *actual* derelicts recruited from the streets of Hong Kong. There was a problem getting actresses to play prostitutes, so real prostitutes were hired. Actress and martial arts champion Angela Mao got only $100 for her two days' work, while chief cameraman Gil Hubbs was making only $250 a week. At $150 a day, the hookers were the biggest wage earners on *Enter the Dragon*, resulting in a lot of ill feeling on set.

While filming the scene where Lee tricks Parsons onto the dinghy that's being towed along behind the junk taking them to Han's Island, the actor Peter Archer almost drowned. Seconds after the scene was cut, the boat capsized, dumping the actor into the churning waters of the China Sea. There were several further accidents, two of which involved Bruce Lee.

In the early part of Bruce's fight with Bob Wall, he kicks Wall over a row of chairs and through a line of Han's men. Wall picks up two bottles, which were there to provide water for the tournament contestants, smashes their ends together and confronts Bruce with a broken bottle in each hand. This being Hong Kong, these were real bottles, not the sugar fake bottles normally used for stunts like this. So far everything had gone precisely as rehearsed, but as Bob Wall moved in, Bruce kicked and then whipped round to punch him, hitting the edge of the broken bottle with his hand. The assistant director, Chaplin Chang, had to rush Bruce to hospital by car where twelve stitches were required to close a deep gash on his finger. He was unable to resume work for several days.

The stuntmen took a dark view of this, convinced that it was no accident. Bruce's deeply superstitious countrymen grew more and more restless until there was a meeting in which he got entangled in their speculation that these incidents might not have been entirely accidental. There was a sense of paranoia in the air. Robert Clouse writes that meanwhile he had received a call from Raymond Chow saying that, in order to save face, Bruce would have to get his revenge on Wall and that it was up to the director to find a way out of the problem. Clouse says that Bruce had intended 'to kill' Bob Wall and the director claims he had to tell Bruce to back off because Wall was needed for further filming and had to stay healthy for the good of the picture.

'Clouse's account is bullshit,' counters Wall. 'We'd already shot that scene seven times before the accident. Not only that, I was breaking real bottles and then having to fall to the ground like a slain ox without being able to look down and see where all the glass had landed.'

Bob Wall is now a real estate broker and entrepreneur in California. When interviewed in his office he recalls the incident and springs up from behind his desk to demonstrate how the fight had been choreographed. He was to lunge at Bruce's chest with a broken bottle; Bruce would block it with a kick to Wall's forearm, then turn quickly to deliver a spinning back-kick. On the eighth take, Bruce's first kick landed fractionally high so he didn't deflect Wall's arm far enough. Then when he spun out of his kick there wasn't enough clearance, resulting in his hand striking the broken glass.

I called Bruce at home and asked him if he'd heard the rumours,' Wall continues. 'He said that he had. I asked him if he intended to kill me and he replied that he'd said no such thing. We could never prove it, but we were convinced that Clouse made up the whole story and spread the rumour. Sure Bruce got cut, but it was an accident. If Bruce had wanted to kill me he had several opportunities. We retook that scene about ten times; all he needed to do was kick me a bit higher or a bit lower than he did.'

Yet on one of those takes Bruce *did* kick Wall so hard that an extra positioned to catch him sustained a broken arm from the impact. 'Bruce knew I could take a good shot,' says Wall. 'He didn't want fake reactions.' Wall took several good shots and emerged covered in red welts, bringing at least some satisfaction to the complaining stuntmen. The fact that there was only one timing-related accident between them shows the phenomenal level of control at which Bruce and his opponents worked.

Jim Kelly was also imposing as martial artist but the same couldn't be said about John Saxon. Robert Clouse wrote that Saxon believed himself to be the 'class' in the film. Like Elvis Presley, Saxon had dabbled in karate to enhance his image, but while the camera pulls back to record the explosive grace of Bruce Lee on screen, Saxon's action sequences require close-up shots to disguise his limited abilities.

Robert Clouse wrote:

> I have been asked many times if Bruce was really as fast as people claimed. All I can say is he had the fastest reflexes I've ever seen. In one shot, Bruce was in a standoff with Bob Wall. In order to see his hand lash out and hit Bob, we had to speed the camera up to thirty frames [a second]. At normal speed it didn't show on film.

The film's editor, Kurt Hirshler, had the perfect opportunity to study Bruce: stopping the film, slowing it down and running it back and forth, just as Bruce had done when studying the actions of boxing champions. Viewing Bruce's standoff with Wall he was intrigued to see that within a single frame of film Bruce's fist had shot out without warning.

A second accident happened while preparing to shoot a scene with a cobra. Before each take, in order to get the hood around the cobra's head to flare out, Bruce would rap the snake across the nose a few times. Finally it struck back. Fortunately, the snake had just been drained of venom, but Bruce was left wounded and shaken. 'Bruce had beaten the snake nine times before it beat him,' adds Bob Wall.

During the last two weeks Bruce stayed on with the director while they filmed the fight sequence between Lee and Han in the mirrored maze. This sequence was not in the original script, which ended with Han impaled on his own metal claw, but was improvised. At one time or another almost everyone except Bruce has taken credit for this idea. A box, about six feet square and faced in mirror glass, was placed in the centre of a room lined with mirrors. From any position in the room there were multiple reflections. Against one wall, three mirrored booths were constructed, which further fragmented the images, and a glass hide was built to cover the camera.

When the sequence was being shot Shih Kien was forced to call out, 'Take it easy, son. It's only a movie!' The actor, who had played the villain in the Master Kwan films Bruce had watched as a boy, was a veteran of some 800 martial arts films and had spent over fifty years training in kung fu daily. Now over sixty, Shih Kien was older than he looked.

Robert Clouse wrote:

In the end, it was all worth it. You couldn't have recreated that Oriental atmosphere in Hollywood for a million dollars. The sights and sounds, even the smells, combined to create a feeling of intense realism for everyone involved in the production and I believed that quality would come over on the screen.

The atmosphere in Han's dungeons must have been pretty realistic; there were hundreds of hookers and tramps pressed together for hours in claustrophobic interiors with no ventilation or air conditioning. The final scenes of *Enter the Dragon* were shot hurriedly as the dungeon scenery began to crack and crumble around them. In the climactic mass fight on the tournament field, the rehearsed encounter rapidly turned into a free-for-all between rival families of Triads who took the opportunity to settle old scores, and the fights continued long after the cameras had stopped filming.

The fight scene in the underground caves ranks as one of Bruce's most stunning sequences on film. Eliminating Han's guards, first in ones and twos, he is soon dealing with them in increasing numbers, now using a series of weapons: the pole, the kali sticks and the nunchakas. To try and describe the complex fluidity and flow would be a long and futile exercise; it is enough to say that as a movie martial artist Bruce's ability had become almost luminous.

The first time he ever saw Bruce Lee in *Enter the Dragon*, the singer songwriter Phil Ochs, a contemporary of Bob Dylan, was moved to write an article for *Time Out* magazine about it:

> It is not the vulgarity of James Arness pistol-whipping a drunken, stubbled stage robber. It is not the ingenious devices of James Bond coming to the rescue, nor the ham-fisted John Wayne slugging it out in the saloon over crumbling tables and paper-thin imitation glass. It is the science of the body taken to its highest form; and the violence, no matter how outrageous, is always strangely purifying.

In *Enter the Dragon*, Bruce Lee moved as fluidly and as gracefully as Ali moved in his prime, but with a rhythm that was all his own. And he was fast, too . . . faster! So explosive were his punches that the camera speed had needed to be adjusted so they could be captured. Even then, you could only see moves begin and end, with nothing in between. Punches and kicks . . . and yet much, much more. Lee's limbs swooped and stabbed in such a poetically precise way that his blows seemed to slice the air into pieces.

Bruce Lee was one of the only genuinely graceful men we had ever seen. Women were often graceful; but men, even the great dancers, almost never were. Lee used hands and feet, knees and elbows, shoulders and head – his entire body – with perfect grace and balance. Pushing the laws of physics and human anatomy to their limits, already larger than life to begin with, but now even three times larger, luminous and incandescent, twenty foot tall on the screen. Even when he was standing still, there was something inside him that shimmered – something so alive it continued to tremble and vibrate.

Yet although he was the little guy who could righteously whip one bad guy after another with unthinkable speed, power, accuracy and dynamic beauty, there was also a kind of eggshell fragility about him. And as we watched, awestruck and enchanted, somewhere at the back of it all we realized . . . that he was no longer alive.

# 23

## *Circumstances*

Anticipating that *Enter the Dragon* would be a massive success, Bruce Lee ordered a gold Rolls Royce Corniche. *The Shrine of Ultimate Bliss* was intended to be Bruce Lee's next film, but before the release of *Enter the Dragon*, and before he could complete the interrupted work on *Game of Death* or take delivery of his new car, Bruce Lee had died.

The *Shrine of Ultimate Bliss* would have pitted Lee against a Western adversary played by James Bond actor George Lazenby, who'd been signed to a three-picture deal by Concord Productions. The film's original tagline was 'It's Lee! It's Lazenby! It's Bruce Versus Bond!'

As with *Enter the Dragon*, Warners were going to co-produce and distribute the film. The planned production budget of $10 million and worldwide marketing budget of a further $10 million were astronomical sums at the time. We can only speculate what Bruce's earnings might have been.

Other projects had also been proposed. There was a possible film starring Bruce and Elvis Presley – the king of kung fu and the king of rock and roll. Sophia Loren's husband, the film producer Carlo Ponti, called and offered 'a substantial sum to be determined' to secure Bruce's name on a contract. One Hungarian producer offered two million dollars for Bruce to appear in . . . anything. There is simply no doubt that Bruce Lee was poised to become the biggest star in the world and well on his way to fulfilling his 'impossible' written affirmation that he would earn ten million dollars by 1980.

But on 10 May 1973, Bruce Lee was in a dubbing room at Golden Harvest studios, looping dialogue for *Enter the Dragon*, repeatedly recording his voice over a short loop of film until the new voice matched the original speech movement as closely as possible. Inside the tiny room it was sweltering, but the air-conditioning unit had been shut down to avoid its noise being recorded. Another typhoon was approaching and the heaviness in the air pressed down on the back of his neck like a giant hand in a wet glove.

Bruce was still drained from the gruelling weeks of filming and had spent many days under these conditions, so no one was surprised when said he felt a bit faint and needed to get out for a minute. He went to a lavatory in the next building and splashed his face with cold water to clear his head, but suddenly he was falling . . . as the scene faded and dissolved to black.

Out of the darkness he heard footsteps approaching as he slowly came round and pretended he was looking for his glasses, which had fallen to the floor. But Bruce had been lying there unconscious for over twenty minutes and the studio assistant who'd been sent to look for him had to help him to his feet. Bruce was pale and sweating buckets, and he had to be helped further as he walked shakily back to the dubbing room. Then suddenly he collapsed again as his body was wrenched into a vomiting fit that left him struggling for breath and feeling as if he were fighting a dark shadow, just as he'd done in the middle of that fateful night in his room above Ruby Chow's restaurant.

Bruce was rushed to the nearby Baptist Hospital where an American doctor, Charles 'Don' Langford, saw that he was running a fever of 105 degrees and wouldn't respond to any stimuli. Now and again, Bruce's eyes would flicker open, though they couldn't focus, and every breath seemed like his last gasp as his body lathered with sweat. Langford immediately summoned neurosurgeon Dr Peter Wu and anaesthesiologist Dr Cecilia

Wong while an anaesthesia machine was improvised as a respirator with a breathing tube into Bruce's throat and an intravenous glucose drip was set up.

Various suggestions about the cause of the collapse were considered in rapid succession – exhaustion, kidney failure, epilepsy – and the appropriate actions were discussed. When a swelling of fluid pressing on the brain was discovered, most credence was given to the diagnosis of cerebral oedema. When Bruce lapsed into complete unconsciousness, it was decided to give him Manitol (a dehydrating agent) to reduce the swelling that had been detected by Dr Wu, and a catheter was set up to drain the flow of urine, which was a side effect of the medication.

Don Langford says, 'From being semi-comatose he suddenly became very agitated – it was almost a seizure – and he could have injured himself, so we had to tape his arms and legs down. Even between four of us we had trouble controlling him. Then we got ready to perform brain surgery should there be no improvement.'

During an anxious two-hour wait, it was obvious to everyone that Bruce was fighting for his life. When he showed signs of pulling back from the brink, he opened his eyes and stared out in confusion.

'By the time we got him into the ambulance,' Dr Langford continues, 'to take him to St Theresa's, where there were beds available, he was still out of it and couldn't speak coherently. Both Dr Wu and I knew that he'd been very close to death.'

The police statement made later by Dr Peter Wu contains the following paragraphs:

8) . . . Mr LEE was interviewed along with his wife in his ward on 13th May, 1973, when he told me that he had taken a piece of cannabis leaf before the onset of his illness on 10th May 1973.

9) Mr LEE requested to be discharged on 13th May, 1973. He refused to take other tests and revealed that he would

be leaving for the U.S.A. in a couple of weeks' time. He stated that he would have the tests in the U.S.A.

10) My clinical diagnosis on Mr LEE were [sic]: (1) cerebral oedema, and (2) poisoning by cannabis suspected.

The doctors agreed that something strange had happened, and along with other information they wanted to know everything that Bruce had eaten around the time of the collapse. When it came to light that one of the things he'd eaten was a hash cookie, it was suggested that he may have had a bad reaction to the drug. He was advised not to eat it any more. He didn't follow their advice.

Two weeks later, Bruce and Linda Lee flew to Los Angeles, checked into a private bungalow in the grounds of the Beverly Hills Hotel, then went to the University of California Medical Center, where a team led by Dr David Reisbord gave Bruce a complete physical examination, including exhaustive brain tests. Eventually they could only accept the diagnosis of the doctors in Hong Kong that Bruce had suffered a convulsion of no identifiable cause, accompanied by excess fluid around the brain. Dr Reisbord prescribed Dilantin, a drug used to calm the brain activity of epileptics, and discharged Bruce with the remark that his body was in superb condition.

During the following week, Bob Wall saw Bruce several times and says:

The last time I was at Bruce's little Japanese house in Kowloon Tong, we'd had a spirited disagreement about the relative merits of wine and hash. I encouraged him to drink wine to relax and told him that a couple of glasses of wine with a meal is considered beneficial, that he didn't have to get drunk and that he could use it without misusing it.

Bruce was enthusing about this article he'd read in *Playboy* about the relaxing effects of hash. Because Bruce neither drank nor smoked, he liked the idea of putting hash in cookies. I told him that there was no way you could know the source or quality of hash, whereas with a bottle of wine there's a label with the name of the vineyard.'

Bruce countered that he only bought the best quality and as I sipped my wine, Bruce ate a hash cookie. As the evening wore on, the spirited debate turned to conversation on the martial arts and philosophy, with Bruce becoming mellow, relaxed and charming.

But later Bruce was miserable; he looked chalky white and thin, nervous and upset. I tried to get him to join me in training but he didn't even go out running once that whole week. That just wasn't Bruce Lee. He told me, 'I'm getting checks poked at me from everywhere . . . people are making up stories about me. Fame isn't what I thought it would be. I haven't got time to train.' Bruce, who was always so clear in his intentions and direction, now seemed jumbled, unsure and just plain worn out. He would repeat himself in a conversation. He told me that his collapse had really scared him and he thought he was going to die. I told him to take a couple of months off, but he said, 'But I've got to promote the film, there's the Johnny Carson Show . . .' He knew it was all finally happening for him and he didn't want to lose it; he was scared that everything he'd worked so hard for was suddenly going to be taken away. Yet at the same time he wondered if it was all worth it. Bruce was putting a lot of pressure on himself.

While in Los Angeles, Bruce went to an early screening of *Enter the Dragon* at the Warners studio. The music soundtrack and sound effects were yet to be added, along with the fades, dissolves and other optical effects, but even so, at the end of the screening, when the house lights came on, Bruce punched the air and exclaimed, 'This is the one!' The Warners executives also knew it was a winner, and even though they'd already gone over budget, they immediately authorized an extra $50,000 to upgrade the music soundtrack and began stepping up publicity for the film's release and the premiere, which was to be held at Grauman's Chinese Theatre in Hollywood on 24 August, to be followed by Bruce's appearance on *The Johnny Carson Show* in New York.

The buzz about *Enter the Dragon* flew around the industry grapevine. Suddenly every studio and producer in the world had a project that was absolutely perfect for Bruce Lee. Warners had already asked him to sign for five more features, offering to pay him $150,000 per film, per year, for life. In truth, he could have got double or treble that, and more.

Aside from personal strain, there were also business conflicts. When Warners decided they wanted to change the title of *Enter the Dragon* back to the earlier *Blood and Steel*, Bruce fiercely disputed it. The studio responded by conceiving a new title that was spectacular in its awfulness, and Bruce was only able to make them back off by threatening never to work for them again. A week later, *Han's Island* had once more become *Enter the Dragon*.

In June 1973 Bruce resumed work on *Game of Death* and picked up his running battle with the Hong Kong press over his relationship with Betty Ting Pei. Golden Harvest's press office responded that many of the rumours and allegations circulating were transparent lies started by unknown persons at Shaw Brothers Studios.

On a business note, Bruce Lee's 'concord' with Raymond Chow was now turning into discord. Even though Bruce was drawing a salary of $HK12,500 a week – with $1,000 for 'living expenses' – not only was he questioning the accounting for *Way of the Dragon*, he was also angry that Chow had gone ahead with foreign release deals while he'd wanted to hold out for better offers. He was also upset by a story that had appeared in Golden Harvest's in-house magazine, which claimed that Chow had not only discovered Bruce Lee but was 'like a babysitter' to him. Bruce retorted that the article made him sound like a stupid child who relied solely on Raymond, and he began to put pressure on Chow by asking Run Run Shaw for $HK2 million to do a film for Shaw Brothers.

Bruce even went as far as shooting some test footage for a film in which he would act traditional Mandarin warrior roles. Of course he had no intention of signing a contract with Shaw or of going through with the project, but he knew that Shaw would trumpet news of the project from the headlines of the Hong Kong newspapers. It was simply a ploy to deliver a straightforward message to Chow.

On 10 July, Bruce Lee was at Golden Harvest studios when he heard that Lo Wei was in the building. Lo Wei, who had incensed Bruce by proclaiming himself 'Hong Kong's first millionaire director' and the 'man who taught Bruce Lee how to fight', found that now he was no longer involved with Bruce, his genius had suddenly deserted him. Even so, Bruce couldn't resist confronting Lo Wei and berating him. He burst into the screening room where the director was viewing a film called *Snake Girl*, along with his wife and Chow's partner, Leonard Ho. As Bruce yelled at him, Lo Wei didn't react, knowing it was futile to fight with Bruce, then Bruce returned to Chow's office.

Minutes later, Mrs Lo Wei appeared to tell Bruce he should behave with more decorum. This had quite the opposite effect and as tempers flared a small crowd gathered. Bruce then charged back to the screening room and denounced Lo Wei further. In the end the police were called after Lo Wei claimed that Bruce had pulled out a short knife concealed in his belt buckle and threatened to stab him. But the police couldn't find the knife and attempted to smooth over the situation rather than make arrests and involve lawyers. Lo Wei insisted that Bruce sign a hastily composed 'cease and desist' letter, promising simply, 'I, Bruce Lee, will leave Lo Wei alone.' The whole studio was in uproar, and in order to get the police and the newly arrived reporters out of the way, Bruce signed the letter. Later he became annoyed when he realized that this gave Lo Wei's version of events more substance.

That evening, when Bruce appeared on *Enjoy Yourself Tonight*, the incident was raised by the show's host, Ho Sho Shin. Bruce explained that if he really wanted to kill anyone, he wouldn't need to use a knife but could simply strike with his hands. But on the TV show, and at the host's insistence, Bruce offered to give a slightly less drastic demonstration of his skills. Although it was only a simple shoulder push, Ho was sent sprawling across the floor. To viewers – unused to the rigours of martial arts training – it looked severe, as if Bruce had slammed into the host hard. This resulted in yet another wave of critical headlines, and worse still, all of them tended to sympathize with Lo Wei and the day's events were cited as further evidence of Bruce's growing arrogance.

Bruce once famously said, 'Circumstances? Hell, I make circumstances!' But now 'circumstances' were becoming ugly intrusions into his life, along with the painful realization that success was not what he'd anticipated it would be. As the cyclone of celebrity began to gather its force he'd started drinking, and at one dinner drank his way through twenty pots of sake. Where once Bruce had supplemented his natural vitality with ginseng and royal jelly, vitamins and herbal teas, now he drank liquidized steak for strength, chewed cannabis and drank sake to help him relax, and his complexion had become pale and dull.

Just as life now offered Bruce Lee its worst, so Bruce Lee was showing the worst aspects of himself. He spent many nights away from home, sometimes at the studio, working through another restless night with ideas for *Game of Death*, while at other times he made his way ... elsewhere. His mood swings also became more pronounced. He'd say he still wanted to act, but not make any more martial arts films, adding that the public would only be interested in kung fu movies for about three years. Then the next day, he'd reaffirm his aim of wanting to educate audiences through the medium of film so that they would understand there was more to martial arts than just fighting.

One minute Bruce could see no end to his possibilities; the next he had no idea if he could maintain the effort needed to realize them. The more he did, the more he felt the need to stretch himself. He would cut people short, telling them that '*trying* to relax' is a contradiction. Even Bruce's friends perceived that he was being pulled in opposite directions: he was either pressed down by a great burden or spiralling away aimlessly. Bruce recalled Yip Man's advice given twenty years before, that nobody can oppose a problem head-on, they have to flow with it.

Attempting to apply this wisdom to his accelerating life, Bruce decided that the answer was to match the speed of change happening around him. Linda Lee later made the analogy that even a car like a Ferrari can't stand being driven with its rev counter permanently over the red line. After all her efforts to get him started on the set of *Enter the Dragon*, she now felt powerless to apply the brakes. Even Linda's mother expressed her concern about Bruce, telling Taky Kimura, 'He's losing weight. Tell him to rest, he'll listen to you.'

All Bruce's relationships had become riddled with suspicion. Bruce told Thomas Chan, an actor who'd had a minor role in *Fist of Fury*, that he had a mountain of money in front of him if he wanted it, but the people who offered the money thought it would buy Bruce; they believed they would own him. 'I must be very, very careful,' Bruce told Chan. Friends could only witness his increasing isolation.

Fred Weintraub says that Bruce was now a different person to the one he'd been only weeks before in Los Angeles, adding that he was no longer so friendly and kept others at a distance.

The actress Nora Miao says, 'Bruce Lee felt lonely in the few months before his death. He was a changed man. He used to phone me and tell me he felt lonely. I told him, "No one dares get close to you!" Confused, he said, "Why? Why do I feel that I don't have a real friend when there are so many people around me?" I said "It's not so strange. You've become an idol. People only flatter you. Then, when they do this, you despise them. On the other hand, if they criticize you, you resent it. You are a victim of fame."'

Perhaps Bruce Lee now had occasion to recall what his mother had told him when he was ten years old, when he'd told her of his ambitions and she'd replied, 'The life of a famous film star is not so comfortable as you imagine. Their lives are abnormal.'

Grace Lee recalls, 'Following his increasing fame, he became thinner and thinner. When he returned to Los Angeles after finishing *Way of the Dragon* he had lost a lot of weight. I told him, "Have a good rest and relax a little." I was really worried about his health. Later, he started filming *Enter the Dragon*. When I saw him in May 1973, I couldn't believe the person in front of me was my son, he had changed so much. He told me that he wouldn't live much longer because doctors in Hong Kong had told him there was a serious problem inside his head. He said, "Mom, don't worry about your future, there will be no money problems." I reproached him at once and told him not to talk like that.'

Maria Yi also noticed a worrying trait: 'Before he died, he developed amnesia. Sometime after filming *The Big Boss*, when I visited him at the studio, he often took out a picture of his car and asked me to admire it. He repeated this action several times a day without knowing that he'd done it before. It was very unsettling.'

On 16 July, as a fierce typhoon approached Hong Kong, Bruce made a rambling $200 phone call to Unicorn, who was in a hotel in Manila where he was working on location. Bruce told his friend he was worried about the headaches he was experiencing.

The feng shui advisor who'd been called in to look over the house that Bruce had bought in Kowloon Tong wasn't happy. The area had a reputation for bringing down wealthy families, symbolized by its situation at the lowest point of a depression in the landscape. The two previous owners of Bruce's house had both suffered financial reversals. Additionally, the house was on the landing approach to Kai Tak airport, meaning that the natural wind currents were disturbed, while the house itself was facing the wrong way. The feng shui man devised a solution: a mirrored figure was placed on the roof of the building to reflect away the bad influences. On 18 July, this figure was blown off the roof by the approaching typhoon.

On the morning of 20 July 1973, Bruce Lee sat down to type a letter to his lawyer Adrian Marshall in Los Angeles. There were possibly some big changes ahead. Bruce wrote about meeting Raymond Chow to 'hear him out'. He listed five deals to be considered and anticipated spending the whole weekend looking at these offers with Marshall, working out a tax plan and endorsement deals for books and clothes. There were details of a hectic promotional tour for *Enter the Dragon*, including the trip to New York for the *Johnny Carson Show*. Bruce added that by 24 August he would be ready to come back to Hong Kong, 'hopefully in one piece'.

That evening, typhoon Dorothy lashed warm rain hard against the windows of the Hotel Miramar, where Raymond Chow and George Lazenby sat in the opulent restaurant. They ordered another aperitif and made small talk as they waited patiently for Bruce Lee and Betty Ting Pei to show up for dinner. It was to be an informal meeting to discuss ideas for *Game of Death*. But at Betty's apartment over on Beacon Hill Road, the actress was becoming desperate as she tried to rouse Bruce from sleep, shaking him and then slapping him across the face. Earlier in the day, Bruce and Raymond Chow had met with Betty at her apartment before Chow left alone. Shortly after, Bruce complained of a headache and, after being given an Equagesic headache pill by Betty, he went to lie on the bed.

Now, at just after nine o'clock in the evening, Chow received a call from Betty. He left the hotel and drove to her apartment, which took some thirty or forty minutes due to bad traffic. When he too could get no response from Bruce, Betty's doctor was summoned and then, after further delay, an ambulance was finally called. The ambulance arrived at the same time as Betty's mother and brother who had been summoned to try to calm the distressed actress. Raymond Chow phoned Linda Lee, telling her to get over to the Queen Elizabeth Hospital where Bruce was being taken.

Linda rushed to the hospital and arrived before the ambulance. There was an aching wait until the doors burst open and Bruce was rushed in, unconscious, on a stretcher, surrounded by a swarm of paramedics, one of whom was thumping on Bruce's chest, trying to keep his heart going. Events blurred – emergency room, stimulant injections, then electric shock pads – but despite the frantic activity, Bruce lay still. After the whirlwind of the past few weeks, hours and seconds, it took an eternity for the truth to hit home.

As the momentum of events picked up gradually, Raymond Chow's wife arrived to collect her husband and take Linda home. There was a long, slow walk down a calm white hospital corridor and suddenly they were confronted by a starburst of flashbulbs and a babble of reporters.

'Every week there would be a new rumour,' Taky Kimura says. 'Someone would say, "I see that Bruce was killed in a tournament last week." I would hear stuff like that from all over. One day, one of my packers told me, "Bruce Lee is dead; it's in all the papers." I didn't even bother to check. Then Linda's mother rang and told me . . .'

Grace Lee also didn't believe the news of her son's death. For months stories had been appearing in the Hong Kong press saying he was dead. She would immediately call up the paper or magazine to see if it was true and it never was. When she told Bruce how much the stories upset her, he would explain the obvious: that they were simply lies to sell magazines. He told her that the next time she heard or read such a story, she shouldn't believe it. When one of Grace Lee's friends called her, crying, with the news that Bruce was dead, she told her friend that it was a lie, but her friend said she hadn't read it in a magazine, she'd seen it on TV. When Grace Lee found out it was true, she said simply, 'Too much work.'

Linda Lee's immediate reaction was to consent to the suggestion that an autopsy be done. In the circumstances, it was deemed important enough for the British Government forensic laboratories to perform it three days later, on 23 July.

In the meantime, speculation was fuelled by Raymond Chow's first account to the press of events on the night of Bruce Lee's death, which implied that Bruce had died at home with his family.

Perhaps Chow was simply trying to spare Linda's feelings, knowing full well what the press would make of the actual situation. In any case, the first reports to be sent around the world said that Bruce had died at home. One paper romanticized things further by reporting that Bruce had died while walking in his garden with his wife. But Henry Parwani, a reporter from *The Star* – the same paper that was the subject of Bruce's legal action – went to the hospital to look over the ambulance call-out records and found the call had not come from Bruce's home but, as he had suspected, from the apartment of Betty Ting Pei. And so, on the day before the funeral *The Star*'s headline blazed: DRAGON KILLED IN BETTY TING PEI'S FRAGRANT CHAMBER.

Like Grace Lee, nobody could believe that the fittest man in the world had died at thirty-two. One could almost hear the anguished echoes from the opening scenes of *Fist of Fury* as Chen Zhen discovers the death of his master: 'How can a healthy man die!' Even on the very day of his death, one of the first rumours to surface was that it was all a publicity stunt to promote *Game of Death*. People were laying bets on whether or not it was true.

Another early headline suggested that Bruce Lee had died of an overdose of the aphrodisiac Spanish fly. Journalists went back through the photo files for any shots of him with a woman. One paper printed five pages of him with different women, smiling with his arm around them, with the implication that every single one had been his lover. Speculation swept through Hong Kong on a tidal wave of high emotion, and word at the Press Club was that Bruce had been involved in a big fight with ten or twenty men who had beaten him to death.

On 25 July, Bruce Lee's 'symbolic' funeral was the largest Hong Kong had ever witnessed. Three hundred police were put on duty outside the Kowloon Funeral Parlour where his body lay in an open bronze casket. Thirty thousand mourners had gathered to fill Maple Street, crowding balconies and lining the roofs as far as the eye could see. Inevitably people fainted and were injured in the pushing and shoving as emotions ran high.

Whenever the crowd spotted Nora Miao, Lo Wei, George Lazenby or other celebrities arriving at the steps of the funeral home, they started clapping and cheering, prompting the *South China Morning Post* to describe the scene as 'a carnival'. Of the gaggle of minor local stars who turned up, some had come to pay their respects, while others just came for the photo opportunity. Two people *not* seen were Run Run Shaw and Betty Ting Pei.

Inside the funeral parlour the midsummer air was thick and stifling with the aroma of flowers and incense. On arrival, each mourner would pay his respects at an altar where small bunches of flowers from tearful children lay next to expensive wreaths. Candles and incense burned before a photograph of Bruce, surrounded by long silk ribbons and flowers, above which hung a banner that read in Chinese: A STAR SINKS IN THE SEA OF ART. Each mourner bowed three times at the altar, then took their place in the hall.

Then came the sad arrival of Linda Lee, red-eyed behind her dark glasses and almost buried in the folds of her traditional mourning clothes: a white burlap robe and headdress. The children, Brandon and Shannon, were each in their own little white robes, blissfully unaware of what was happening as they took their places. To their side sat Bruce's mother Grace, his brother Peter and Unicorn, who had returned from Manila.

The band struck up the traditional funeral song. Now Bruce's coffin was brought in and situated near the altar for the mourners to file past. His body lay swathed to the chin in white silk and his face looked grey and somehow distorted under heavy make-up. In the pocket of his suit were his broken spectacles. Long after the funeral was over, police with loudspeakers patrolled the streets, urging people to go home.

The day after the ceremony in Hong Kong, Linda left for Seattle with Bruce's body. At Kai Tak airport, Linda, now dressed in black and her face strained with sorrow, read out a press statement in an attempt to stop the mounting controversy surrounding Bruce's death. Linda said she knew what made good headlines, and asked what difference it made anyway.

The tickets that were to have been used to travel to New York for Bruce's appearance on the *Johnny Carson Show* had been traded in for tickets to return his body to the United States. The funeral in Hong Kong had been for his family, friends and fans there, but because his happiest times had been in Seattle, his family decided to bury him in peaceful Lake View Cemetery, where he used to enjoy walking alone in the rain.

On 31 July, a small crowd of twenty people gathered outside the Butterworth Funeral Home on East Pine Street to watch colleagues and friends arrive for Bruce's funeral. But during the journey, the coffin had been damaged. This was taken by some to be an omen that his soul was not at peace, and with all the controversy raging, it's hard to see how it could have been. The new coffin was covered with red, yellow and white flowers, making up the yin-yang sign he had first adopted as an emblem for his gung fu institutes.

The pallbearers were Robert Lee, Taky Kimura, Dan Inosanto, Steve McQueen, James Coburn and family friend and actor Peter Chin. As Bruce had wished, there was no traditional music. The music played was Frank Sinatra's version of 'My Way', Tom Jones singing 'The Impossible Dream', Sergio Mendes' 'Look Around', and the Blood, Sweat and Tears song, 'And When I Die'. Though all of these songs have since become clichéd cliché, and seem rather mawkish and sentimental, Bruce Lee more than most could at least claim to have lived life his way by attempting to achieve an almost impossible dream.

Linda Lee spoke first: 'He lived every day as a day of discovery. His thirty-two years were full of living. Bruce believed that the individual represents the whole of mankind, whether he lives in the Orient or elsewhere. He believed that man struggles to find a life outside himself, not realizing that the life he seeks is within him.'

Taky Kimura said simply that Bruce had inspired good in others, while Ted Ashley expressed a more businesslike philosophy: 'It could be viewed as a pity that Bruce passed on right at the beginning of his realization that he would make it big. I have a sense of sadness mingled with the realization that, while he may not have gotten up the ladder, he at least got his foot on it.'

Finally, at the side of the grave, James Coburn made the last short speech: 'Farewell, my brother. It has been an honour to share this space and time with you. As a friend and as a teacher, you have given to me and have brought my physical, spiritual and psychological selves together. Thank you. May peace be with you.'

The coffin was lowered into the grave along with the pallbearers' white gloves.

# 24

## Inquest

On 3 September, the inquest opened in Tsunwan, under the directorship of coroner Egbert Tung. At the start of the inquest, police barricades had been set up to deal with the crowds who came to get a glimpse of Betty Ting Pei, but once the medical testimony began, the crowds drifted away. The 23 July autopsy had found traces of cannabis in Bruce Lee's stomach and the accompanying headlines now suggested he'd died a drug addict, while others suggested he'd needed drugs to accomplish his extraordinary physical feats.

The cannabis question had also become important because of the attendance at the inquest of David Yapp, of the American International Insurance Company. The company had seen a possible way out of paying up on Bruce's life insurance policy if it could be shown that Bruce had taken cannabis before he had filled out the application form and answered the question of whether he had ever used narcotics with a 'no'. Various tests for evidence of poisoning, made at the request of detectives, all proved negative. The only further finding was that Bruce had taken the equivalent of one tablet of the aspirin compound Equagesic.

Dr R. R. Lycette, the clinical pathologist at the Queen Elizabeth Hospital, told the hearing that death could not have been caused by cannabis but was due to hypersensitivity to one or more of the ingredients of Equagesic. While the doctor had found no injuries to the skull and no evidence of a brain haemorrhage, Bruce's brain had swollen very rapidly from its normal weight of 1,400 grams to 1,575 grams.

Ronald Teare, a professor of forensic medicine at the University of London, was flown in as the inquest's heavyweight. Over the course of thirty-five years Teare had supervised nearly 100,000 autopsies and provided evidence for almost 20,000 inquests. The professor said that the presence of cannabis was a mere coincidence, adding that it would be both 'irresponsible and irrational' to say that it might have triggered either the events of Bruce's collapse on 10 May or his death on 20 July. Although it was a rare and unusual case, he said, the only conclusion that could be reached was that death was caused by an acute cerebral oedema due to a reaction to compounds present in the prescription painkiller Equagesic.

Bruce Lee's doctor Charles Langford left Hong Kong in 1989 to head a medical faculty in Lafayette in his native Louisiana. Also a Baptist minister, he speaks in the measured tones of a Southern gentleman, recalling:

Neither Dr Wu nor myself ever saw Bruce with cannabis, but he told us that he used to chew the root. He did say that it made time slow down for a little while. I can see why it had appeal for Bruce; cannabis would induce a sense of timelessness that might relieve some of the pressure from deadlines that he was under. Bruce was in touch with reality in every way; he had a very realistic self-view. He didn't think that he was more than he was.

Bruce Lee was a man of unusual ability, but the opportunities, his importance and his fame all arrived in such a deluge that he literally didn't have the time to cope with it. From being a minor TV star he suddenly leaped to being the biggest thing in the world. If he hadn't had to deal with all the phoniness of that world, I think he could have coped. But what he was given to deal with was more than any mortal could have coped with. Even up until the time that I left Hong Kong, I would stop every day at my local newsstand and scan the covers of the papers and magazines. There wasn't one single day when Bruce's face wasn't on at least one cover, even sixteen years after his death.

The negative light in which the use of cannabis was viewed in Hong Kong can not be overstated. It was seen as far worse than the use of heroin or opium. The situation between East and West is reversed. While the Chinese view opium liberally, cannabis is considered a 'foreign' drug with sinister and evil overtones. Bruce's father and even his wing chun master Yip Man were no strangers to the opium pipe, but cannabis was associated with the 'hippie-tourist foreign devils', and this view had a massive impact on the official findings.

Dr Peter Wu's recommendation to the coroner reflected this cultural and even political pressure that the cause of death was due to hypersensitivity to Equagesic *or* cannabis. As the cause of death wasn't clear and cannabis was present, realistically, this possibility couldn't be denied, but the official verdict went on to name *only* Equagesic as the presumed cause.

When first interviewed by me in 1992 at his clinic in Hong Kong, Dr Wu still echoed his original opinion: 'Professor Teare was a forensic scientist recommended by Scotland Yard; he was brought in as the expert, so we can't contradict his testimony. The dosage of cannabis is neither precise nor predictable, but I've never known anyone to die simply from taking it.'

Dr Don Langford reminds us of the further reason for the verdict that was eventually reached by the inquest:

There was a great deal of concern because of Bruce's life-insurance policy. For a long time I believed that if I said anything the case might be reopened. I even took Bruce's notes out of the file at the Baptist Hospital in case someone might attempt to get to them. Cannabis has a known chemical alkaloid that can produce seizures: it can be extracted and administered to produce that effect. Equagesic was not at all involved in Bruce's first collapse. Thousands of people take Equagesic with no adverse effects, whereas people can be adversely affected by cannabis. It doesn't even need a hypersensitivity to it, simply exposure, and it's impossible to determine the dosage. There's not a question in my mind that cannabis should have been named as the presumptive cause of death. I would like to have seen a truer verdict rendered. But the whole world was watching this inquest to see if a precedent would be set. If cannabis had been ruled as the cause of death it would have opened up a real can of worms, because no one had ever before said it had that potential. Hong Kong didn't want to set that precedent, particularly in view of the fact that the coroner was a layman.

The coroner Egbert Tung was a lawyer with no scientific background, and by all accounts the inquest was something of a shambles and not without its comic moments.

Dr Langford adds:

He would stop us and make us spell medical terms for him, which he would then write out in long hand. It was ludicrous. . . . Does all this make Bruce Lee out to be some raving drug fiend? Of course not! He had the money and access to anything he wanted. Opium was more plentiful, and drugs would certainly have not been frowned on in entertainment circles. In my opinion, Bruce had simply taken practical steps to seek out something that would alleviate a little of the great pressure he was under.

With the passage of time, both Dr Langford and Dr Wu now feel freer to expand on their earlier opinions.

Don Langford states plainly:

He was the fittest man I've ever seen. A headache tablet didn't kill Bruce Lee. But he didn't think there was anyone who knew what was best for him, except himself. The factors that caused his collapse in May are the same as those that caused his death in July. Bruce was affected by one or more of the alkaloids in cannabis. The official verdict wasn't so much a cover-up as an attempt to produce a verdict that was more socially acceptable.

Dr Wu echoes this:

Bruce Lee could have died in May; he was in a very critical condition. It was sheer luck that there was someone there to help him. A lot of Nepalese hashish was taken from his stomach. Not wanting to damage his health by smoking canna-bis, he chose instead to eat it. Unfortunately, this overloads the body with the active ingredients far quicker than they can be processed. And his very low percentage of body fat, along with all the stress he was under, made him even more vulnerable to the drug and dramatically intensified its effects.

We gave him a good talking to before we discharged him from the hospital [in May] and told him not to eat the stuff again. Since he'd had such a bad reaction to it, we told him that if there was a next time the consequences might be even more severe. But I knew he wasn't listening. He was convinced that he was invincible . . . immortal.

By the end of the inquest on 24 September 1973, only a handful of reporters approached Linda Lee for her comment on the verdict of 'death by misadventure'. Once again, she could only ask them what difference it made.

After being introduced to cannabis by Steve McQueen, Bruce Lee started using it while he was in Los Angeles, and both Joe Lewis and James Coburn witnessed it. Bob Wall says that Bruce was using it while filming *Enter the Dragon* and kept a jar of hash brownies on his desk to nibble between takes. Between 1971 and 1973 Bruce's weight had dropped from 145 to 122 pounds, due to a punishing exercise regime and workload that resulted in his body fat content falling to the seemingly impossible figure of less than one per cent. On production stills taken on the set of *Enter the Dragon* it is even possible to see the individual clusters of muscle fibre, particularly on his shoulders, arms and chest.

On the film set, Bruce invited Ann Clouse, the director's wife, to feel his biceps. 'It was like feeling warm marble,' she commented. She also recalls that Bruce told her he would be dead before his next birthday and wondered just how much more he could push his body.

As an athlete, Bruce always drove himself higher, further and faster, but towards the end he was trying to do so while chained to the heavy load of stardom. Even if he'd had the opportunity, he never seemed to have the inclination to rest, just to try and 'stop time' for a while. Only once did he ever speak on the subject of rest, saying he saw it as a not particularly desirable state, but as somehow static, frozen and lifeless.

Bob Wall explains, 'He built himself. He took this skinny weakling body and turned it into something incredible. He put in hours of training, very intense, very complete. I don't know what motivated him to do it.'

Golden Harvest's Russell Cawthorne adds, 'I think the first impression you'd get from Bruce would be the incredible aura of energy that surrounded him, like an energy field. In fact, he seemed much bigger than he was physically. You almost got the impression that his feet never really touched the ground; he seemed to be standing about six inches above it. It was quite a remarkable experience just meeting him. The intensity you see in his films is just a watered-down version of what he had in real life. Bruce always stays in my mind as someone of incredible intensity, force and power, so motivated and so forward-driven you'd almost believe he could fly!'

Another Golden Harvest executive, Andre Morgan, remembers, 'He spent a whole morning doing one fight sequence, something like a dozen takes. We viewed the rushes and the third, fourth and fifth takes were all good, yet he went on and did a sixth, seventh and eighth, because all the time he didn't feel comfortable about them. As a person he was very intense. That was part of the problem. He was always going off in too many directions at once, to find out about everything as quickly as possible, always in a hurry.'

Chinese medicine, philosophy, religion and martial art – every aspect of its traditional culture – recognizes that there are channels through which life energy flows. This energy, chi, is not secondary to life but is fundamental to existence. The flow of chi is the very basis of life itself, as if our bodies and our personalities themselves are formed from its condensed ripples and patterns. These channels extend far beyond everyday physical reality; they move not only within the nervous system and the psychological realm, but ultimately throughout everything that exists.

Occasionally someone with a phenomenal concentration of will power, emotional intensity or physical determination strives to go beyond the normal uses of the body and mind, and beyond normal human needs. Such a person begins to open him- or herself up to these greater, more universal energies. This can happen through intense creative or physical effort done with great motivation or intent. To different degrees, this process can be seen in the lives of many of the great composers, writers and artists, as well as in the lives of spiritual masters and powerful dictators.

But some people may get to the point where this energy overwhelms them and they cannot channel it any more. For example, the painter Vincent van Gogh attempted to transfer onto his canvas the intense world that blazed before his eyes before it all became too much for him. There is a Greek myth that describes this situation: Prometheus steals the fire of the gods from heaven to bring back to earth, but ends up being consumed by the flames.

So did Bruce Lee simply burn out? Did the 'unlimited expression of his being', which Bruce found in his martial art, implode? Was the boy who could 'never sit still' not able to handle what was happening in his body as it came under increasing pressure? Was it simply pushed beyond the limits?

To use Western terminology for a moment: Bruce Lee was able to channel the archetypal energies that exist beyond the energy bound up in the everyday personality structure. He succeeded in accessing *extra*ordinary or even *super*natural levels of energy in a process that has been described in other ways by many different traditions.

For example, in tribal cultures a shaman is someone who is skilled in moving in dimensions of reality outside of the norm. The medicine men of the Plains Indians would use various disciplines, rituals and meditations to carry out 'vision quests' to acquire knowledge and power. In a similar way, the Chinese warrior priests found that lessons and techniques in martial arts could be transferred from the depth of the unconscious – even though this might later be described as a meeting with the spirit of a power animal, such as a tiger or a crane, or as some other supernatural force or being . . . maybe even a demon or dragon.

We can now appreciate the significance of that fateful night in Bruce's room above Ruby Chow's restaurant – his encounter with the archetypal energies that are the basis of human life – when, at the age of nineteen, he did battle with a dark force and came face to face with energy from the depths of the collective unconscious. The result of this encounter was that he became *more* motivated and driven, and it was this force that drove him to his great achievements, and on to the limits of what is humanly possible.

We get a taste of this energy when we watch Bruce on film, receiving a kind of secondary charge from him that has a curiously uplifting quality. Fred Weintraub recounts a telling incident at the premiere of *Enter the Dragon*, when a friend of his was so charged up by the end of the film that he told his wife to drive back alone to Beverly Hills because he wanted to *run* back.

Given the overload of pressure and phenomenal outpouring of energy in the last two years of Bruce's life, something had to give. There was the sheer physical effort of fighting in stupefying heat and humidity, doing take after take while writing and directing at the same time, as well as constantly turning over thoughts about what direction he should take next, and the strain created by his instant celebrity and constant intrusions into his personal life.

Too many people looked at Bruce and saw only dollar signs. While he tried to go with what was happening to him, it was all too much, too fast. Not only had he stopped training, in the end he'd stopped laughing, too.

James Coburn, says 'Wherever we were, he had to be at the centre of attention. He was always demonstrating his ability to control people, and when he wasn't in control, he left. But that still point, that still point in the middle of the action, I don't think he ever found that.'

Taky Kimura recalls, 'Just after his collapse, Bruce called me from LA and said, "You never write, you never call me." I said, "I'm enjoying what you're doing, you don't need me." He replied, "If I can help you, Taky . . . You're still my number one friend and don't you forget that. Let me know what you need. Anything you want. I haven't changed. I'm still the same guy." He never forgot that I'd helped him out in the past and that I never asked for anything. He told me to send the old plane ticket that he'd given me – to go to Hong Kong to start work on *Game of Death* – and he'd replace it.'

Taky may have been happy to see Bruce doing well, but he was wrong when he said Bruce didn't need him. At the end, what Bruce Lee needed wasn't a wife who supported but didn't challenge him. Nor did he need people who looked at him and saw only money, or fans who looked at him and saw a superman. What he really needed was an old teacher like Yip Man, or a genuine friend like James Coburn or Taky Kimura. He needed someone, *anyone*, who could have helped him to reconcile it all.

The last time Bruce spoke to Yip Man, he asked him: 'Do you still regard me as your student?'

Yip Man's response was to ask Bruce, 'Do you still regard me as your teacher?'

They laughed, but the silence that followed spoke for itself.

In the end, Bruce isolated himself through his own fierce

autonomy. And instead of being full of 'the love of life and the power of all things', he succeeded in his ambition to become a totally self-made man. . . . But one who had nowhere left to turn but to his creator. It turned out that behind the dazzling brilliance of his creation he was just as human as we are. He shared our vanities and flaws, just as we all share his unrealized potential.

The 'what if?' questions will never go away, and his unrealized potential will forever be the footnote to the legend and the icon. Of course Bruce had big personal ambitions, more than the occasional ulterior motive, and ambivalent goals. At the end of his life, Bruce was trying to reconcile the two most opposite human pursuits: the preoccupations of Hollywood, celebrity and wealth with the disciplines found in a Taoist monastery. Put bluntly, there are not many gold Rolls Royces parked outside the Shaolin temple.

It's almost as if Bruce had trained and dedicated himself for twenty years to become the ultimate screen hero for just one film. *Enter the Dragon* took Bruce to within touching distance of the seemingly impossible statement where he affirmed that he would become the first genuine international Chinese star and make $10 million in ten years.

Bruce's finger may have been pointing to the moon and all its heavenly glory, but he had also taken to wearing a full-length mink coat and enough aftershave to bring down a swarm of tsetse flies. And in the end, the master of unarmed combat had taken to carrying an illegal handgun whenever he left his house in Kowloon Tong.

How could he possibly have carried on writing, choreographing, directing and starring in films, training as consistently and intensively as he needed to, eating the right foods, flying around the world to meetings to set up new deals, endorse new products, appear in ads, do interviews, promote films . . . and still spend time with his family? Something had to give, and it did. The fittest man in the world, it seems, had one weak spot.

The hyperactive child, the dancer, the innovative teacher, the philosopher, the star, the fiercely autonomous individual, the prophet of kung fu – these were all roles that Bruce Lee was forced to carry, sometimes simultaneously, by his own sense of destiny. At its climax, this destiny saw intense discipline and unique ability being worked out on the world stage for millions. In the end, the ultimate impossibility of this combination of energies is probably what killed him.

And if it did, then Bruce Lee died the death his whole life had been preparing him for: a death that went beyond the limits of identity.

> If you always put limits on yourself and what you can do, physical or anything, you might as well be dead. It will spread into your work, your morality, your entire being. There are not limits, only plateaux. But you must not stay there, you must go beyond them. If it kills you, it kills you.
>
> *Bruce Lee*

# 25

## Rumours and Lies

Predictably, the inquest did nothing to quell the rumours that sprang up immediately after Bruce's death and which become ever more extravagant year on year.

It's true that there were probably many people with whom Bruce Lee had no personal connection who wished him dead. There were suggestions that Bruce had been murdered by members of the Triads he had crossed or offended, or that he perished at the hands of Japanese martial artists who were tired of his dismissive attitude towards karate. Others suggested that kung fu masters had killed Bruce with a secret death-touch technique because he had exploited the art and, in his dealings with Hollywood, brought the martial arts into disrepute.

Kung fu fanzines looked in desperation for any angle on which to hang a story. Astrologers were hired to say why everyone should have seen it coming and to speculate on what Bruce would have done had he lived. Some even believed that Bruce was not dead at all and had retreated to the mountains ready to make a messianic reappearance at a later date.

The theories became ever more outlandish, including one that Bruce had died from having his sweat glands removed so that he'd look good on camera. The Chinese whispers spread until, months later, Golden Harvest's Andre Morgan received a letter from a woman in Goose Bay, Labrador, saying that her family had just seen one of Bruce's films and understood that he was now dead. She asked Golden Harvest to confirm the rumour that the mafia had shot Bruce because he was too big to control any more.

Much was also made of the signs and omens surrounding Bruce's death. Journalist Mel Tobias observed that Kowloon, where Bruce's house was situated, means Nine Dragon Pond, and speculated that the big dragons did not like having a Little Dragon in their midst, so devoured him, while another Chinese superstition has it that one should never put the word 'death' in the title of a book or film.

Bruce Lee's friends and colleagues have all expressed their opinions about his death. Doug Palmer wrote:

His broadmindedness made him impervious to any restrictions, whether on martial arts techniques or the conventions surrounding them. He was the first to teach gung fu to non-Chinese, at a time when he risked criticism and even ostracism from the Chinese community. Ultimately, coupled with the jealousies of his overwhelming skill and popularity, was the effect of his impatience (some called it arrogance) with those who relied on cant and tradition instead of merit and ability. All this, I believe, led to his death.

In August 1972, Bruce appeared on Hong Kong's TVB channel, as part of a benefit which raised over $5 million on behalf of the victims of a recent typhoon. Several masters from other schools were on the show. The mutual dislike between him and some of the more-traditional masters in Hong Kong had grown as fast as Bruce's reputation. At any rate, one of the other masters was bragging about his inner power, goading Bruce and challenging him to strike him in the stomach. The master stood in the ready stance, one arm at his side and the other pointing at his stomach, insisting that Bruce hit him there, adding that it was impossible to hurt him. Bruce approached and struck him on the nose. The master jumped back startled, then incensed, and demanded to know what Bruce was doing. 'It's easy to defend, if you dictate how you are going to be attacked,' said Bruce. 'Anyone can learn to resist a blow if he is prepared for it. A gung fu man must be prepared for the unexpected.'

The last time I saw Bruce was while he was filming *Game of Death*. Sure he was thin, but he was very fit. I don't believe that he was working himself to death. Bruce made many enemies in Hong Kong for openly flouting tradition and causing loss of face – that TV show was seen by three million people. Nobody could openly challenge Bruce; no one could beat him one-to-one: so the only way to get rid of him, without leaving any evidence, would be to poison him.

Another of Bruce's early students, James DeMile, was so convinced that foul play was involved in Bruce's death that he mounted his own investigation. DeMile's first suspicion was also that the Chinese wing chun clans were unhappy about Bruce westernizing the art. In Hong Kong people took up a fighting style as part of a deeply ingrained family tradition. Unless you are privy to that tradition it is difficult to understand the depth of feeling involved, just as it is hard for some cultures to comprehend that in Europe violent deaths occur as a result of rivalry between fans of competing soccer teams.

Later DeMile revised his thinking, saying that he believed Bruce had been poisoned by people he'd antagonized in the Hong Kong film industry, because Bruce's independent attitude had made too many waves in an exploitative industry that had previously run like clockwork.

In *Bruce Lee, King of Kung Fu*, Felix Dennis wrote:

Bruce Lee destroyed face like a leprous aftershave. To many of those beaten by Lee, in business or in the ring, his superman self-confidence was unbearable, his blunt candidness an insult. Then again, Lee cost many of his rivals large amounts of money. Besides siphoning off much audience support from the established studios, there were numerous complaints that, under competition from the Lee films, smaller production companies floundered and were squeezed out of the race.

Lee irrevocably altered not only the products of the Mandarin film industry, but also the structure of the industry itself. As the first Mandarin actor to take control of his own career, he showed the way to a more equitable share of the profits for his fellow performers. Certainly, in Hong Kong, in the early months of 1973, there were many people who would have been more than happy to bring down the curtain on the meteoric rise of Lee's star.

Alex Ben Block, then the entertainment editor of the *Miami News*, wrote *The Legend of Bruce Lee*. Despite the fact that Block had no experience at all of the martial arts, it is mainly from this book that all the tales of clandestine assassination squads and jealous kung fu masters arose. Block made many suggestions: Bruce Lee was murdered by those who hadn't wanted kung fu made public, by people jealous of his fame, or by those angry that he wouldn't endorse their products. Block leaves it for us to decide whether the assassination itself was done by 'one talented enemy with the knowledge and the will', 'by ninja poisoners using cannabis', by Malaysian martial artists using a 'vibrating palm' technique, or by Shaolin monks who were upset with Bruce and used the delayed death-touch known as dim mak. This was the technique Bruce had first seen demonstrated by the praying-mantis master Gin Foon Mark in New York; it works as a kind of reverse acupuncture, to disrupt energy and to harm, rather than to balance and to heal.

The wild speculation in Block's book was soon being quoted as authoritative, well-researched fact. While *Popster* magazine promised to reveal that Bruce was killed by unknown assassins using a secret death-touch, on the following page it attempted to answer the rather more basic question, 'What is Kung Fu?'

Alex Ben Block, former editor of the *Hollywood Reporter*, now says, 'Have I revised any of my opinions? To a certain extent I have, though personally, I always believed Bruce Lee died of natural causes. I wrote that book in a matter of weeks, when nobody really knew what was happening, so I just threw out everything I could that might offer some explanation. I don't, for example, believe any of that stuff that Goldman wrote in *Penthouse.*'

Ben Block is referring to the two-part article by Albert Goldman which appeared in the January and February 1983 issues of *Penthouse.* In this article Goldman asserts that Bruce Lee showed all the classic signs of the cowardly bully, calling him an overrated showbiz brat, a fortune-cookie philosopher and a control freak who'd become addicted to a powerful Nepalese hash resin which eventually killed him. Goldman's thesis was concocted from two phone conversations, one with Bob Wall and one with Bruce's doctor, Charles 'Don' Langford.

'Goldman talked to me once on the phone,' says Bob Wall, 'then misquoted everything I'd said from the most negative point of view.'

Don Langford also recalls the Goldman article in which he is 'quoted' as calling Bruce a hysteric and in which Bruce supposedly presented both Dr Langford and his colleague Dr Peter Wu with a sample of cannabis while exclaiming hysterically, 'It's the only thing that stops time!'

Langford recalls, 'My first contact with the Lee family was when Brandon was brought to me because he'd injured his hand when he trapped it in a folding chair. I didn't know who Bruce was; I simply remembered Brandon's father as being a muscular and intelligent man. Then a nurse said to me, "Don't you know who that is?" When I realized that the family lived nearby I started to notice Bruce jogging every morning. After that, I treated Bruce whenever he'd been injured on the set.

'That article caused me some embarrassment. I remember with some disappointment that Albert Goldman's data was incorrect. Bruce was certainly made to look like less than he really was. Bruce was theatrical rather than hysterical; he was a dramatic person, an actor, and he used to act out the events of his injuries. Bruce and I even talked about it; he said that when he was acting he became the part, and I guess that was what he was doing when he was in the surgery. But he was always in control. I think Goldman's account was over-dramatized.'

Albert Goldman also wrote similarly cynical biographies of Elvis Presley and John Lennon. As with his treatment of their lives, his account of Bruce Lee's life reveals less about its subject than it does about the writer's own ugly psyche. In Goldman's world, Bruce Lee worked out with 'grimy punch bags' and 'bizarre dummies'. Goldman was even capable of imbuing martial arts training with a sleazy atmosphere. The writer appeared quite literally to hate his work, despising those popular heroes he wrote about while resenting having to feed off their achievement to make his own living. Behind Goldman's portrait of Bruce Lee – and the loaded questions and misquotes – one can always sense the writer's heartless, unfulfilled self. Just as the truth is that foul play did not kill Bruce Lee, so Goldman's brand of foul play has always been a failed attempt to kill the truth. When the writer died later on a transatlantic flight, no one could be found who was willing to take responsibility for his body or pay the funeral expenses: a fitting legacy.

Bruce's younger brother Robert has always said that he believes Bruce died as a result of foul play, and there are always interviews on Bruce Lee websites to that effect. Robert adds that the Lee family is united in these beliefs, but by 'the Lee family', Robert means himself and Bruce's other siblings, who have never been on the best of terms with Linda's side of the family. While their antipathy falls short of an outright feud or open hostility, it would be fair to say that not many Christmas cards are exchanged. Robert cites Bruce's rapid weight loss prior to his death as significant, saying that 'other factors' were involved and adding that when the time is right the details will be made public – though 34 years and counting seems like a long time to wait for the time to be right.

We must also take into account the material presented by Tom Bleecker, Linda Lee's second husband, in his book, *Unsettled Matters* (1999), which he wrote after their divorce. Bleecker states plainly that at the time of his death Bruce was not 'the world's fittest man' and was gravely ill from abusing his body. His baldest assertion is that Bruce's dramatic mood changes and physical condition came about from using anabolic steroids, which Bleecker says he probably began using in the late Sixties.

There is absolutely no evidence to this effect, other than Bleecker's own testimony, and *nobody* else anywhere has repeated or endorsed his claim. At the time in question steroid use wasn't illegal, so this isn't the issue. The main 'evidence' that Bleecker presents is Bruce's sometimes alarming mood swings, but they were always evident and a manifestation of his driven and, at times, impatient perfectionism. The fact is that during the last two years of his life Bruce lost weight at an astonishing rate. Linda Lee has never commented on any of Bleecker's assertions, but it's certainly possible that some of Bleecker's material may be fallout from his failed partnership with Linda.

Bleecker says, 'The issue of Lee's steroid use is complex, but the main thing I wanted to get across was that steroids damaged Bruce physically and emotionally. Like so many athletes who have used them, Bruce paid a heavy price. I know that there will be those who'll scream and yell that never in a million years would Bruce use steroids. He still had to do the workouts – it's not that he was cheating – but it does explain a lot of his erratic behaviour. I felt it was important to give a credible explanation of many of Lee's violent outbursts, and these had more to do with "roid rage" than any stresses of the business, or displays of his natural personality.'

One such violent outburst was the 'Lo Wei incident', when the director claims that Bruce pulled a knife and threatened him. In a later search no knife was found, but Bleecker claims that Linda told him she quietly removed the knife from the screening room.

The final bomb that Bleecker drops concerns Bruce's extra-marital affairs: 'Bruce Lee was well known for cheating on his wife, both before and during their marriage. It's also well known to those close to him that his marriage was heading for the divorce court and many have said that Linda was greatly relieved when Bruce died.'

The respected author Davis Miller has endorsed this view in interviews for his proposed book *The Last Days of Bruce Lee* – as yet unpublished – in which he says Bruce had been having sexual relationships with women, including some of his leading ladies, as far back as 1967, adding, 'In Hong Kong, he was much more of a tomcat.'

Hedging his bets, Tom Bleecker believes that Bruce had a massive adrenal failure due either to steroid or drug abuse . . . *or* that he was poisoned.

There are bound to be many theories about the premature death of one of the world's fittest men, but since Bruce had suffered a serious brain trauma only two months before he died, this weakness was evident. Whether it had been present from birth or had been brought about by injury should be the first point to consider. At the coroner's inquiry, Raymond Chow testified that during the course of making his films, Bruce had taken many blows that were not included in the scripts, and Chow added that some of these accidental blows had been quite severe.

In truth, the greatest element of foul play surrounding Bruce Lee's death seems to be people's willingness to exploit the circumstances of it. In the end, most of the confusion and conjecture stem from Raymond Chow's attempts to cover up the true events.

Thereafter, a bewildered and defensive Betty Ting Pei was left to face the press alone. She made things worse by lying, claiming, 'On the night he died I was not at home. I had gone out with my mother. I last saw him several months ago, when we met by chance in the street.' But journalists who spoke to Betty's neighbours found out that Bruce had been a regular visitor to her apartment for months prior to his death.

Betty stayed away from Bruce's funeral, and when questioned about their relationship she spoke evasively, implying that they had a special friendship. 'Silence is the best answer to scandalous rumours,' she protested. 'Because I treasure his friendship, I put up with the gossip.' The actress then threatened to sue the press if they persisted with stories of an affair. 'It seems people want me to die,' she told *The Star*. 'Bruce is dead. Why don't you just leave it at that?' One paper retorted with the headline: 'BETTY TING, SUE US!' and printed a fresh list of disclosures as the besieged actress went into hiding.

The best witness to these particular events is Felix Dennis, who was one of the very first to speak to Betty after Bruce's death. According to Dennis, Betty told him that she and Bruce had been having an affair, and their friends openly confirmed that it had been going on for about a year. At one point Bruce had attempted to end the affair, resuming it only after Betty broke down and was admitted to hospital. The general feeling was that Bruce was not as worldly as Betty when it came to sex and that he'd been getting a bit of an education. 'She's a revelation with her cleverness,' Bruce had told friends shortly after he and Betty met.

It seems it was never 'true love' but whatever the case, the relationship was obviously more than a brief or casual fling.

As for Betty's delay in calling an ambulance, again one can't underestimate the role that 'loss of face' plays in Chinese culture. There can't be many worse scenarios than having the dying husband of another woman in your apartment.

Felix Dennis adds, 'Although Betty initially admitted that she and Bruce had been having an affair, she later changed her account because she felt 'responsible'. If Betty had picked up the phone the moment Bruce collapsed, he might have been saved, but she panicked, hoping he would recover, then waited too long before calling Raymond Chow, who was on the other side of Hong Kong. By the time Chow had fought through the traffic it was too late. Bruce wasn't dead on arrival at hospital, but the doctors were astonished that he'd lasted as long as he had.'

# 26

## Afterwords

In the weeks after Bruce Lee's death, as grief and controversy raged across the world, Bruce crossed the line between being the film industry's hottest property and becoming an icon. The Bruce Lee cult had arrived and fans began flocking to showings of the B-feature *Marlowe*, which had flopped when first released but was reissued immediately with Bruce given top billing.

A month after Bruce's death, *Enter the Dragon* was released. In London it monopolized three West End cinemas for five weeks before becoming a sellout throughout Britain, Europe and the US. Although reviews in the West thought that Bruce Lee had played in little more than a James Bond pastiche, in the end the film worked to his advantage, as it is his appearance alone that lifts *Enter the Dragon* out of the ordinary, making it the genre's greatest movie.

The finished version of the film is significantly different from the original drafts, and Bruce was successful in using the film as a vehicle for expressing elements of his culture, rather than just another action movie. Based on a cost-to-profit ratio, it is also the most successful film ever made. In 2004, it was deemed 'culturally significant' and selected for preservation in the US National Film Registry. *Enter the Dragon* could have been just the beginning for Bruce Lee, and even though it wasn't, it is nevertheless a fitting legacy.

*

Bruce Lee lived an extraordinary life: he bridged cultures, revolutionized the martial arts, taught a fierce philosophy of individualism, remade the image of the Asian man in the West and, in the process, became unforgettable. Few lives in modern times have provided so much to study and reflect on, yet few lives have been so obscured by fantasy and B-movie-grade tack.

In 1975, the Shaw Brothers' film *Bruce Lee and I* showed Betty Ting Pei romping semi-nude while 'Bruce' clutches his head in agony. After Bruce's death, Betty tells a barman she is forced to leave town because of the hate directed at her from his fans, then the barman beats up some thugs and tells them to respect Bruce's memory. Though if respect for Bruce's memory were the issue, the film would never have been made. Not only did Betty get a writer's fee, she also persuaded Run Run Shaw to shell out $20,000 for twenty dresses – ten times as much as Shaw had originally offered Bruce to star in one of his pictures. In the light of this, it's hard to believe that this is the same woman who protested, 'I didn't gain anything because of him, be it in name or profit. Each day I confined myself to my room, blaming myself, cursing myself, my feelings numb.'

After making this film for Shaw, Betty Ting Pei made more bad films, married a wealthy Taiwanese businessman, ran two clothes shops, bought a Mercedes sports car similar to Bruce's, divorced, then became a nightclub singer and a vegetarian.

Almost twenty years later, in 1993, Universal released its Bruce Lee biopic *Dragon: The Bruce Lee Story*. The director, Rob Cohen, bought the option for Linda Lee's biography, written with second husband Tom Bleecker, and threw the script together in three weeks flat. Cohen was certainly accurate when he said that he was doing a 'fictional version of a non-fiction story – neither a true story nor a documentary', because it bears no resemblance whatsoever to his *actual* life.

The story of *Dragon* centres on a highly romanticized account of Bruce and Linda's relationship. Not only does it take far too much latitude with the characters, it stretches artistic licence to breaking point. To list the absurdities and errors in the story would fill an entire book, and in a special supplement printed in June 1994, *Martial Arts Illustrated* magazine did exactly that.

*Dragon* was a commercial success, but unlike Betty Ting Pei's film, and the countless exaggerated biopics that emerged from Hong Kong in the 1970s, it is difficult to excuse such lazy exploitation from mainstream Hollywood. Contemporary films on the lives of Malcolm X, Jim Morrison, Tina Turner and Geronimo all use some artistic licence, but even so they treat their subjects with a great deal more accuracy and respect. Bruce Lee deserved far better.

Fortunately Bruce Lee's work is more significant and still hugely popular, so it will outlive all the exploitative dross, as his own films are discovered anew by each succeeding generation.

After Bruce's death, Linda and the children returned to Seattle before eventually moving to the upmarket Rolling Hills Estate, south of Los Angeles. However, Brandon had trouble adapting to life in America and became angry and withdrawn for a while. His heritage meant that he was constantly challenged at every school he attended, and he spent time at nearly every school in the South Bay area. Unsurprisingly, he rebelled against his image as Bruce's son and strived for his own identity, getting involved in teenage crimes, joyriding in a stolen car and once even impersonating a driving test examiner. He spent a couple of years on the road exploring the West Coast, and four months before graduation he was expelled from college. Finally, when he was fifteen, Brandon spent a year training with Dan Inosanto and Ted Wong.

Brandon recalls, 'I had a bit of a love-hate relationship with the martial arts. There was a year where I was very involved, then a period where I said, "Hey, I don't have to do this." About the only constant throughout that period was acting. My dad never told me to get into acting, and neither did my mother, but even as a little boy, it's all I wanted to do. I never thought about anything else.'

In the 1980s, Brandon moved to Boston to study acting at

Emerson College, with the aim of becoming an actor who could do realistic fighting, rather than becoming a martial artist who could act. However, his name opened no doors and he was working as a script reader when a casting agent finally got him his debut in *Kung Fu*, a movie spin-off from the TV series. Further roles did not materialize, and like Bruce, Brandon broke into films in Hong Kong, where he made a low-budget film called *Legacy of Rage* followed by *Laser Mission*, which was made in Germany. He made his first US feature, *Showdown in Little Tokyo*, with Dolph Lundgren in 1991.

Inevitably Brandon's work was compared with his father's, and for a short time it looked as if Brandon might be his father's heir on screen too.

'In a perfect world, I'd rather that comparisons to my dad didn't happen,' Brandon says, 'but I'm lucky; he's somebody that people admire a lot. I've met a lot of people who've been really positively affected by his film work, people who say, "It changed my life after I saw one of your dad's films." So long as people are respectful about my dad, I try to be respectful to them as well.'

Brandon's second feature, the martial arts action movie *Rapid Fire*, showed he was more willing to embrace his heritage. While the film's props master listed fifty-six guns, in a weapons count that ran to six typed pages, there is no shortage of hand-to-hand fights choreographed by Brandon and Jeff Imada, whom he met at Dan Inosanto's academy.

Like his father, Brandon was also given to showing off and tearing down Mulholland Drive, not in a Porsche, but on his motorcycle. Comparing Brandon with his father, producer Robert Lawrence said, 'His father had a burning intensity; Brandon is more fun. He's freewheeling, hip and more tongue-in-cheek.' Little did anyone know that Brandon was soon to share his father's tragic fate.

Filming of a new movie, *The Crow*, began in Wilmington, North Carolina, on Brandon's twenty-eighth birthday, 1 February 1993. The story is of a murdered rock star who returns in the form of a crow to exact retribution. From the very start the set was plagued by mishaps and the crew began to speak openly about the 'curse of *The Crow*'.

On the first day of shooting a carpenter had to be hospitalized with burns over ninety per cent of his body after his crane ran foul of a live power cable; a construction worker slipped and drove a screwdriver through his hand; a disgruntled set sculptor went berserk and drove a car through the props room, destroying it, and on 13 March, a storm wrecked most of the set.

In the early hours of 1 April 1993, I received a phone call from a friend in Los Angeles who was helping me set up an interview with Brandon. Instead of news of the proposed meeting, the message was that Brandon Lee had just been killed on the film set. TV news bulletins soon confirmed the astonishing news that Brandon Lee was dead.

Just before the incident that resulted in his death, Brandon expressed his concern that the crew were so tired. Shortly after midnight on 31 March, they had just finished another gruelling day. The next scene to be filmed was Brandon's death scene, in which he was to be shot, with special effects used to simulate the bullets hitting him. As the cameras turned, a fellow actor fifteen feet away fired blanks from a Magnum 44 and Brandon slumped to the ground. So convincing was his performance that the crew broke into spontaneous applause, then, slowly, onlookers realized the true situation. Brandon was rushed to Wilmington Medical Center where doctors gave him fourteen pints of blood and fought for twelve hours to save him. Just as she had done twenty years earlier, Linda Lee heard herself requesting an autopsy.

Later the cause of death was established: the dummy bullet that had been loaded for the close-up scene had become lodged in the gun. Subsequently a blank charge used to simulate gunfire had shot the fake bullet with enough force to cause the tragedy. Just as happened immediately after Bruce's death, the tabloids had a field day. Early stories told of Brandon being killed by yakuza (Japanese mafia) assassins or jealous lovers. It was even speculated that he had been killed by the same black demon that had pursued his father. On 3 April Brandon was buried in Lake View Cemetery, alongside his father.

In May 1994 *The Crow* went on general release where it went straight to number one at the box office. Though the external baggage that went with the film may have drawn some curiosity seekers, the completed film avoids being exploitative, but this doesn't make the death scene any easier to watch. Brandon received widespread acclaim for his performance, with *Rolling Stone*'s Peter Travers describing Brandon's acting as having a probing intelligence and passionate heart. He added, 'Lee is sensational on all counts in a final performance that brims over with athleticism and ardour.'

In *LA Weekly*, Manohla Dargis wrote, 'If Brandon Lee hadn't died, it's likely that *The Crow* would have been a great movie; as it is, it's implausibly great. Inevitably, Lee will be folded into the same history as his father, Bruce. But Brandon Lee deserves to be remembered for himself.'

Although Bruce will always be the unparalleled genius of martial arts on screen, Brandon had become a confident, compelling and convincing actor and martial artist in his own right. His father would have been very proud of him. Brandon's enduring memory of his father was of a hard-working man: 'He always impressed upon me that there isn't an endless amount of time. I've always remembered his words and try, consciously, not to waste any time.' His words seem all the more poignant now.

Immediately after Bruce's death the house at 41 Cumberland Road, Hong Kong, became the focus for his many 'disciples'. Fans who today make the pilgrimage to the house he named 'The Crane's Nest' will be disappointed to find that it is being used as a 'romantic hotel'. Rooms with TVs showing round-the-clock porn can be rented by the hour, with condoms discreetly provided in the bedside cabinet. Thankfully the hotel doesn't use Bruce's name to promote itself, though most people are aware that he lived there. The house has been used as a brothel for many years and was already being used in this way when I first visited Hong Kong in the 1980s, when it was called the Kam Wah Gardens. Most of the luxurious homes in the area are no longer private houses, but brothels, children's nurseries, wedding chapels, retirement homes and funeral parlours. It might even be possible to be hatched, matched and dispatched without ever leaving Cumberland Road.

Today Bruce Lee still attracts fans who fail to see the irony of belonging to a club that has the motto, 'Towards Personal Liberation'. It's not unlike the fans of *The Prisoner* TV series who fail to see the contradiction in joining a club devoted to a character whose tag line was, 'I am not a number: I am a free man!'

Bearing in mind that the word fan is also the root of the word fantasy, what do we make of the following members of the *geek kune do* fraternity unearthed by Davis Miller in his excellent book *The Tao of Bruce Lee*?

Mike Miyazaki is the kung fu pyjama-wearing son of a Japanese businessman who used his father's wealth to turn his apartment into the set of *Enter the Dragon*, where TV sets playing non-stop Bruce Lee movies were mounted in the ceiling and walls. An American, Blade Leong, claimed to be a reincarnation of Bruce Lee because they shared the same initials – no mention was made of Buzz Lightyear. Leong's unfortunate wife was made to wear Linda Lee shift dresses, circa 1960, and sculpt her hair into a beehive. Dalton Lee claimed to be the love child of Bruce Lee and Lindsay 'Bionic Woman' Wagner. He moved to the motel near Lake View Cemetery in Seattle, where Bruce is buried, and proceeded to mail videos of himself performing various action routines to the long-suffering Linda Lee. Linda's attorney, Adrian Marshall, sent notice that under no circumstances was he to approach her or the children. One confused individual from Idaho named his son Brandon, his daughters Shannon and Lisa Marie, and changed his own name to Jesus Lee Presley.

In London in the late Seventies, a young man who realized what the initials of the movie *Game of Death* spelled out, hijacked a bus and rammed a shop front while screaming, 'I'm Bruce Lee, I'm God.' And in 1986, on 20 July, Betty Ting Pei gave birth to a son on the thirteenth anniversary of Bruce Lee's death. Ms Ting Pei informed friends that she was the proud mother of (yet another) reincarnation. On the twentieth anniversary of Bruce's death in 1993, a retired Mongolian doctor, Ichinorov Dendrev, undertook a nine-month pilgrimage in which he and two other gentlemen made an unsuccessful attempt to walk from Mongolia, by way of Siberia and Alaska, to place a bunch of flowers on the grave in Seattle.

There is a history of ill feeling between Linda Lee and Bruce's siblings, but on 28 April 1993, the family kept the peace for long enough to gather and celebrate Bruce being awarded a star on Hollywood Boulevard's Walk of Fame. Linda, *Dragon* director Rob Cohen and Mayor Bradley spoke before the assembled guests at a VIP dinner, followed on 7 August by Linda's auction of Bruce's possessions, which she had lent for the filming of *Dragon* – adding the only note of authenticity in the film. Bruce's Hong Kong driver's licence fetched $7,200. His Kato cap and braces went for $8,600 – only a little short of what he netted for the entire *Green Hornet* series. By far the biggest money-spinner was Bruce's written affirmation 'My Definite Chief Aim', in which he vowed to achieve world fame as the highest-paid Chinese super-star by making $10 million between 1970 and 1980. This item, handwritten on a single sheet of paper, was bought for the Planet Hollywood restaurant for $29,000.

One afternoon in July 2003, close to the thirtieth anniversary of Bruce's death, I was passing a shop on the Strand in London, which sells memorabilia and autographs. I went inside and began talking to the owner. I asked him whose signature was worth most these days, and he replied that the Beatles were always good value, or the three astronauts who went to the moon, but that anything with Bruce Lee's signature on it started at about £5,000. At the time of writing Bruce's signed *Green Hornet* contract was being advertised for $30,000.

Also at the time of writing, a $25 million theme park is planned to open at Bruce's ancestral home in Shunde, a town of canals and bamboo gardens northwest of Hong Kong, the bucolic area that Bruce's grandfather left in the late nineteenth century. Betty Ting Pei and Bruce's younger brother Robert attended the ceremony to lay the foundation stone. London's *Sunday Times* reported that the park will be patrolled by Bruce Lee 'mannequin robots', radio-controlled from inside a giant statue of the late film star, and that a rollercoaster will make his signature screams and grunts. Officials named a street in Hong Kong after Lee and turned a tea shop into a museum, packed with letters and photographs of uncertain provenance, to which Betty Ting donated a set of 'nunchucks' [sic]. They are also discussing plans for a memorial hall and a monorail to connect the town centre with the theme park. However, all this may be brought to a halt by Shannon Lee, the actor's only surviving child, who plans to visit Shunde in 2008 'to find out what else they are dreaming up over there'.

After a sketchy career as an actress and singer, Shannon and her lawyer husband, Ian Keasler, now control the Lee estate. Shannon has her own plans, which include a television series that will use computer graphics to recreate her father. 'The technology is nearly here to make it look as if he's back,' she's reported to have said. She has also authorized a Broadway musical of Bruce's life and hopes to work with the Chinese government, which is in discussion with the BBC to make a documentary about Bruce. Meanwhile, Robert Lee is preparing his own cinematic version of the much-filmed Bruce Lee story, which may yet lead to a direct confrontation with Shannon.

After thirty years, no human has yet been able to emulate Bruce Lee's screen performances, so producers are turning to technology to do the job. A movie provisionally titled *Dragon Warrior*, which will take three to four years to make with a budget of $50 million, will recreate Bruce Lee using computer-generated imagery and voice-simulation technology. The movie's mastermind, Chul Shin, head of the Korean-based Shincine Films, has promised both A-list supporting actors and an A-list director. 'We chose this film as our first international project,' says Shin, 'because we have the resources and the technology to make it work. There is no figure who commands more respect and excitement than Bruce Lee, who is included in *Time* magazine's list of The 100 Most Influential People of the 20th Century' – an accolade that puts him alongside the like of Charles Lindbergh, Muhammad Ali, Marilyn Monroe, the Kennedys and the Beatles. For their part, Linda and Shannon Lee agreed to the project because 'we believe in Shincine and Mr Shin's enthusiasm and commitment to making a first-rate film'.

On 30 August 2002, Universal's games division launched an action-adventure game, *Bruce Lee: Quest of the Dragon*, 'inspired by the legendary martial artist' for Microsoft's X-box™ video game system. The game's storyline sticks closely to the intended theme of *Game of Death*, where Bruce Lee would have had to complete seven levels in order to finish the 'game'. In the video game Bruce has to battle multiple opponents in order to rescue his kidnapped father and retrieve a mystical golden relic that holds the secret to all the martial arts. It hardly needs to be said that actual martial arts training will get you a little closer to this secret than playing a video game ever will.

Players have to perfect a variety of martial arts styles, including some of Bruce Lee's signature jeet kune do moves, as they travel through the levels. Over a hundred moves were 'motion captured' with the help of one of Bruce Lee's last students, Jerry Poteet. The game is set not in a pagoda, but in various locations from Hong Kong to San Francisco and spans not seven, but thirty levels of opponents. According to Universal Interactive president Jim Wilson, the game matches Bruce Lee for speed, featuring 'lightning-fast play at blistering frame rates and is the experience Lee fans have long been waiting for'.

Bruce Lee's image has appeared on postage stamps in China, as well as in Gambia, Madagascar and many other African countries. Asian *Time* magazine placed him on a list of heroes who have helped Asia rise 'from poverty to powerhouse'. There are plans for a Broadway musical and, as a prelude to the 2008 Beijing Olympic Games, a forty-part TV biography *The Legend of Bruce Lee*, with a $6.5 million budget is scheduled. Had he still been alive perhaps – as Muhammad Ali did in Atlanta – Bruce would have been lighting the Olympic flame in Beijing.

There have been many dubious tributes and accolades to Bruce Lee's memory over the years, but Bruce himself would have been touched by recognition from his childhood hero, China's first martial arts screen actor, Master Kwan.

When journalist Bey Logan asked Master Kwan what he thought of Lee Little Dragon, Master Kwan walked off towards his inner sanctum. Even though he was in his eighties, he still had a clear gaze and walked with a straight posture. When he returned he had a book on Chinese movies in which both he and Bruce appeared. 'Maybe you can get this book in the library,' he said, modestly acknowledging the recognition they shared.

Bruce Lee expressed regret that after he died people would probably hang pictures of him in their schools and bow to him. One Ohio karate instructor went one better than this: he claimed he had a pair of Bruce Lee's old trainers that he would bring out and hold up in front of the class. The students duly bowed to the shoes, while the teacher talked about their aura and the chi the students would absorb from them.

For their part, Linda Lee and biographer John Little present Bruce in a somewhat sanitized and sanctified light; but the Bruce Lee Fan Club of India goes considerably further by attempting to deify 'Him' as a bona fide messiah to be worshipped and adored.

Davis Miller writes:

In music certainly, there can be life. But there's death in music, too. That plaintive stuff you hear as fat-ass congregations of white folks sing sorrowfully, obligingly, of Christ bringing them alive. Maybe Jesus had something going. But Christ, how can any sane person take anyone's followers seriously?

Most relevant and touching is the simple tribute of Shanlon Wu, a Chinese-American who grew up in suburban New York in the 1960s. He had no Asian heroes to use as role models until he saw his first Bruce Lee movie. He described his subsequent experience of dawning self-awareness in a 1990 article for the *New York Times*:

I was born in 1959, an Asian-American in Westchester County, NY. During my childhood there were no Asian sports stars. On television I can recall only that most pathetic of Asian characters, Hop Sing, the Cartwright family houseboy on *Bonanza*. But in my adolescence there was Bruce.

I was fourteen years old when I first saw *Enter the Dragon*, the granddaddy of all martial arts movies. Between the ages of fourteen and seventeen, I saw *Enter the Dragon* twenty-two times before I stopped counting. During those years, I collected Bruce Lee posters, putting them up at all angles in my bedroom. I took up the Chinese martial arts and spent hours comparing my physique with his. I learned all I could about Bruce.

My parents, who immigrated to America and had become professors at Hunter College, tolerated my behavior, but seemed puzzled at my admiration of 'an entertainer'. My father jokingly tried to compare my obsession with Bruce to his boyhood worship of Chinese folk-tale heroes. But my father's heroes could not be mine; they came from an ancient literary tradition.

After college, I competed as an amateur boxer in an attempt to find my self-image in the ring. It didn't work. My fighting was only an attempt to copy Bruce's movies. What I needed was instruction on how to live. I quit boxing after a year and went to law school.

One grey morning, many years later, Shanlon Wu visited Bruce Lee's grave:

The headstone is red granite with a small picture etched into it. The picture is very Hollywood – Bruce wears dark glasses –

and I think the calligraphy looks a bit sloppy. Two tourists stop but leave quickly after glancing at me. I realize I am crying. Bruce's grave seems so small compared to his place in my boyhood; so small in comparison to my need for heroes. Seeing his grave, I understand how large the hole in my life has been, and how desperately I'd sought to fill it.

I had sought an Asian hero to emulate. But none of my choices quite fitted me. Their lives were defined through heroic tasks – they had villains to defeat and battles to fight – while my life seemed merely a struggle to define myself. But now I see that the very struggle has defined me. I must be my own hero even as I learn to treasure those who have gone before. Their lives beckon like fireflies on a moonless night, and I know that they, like me, may have been flawed. Still, their lives were real. They were not houseboys on *Bonanza*.

*Legacy*

# 27

## Quite a Hero

When I look around I always learn something and that is to be
yourself always, express yourself and have faith in yourself. Do
not go out and look for a successful personality and duplicate it.
Now that seems to be the prevalent thing happening in Hong
Kong, like they always copy mannerisms but they never start
from the root of being and ask, 'How can I be me?'

*Bruce Lee*

Despite this hopeful advice, Bruce Lee made such an impact on
the film industry, then left such a vacuum that, in the East, a
multitude of imitators appeared. Bruce Le, several Bruce Lis,
Bruce Leong, Bruce Rhe and Myron Bruce Lee; not to mention
Tarzen Li and Tarzen Lee, Kowloon Li and Hong Kong Lee,
Rocky Lee, Jet Lee, Bronson Lee, Dragon Lee, Conan Lee, Clint
Lee and even one Gypsy Lee. Those few who didn't actually
change their names were usually billed as 'the new Bruce Lee'.
Dozens of films worked the name of Bruce Lee into their titles
and used deceptive promotional material, while other films used
every possible combination of 'Fist', 'Fury', 'Game', 'Dragon' and
'Enter' in their titles. There was even a sci-fi-plotted film that
involved clones of Bruce Lee.

For any good kung fu movie there were a hundred with bad
plots, bad acting and bad production, all with titles like *Kung Fu
Exorcist*, *Kung Fu Zombie* and even *Kung Fu-ry*. When the honey-
moon with kung fu was over, there was a brief flurry of ninja
films, depicting the exploits of the black-hooded martial artists

presented as a hybrid of Spiderman and James Bond, equipped with all kinds of weapons and gadgets.

In the West the history of martial arts movies is very simple: there is no 'before Bruce Lee'. Only two Western actors have forged careers as martial arts heroes, but although Steven Seagal and Jean-Claude van Damme have enjoyed successful film careers they are less convincing as martial artists than those who are generally considered to be Bruce Lee's true heirs.

By coincidence, Jackie Chan and Sammo Hung, two of the best martial arts actors to emerge since Bruce's death, both made early cameo appearances alongside Bruce. Having previously acted together in the Peking Opera, both men worked on *Enter the Dragon*. At the beginning of the movie, Sammo Hung appears as Bruce Lee's sparring opponent, while Jackie Chan appears briefly in a couple of scenes, first as one of Oharra's henchmen and later on when he gets his neck snapped by Bruce during a battle with several guards.

Born in 1954, Jackie Chan spent his youth in a Peking Opera school where he studied gymnastics, acrobatics and martial arts. Like Bruce, he was also a child movie actor. As a stuntman Chan appeared in *Fist of Fury* and *Enter the Dragon*, before Lo Wei – who was looking for a new Bruce Lee to net him further millions – cast him in the 1976 movie unimaginatively titled *New Fist of Fury*. Inevitably, Lo Wei billed Jackie Chan as 'the new Bruce Lee' for eight movies, until Chan discovered and developed his own screen personality, with a fighting style that owes as much to Buster Keaton as it does to Bruce Lee.

Chan's real success began when he started to write his own scripts for films like the slick action-filled comedies *Armour of God* and *Police Story*. Though Jackie Chan's fights have an element of slapstick to them, there is also a satisfying level of skill. He works closely with a regular team of highly trained stuntmen to create an immaculately choreographed and slickly edited blend of comedy, fighting and stunt work. Chan, who insists on doing all his own stunts, has nearly killed himself three times, once in a fall of over forty feet, which was broken only by a single sheet of canvas. The audience's knowledge that Chan is risking his life is what brings them to see his films, and each one features an epilogue of out-takes, showing the stunts that went wrong, with Chan limping away, wincing in agony.

Sammo Hung, or Hong Jinbao as he was known then, was born in Hong Kong in 1952. Both of his parents worked in the local film industry, and guardianship was thrust upon his grandparents. Hong joined the Opera Academy in 1959 after his grandparents heard about the school from their friends. As one of the Seven Little Fortunes performing group, he established a school rivalry with one of the younger students, Yuen Lo, who later became Jackie Chan. Hong departed the Academy after an injury left him bedridden for an extended period, during which time his weight ballooned. He eventually returned to work in the film industry as a stuntman and was given the name Sam Mo after a portly Chinese cartoon character. He later anglicized this to Sammo Hung.

With *Warriors Two* (1978) and *The Prodigal Son* (1981), Hung made two movies that are considered to contain the best examples of wing chun on film. In 1988, he starred in Alex Law's *Painted Faces*, a dramatic retelling of his experiences at the Peking Opera School, where students were made to perform hundreds of acrobatic back flips and hours of handstands against a wall. Despite some of the more brutal exercises and physical punishments shown, Hung and Chan consider the movie a toned-down version of their own experiences.

Hung became one of the pivotal figures to spearhead the Hong Kong new-wave film movement of the 1980s, which helped reinvent the martial arts genre. He is best known in the West for his starring role in the US television series *Martial Law*, in which he reportedly recites his English dialogue phonetically.

Mention should also be made of Tony Jaa, who was born in Thailand in 1976 and grew up in a rural area where he saw films by Bruce Lee, Jackie Chan and Jet Li at temple fairs. While doing chores or playing with friends, he would imitate the martial arts moves he had seen in the films. 'I practised until I could do the move exactly as I'd seen the masters do it,' he told *Time* magazine in 2004. Tony Jaa has become best known for his breathtaking stunts and mesmerizing fighting techniques in the art of muay thai. He too initially worked as a stuntman, and even doubled for Sammo Hung when the actor made a commercial for an energy drink that required him to grasp an elephant's tusks and somersault onto its back.

Jaa's work eventually led to his breakthrough role as a leading man in the film *Ong-Bak* (2003), where he does all his own stunts without mechanical assistance or computer-generated effects in a style of extreme acrobatics and speedy dance-like moves. This film led to him being hailed as Asia's next martial-arts film superstar. As Jaa gained popularity, his films captured the attention of his hero, Jackie Chan, who asked his director to cast Jaa in one of his films, *Rush Hour 3*, though this role never materialized.

A second development in post-Bruce Lee martial arts' cinema harks back to the old 'unrealistic' style of film featuring the kind of impossible feats Bruce himself would have watched as a boy, although now at least they were accompanied by strong storylines and extremely high production values. These epic films use a lot of sophisticated aerial 'wire work' or computer-generated imagery and have as much in common with myth and fairy tale as martial art.

In the *Matrix* series of films, directed by the Wachowski brothers and begun in 1999, the hero has martial arts abilities downloaded directly into his nervous system. It's an impressive movie that owes everything to the brilliance of its cutting-edge special effects, for which it won an Academy Award. The films depict a complex science fiction story incorporating many elements, including cyberpunk, mythology, Hong Kong action films and virtual reality. Several philosophical concepts are also explored, including Hinduism, Christianity, Gnosticism and Buddhism, along with the concept of artificial intelligence overthrowing or enslaving mankind, a theme that's previously been touched upon in many science fiction stories.

*Crouching Tiger, Hidden Dragon* (2000) is a wuxia (chivalric martial arts) film directed by Ang Lee and featuring an international cast of Chinese actors, including Chow Yun Fat, Michelle Yeoh, Zhang Ziyi and Chang Chen. Made on a mere US$15 million budget with dialogue in Mandarin, *Crouching Tiger, Hidden Dragon* became a surprise international success and won the Academy Award for Best Foreign Language Film as well as being nominated for Best Picture and winning four other Academy Awards. The fantasy aspect of the film comes into play whenever the main characters fight: they possess seemingly magical powers, soaring through the air as they vault across roofs, running up walls and moving with superhuman ease. These powers are never clearly explained in the movie, but the implication is that they come from the training and secret knowledge of the Wudang school of martial arts. The film's enigmatic ending hints that, under the right conditions, one might even acquire the ability to fly.

Told in flashbacks – and even flashbacks within flashbacks – *Hero* (2002) is another wuxia film, starring Jet Li as the nameless leading character. Inspired by acclaim for *Crouching Tiger, Hidden Dragon*, it failed to achieve the same success, due in part to overseas criticism of its perceived pro-Chinese communist subtext.

*Kill Bill* by writer-director Quentin Tarantino was originally conceived as one film but released in two separate volumes (2003 and 2004) due to its running time of approximately four hours. The movie is an ambitious epic-length revenge drama, told with extensive use of flashbacks and flash-forwards, which nod in the direction of film genres such as Hong Kong martial arts movies and Italian spaghetti Westerns, accompanied by much use of popular-music and pop-culture references and deliberately over-the-top bloodletting, not to mention dialogue lifted from *Fist of Fury*. Notably, Uma Thurman stars in a *Game of Death*-style yellow and black catsuit.

*House of Flying Daggers* (2004) is a wuxia film that's more of a love story than a martial arts film, and the use of strong colours is a signature of the director Zhang Yimou: several scenes in a bamboo forest completely fill the screen with green. Near the end of the movie, there's a fight scene in a blizzard, with the actors set against a completely white background, while another scene uses bright yellow as its colour theme. The costumes, props and decorations are taken from Chinese paintings of the period to add authenticity to the look of the film, making it a visually stunning film. Chinese critics, however, have carped that Zhang was simply trying to appeal to Western audiences with heavily choreographed fight scenes and extensive use of computer-generated imagery.

In real life the best martial artists do not always make the best film performers, and vice versa. The very qualities that make a good fighter make a poor screen fighter. Speed, the ability to hide emotions, disguising the effect of blows received and not telegraphing moves all have to be reversed so that audiences can *see* what is happening.

Bruce Lee set modern screen fighting standards with his many innovations, technical mastery, inventive choreography, dramatic pauses and humour, and these innovations successfully spawned a further form of martial art. While Bruce often said that acting was his career and martial arts his real love, for a few glorious moments his ambition and his vocation became one and the same thing.

Bruce Lee was unique as a screen fighter because he was the first and best 'real' fighter any of us saw. My own kung fu teacher Derek Jones told me how, as a young boy, he would sit through every showing of *Enter the Dragon*, remaining in the cinema all day, watching the film on rotation, because each time he saw it he would learn something new. These repeated viewings in no way diminished Bruce's abilities, but served to enhance them. Nobody ever sat through repeated showings of Roger Moore or John Wayne: John Wayne was big and slow and won fights only because it said so in the script, while the exploits portrayed in the Bond films were little more than escapist schoolboy fun.

The most recent generation of martial arts films owes everything to contemporary filmmaking technology, but to see Bruce Lee on film is to see a human body brought to a level of supreme ability through a combination of almost unique talent allied to a lifetime of hard work. Bruce was blessed with abilities and a screen presence that few have enjoyed, but he became imprisoned by his own success and the need to be what everyone wanted him to be. There is no doubt that the typhoon of super-celebrity affected him deeply, and having suddenly achieved almost all his ambitions, he was faced with the question of what to do next.

Bruce guessed right when he said that that kung fu films would enjoy mass appeal for only a few years. Fred Weintraub had already explained that too much philosophy in his films wouldn't appeal to the mainstream, and he was also beginning to suspect that he might not be able to maintain the level of physical performance needed. Yet still he couldn't resist the urge to forge ahead. Bruce refused to step back, rest and recharge himself. At the same time there were other pressing decisions over career direction. Would he play roles outside of the martial arts? Would he consider parts that showed some vulnerability or denied his athletic abilities? Would working with better-quality scripts and actors, directing or doing non-martial art dramatic roles, have been the challenge he needed? Might such roles reveal that his acting was too unrealistic for Western audiences?

Brandon Lee believed his father would have met these challenges:

When I see his films, I can see that he acted sincerely. He put over what he really felt, neither more nor less. When he was filming, I remember that he never overacted to make an effect, it would have rung false. He was a very intense man and that's why he only did what he believed he had to do. His performances were a pure expression of something he had deep within himself. He never tried to portray something he didn't feel, and even less to imitate someone else. I hate that bunch of Chinese actors who try to act like my father did. He was naturally great. If he had lived, I am sure he would have made other films, without restricting himself to kung fu films. In any case, he would have made other films.

Honestly, you have to admit that, apart from *Enter the Dragon*, the others are not particularly good films. I mean by that that the stories were very poor. The actors couldn't act and even *Enter the Dragon* was, all in all, let us say a rather simple film. Were it not for his presence these productions would not have made a cent, they would be nothing today. My father would certainly have made films that could stand on their own, by the story and by their acting. The problem is my father disappeared at the moment when he could have done great things.

Like everyone, I was real respectful towards my dad. He was quite a hero, but he wasn't superhuman, just a guy.

Like a handful of others, Bruce Lee has become larger in death than he was in life. James Dean represents the restlessness and rebellion of youth. Monroe is Hollywood's goddess. Despite everything, Elvis will always be the king of rock and roll. John Lennon epitomizes the optimism and freewheeling ideas of the Sixties. All have become icons: fantasy images or symbols of an ideal. All are unique. And just as Anna Nicole Smith was no Marilyn and Liam Gallagher is no John Lennon, so there will never be another Bruce Lee.

All of this was summed up perfectly in the telling reply that followed when someone was once asked, 'Who is the next Bruce Lee?'

'Why?' came the response, 'wasn't the first one good enough for you?'

# 28

*Roots . . .*

A comprehensive list of all the martial arts in the world would be several pages long, while a description of each of them would fill an entire library. Among the many fighting systems evolved by different cultures – Japanese, Chinese, Korean, Filipino, Brazilian and so on – there's an almost endless variety in the techniques used. But there are also broad similarities between these arts and a number of ways of categorizing them: such as internal or external, hard or soft, striking or grappling, hand-to-hand, weapons-based and so on. Of course, all systems will include one or more of these elements. For example: boxing is principally a striking art, but it involves grappling when boxers hold each other to smother their opponent. Wing chun has both blocking and striking at the same time. Wrestling and judo are grappling styles, but there can be strikes, and so on. Beneath all of these ways of analysing the fighting arts, however, there are core principles, what Bruce Lee called 'the roots of combat'.

The foundation of Bruce's martial art was the Shaolin 'master martial art' that evolved into wing chun and became the root of jeet kune do. The most vital aspect of this art derived from the practice known as chi sao – usually translated in the West as 'sticking hands' – a practice that initially trains the 'contact reflex' through which physical contact with the opponent's limbs allows one to sense the right moves and act spontaneously and instinctively.

Sticking hands practice develops a kinesthetic awareness – what Bruce Lee called 'body feel' – that far outstrips our normal perception. Usually, we perceive what is happening around us mainly through our eyes, coupled with the process of recognition in the brain, both of which are interconnected through the same neurological circuits. An impression perceived through touch doesn't travel through the same neural circuitry as a visual impression; it travels through the same circuits that control physical movement. In this way, the martial artist learns that the best way of recognizing and responding to attack is directly, through physical sensation, rather than through the eyes and thoughts. The seeing-recognizing-calculating-acting process is far too slow and complicated to be of any use in physical confrontation. As Bruce Lee put it, 'From the eye to the hand, how much time is lost?' Developing kinesthetic awareness through the contact reflex is vital to an efficient response when being confronted or attacked.

At first this ability is developed slowly and methodically. To develop 'muscle memory' using simple preset moves involves all the possible combinations of arm-to-arm contact that can be made between two people. From practising these predetermined moves, I am eventually able to deal with random interaction.

It's not difficult to see the similarity between the way the musician begins by learning chords and scales before he can improvise, and the way the novice driver learns the various skills of driving before she can drive and hold a conversation at the same time. The learning process allows you to progress a skill from the thinking function to the instinctive function. Sticking hands practice was the foundation and cornerstone of Bruce Lee's martial art, making it impossible for his ordinary thought processes to dictate his movements. Or as he put it, 'I don't hit. *It* hits!'

As his character explains in *Enter the Dragon*, 'When the opponent expands, I contract, and when he contracts, I expand. And when there is an opportunity, I do not hit, *it* hits all by itself.'

The actions of the contact reflex can be seen in those that *expand* on contact and those that *contract*. To repeat an earlier example: this is what happens when I ride a bicycle. When I push my foot down (expand) on the right pedal, I have to simultaneously release (contract) the pressure on the left pedal, and vice versa, to allow the cranks to turn, otherwise there is no forward movement.

In a combat situation, if you feel your opponent withdraw his arm – by sensing a decrease in the pressure or intent coming from it – this automatically sends your arm out to strike him or her. Conversely, if the opponent presses in on you, the increased pressure again automatically triggers the technique to dissolve or deflect this excess force. This principle doesn't only apply to kung fu, there is a similar maxim in judo: 'Push when pulled, pull when pushed'. In aikido, it translates to 'Turn when pushed, enter when pulled.' In judo the response is linear, while in aikido it's circular, but the intention is exactly the same.

Whatever happens, I can stay one step ahead of the opponent. In the children's' game of stone, scissors and paper, if my opponent gives me paper, then I cut it with scissors. If my opponent gives me a stone, then I wrap it in paper. And if he gives me scissors, then I jam them with a stone, and so on. There is no right or wrong, I simply allow my opponent to dictate my moves, as he strikes (expands) or pulls away (contracts). As this process further refines itself, I can begin to sense subtle shifts in my opponent's emotional state, his level of commitment, or even 'read' his thoughts and intention without making physical contact.

As a young man, Bruce Lee wrote:

The important thing is not to attempt to control the attack by resisting it with force, either physical or mental, but rather to control it by going with it and not asserting oneself against nature. This is simply based on the harmonious interchanging of the theory of yin [contraction] and yang [expansion]. As long as we plan our actions, we are still using strength and will not be able to feel our opponent's movements, thus failing to comprehend the true application of yin and yang. In view of this, the two practitioners are actually two halves of one whole.

... When you understand the root, then you understand all of its blossoming.

Bruce Lee's martial art concept of jeet kune do is the blossom on a tree that has very deep roots. Far too many people try to explain Bruce by looking at the almost limitless ability he possessed at the height of his powers, but it simply isn't possible to understand Bruce's genius as a martial artist without looking at how he got there.

Bruce's unique skills and abilities were rooted in his mother art of wing chun. Wing chun principles, structure and energy are present in everything he did subsequently. Bruce Lee spent five years rooting himself in wing chun before allowing any branches to develop, and only then, once he had understood and *embodied* the principles of one martial art, was he able to understand and incorporate the principles of other martial arts.

By the time Bruce arrived in the US and began teaching his art, its principles had already become part of him. He didn't simply know what he was doing, he had *become* it. Bruce said that only martial artists who were already experienced and well grounded in their own disciplines could learn from him. That's why Dan Inosanto, with his Filipino martial art, and karate champion Joe Lewis were both able to benefit from what Bruce had to offer. Bruce inspired them to greater levels of performance, achieving similar standards but from different foundations.

It's sheer folly for anyone to think that he can begin from the almost limitless freedom that Bruce Lee took his entire lifetime to realize. Trying to graft together cuttings from several traditions without having a solid, stable root would be futile and pointless. You must begin with some form of martial art, before you can grow into having no particular or *fixed* form. You can't just begin with no form at all. This is what Bruce means by his insistence on recognizing the difference between having 'no form' (no rigid or dogmatic form) and 'having no form' (being without any form at all).

As Jhoon Rhee said, 'It was possible to show Bruce Lee a move once and he would do it as if he had mastered it for years.' Bruce's understanding of core principles was a touchstone that allowed him later to integrate aspects of every martial art he ever encountered. And it seems that he achieved this ability so early that he may well have been blessed with it from the very beginning.

Bruce Lee synthesized many arts – Chinese, Japanese, Korean and Filipino – as well as Western techniques such as fencing and boxing, into one seamless, homogenous, fundamental understanding. In essence, this was a completely new conceptual approach to the subject: jeet kune do.

'The mastery of any art transcends the art,' said Bruce Lee. Because of this principle we can make connections between a martial art and any other art. Like an artist creating a landscape by choosing forms and mixing colours, the martial artist can choose from a palette of kick, punch, block, advance and retreat, creating any strategy under the sun. It is only a matter of knowing how to blend the components.

If Bruce had taught music instead of martial arts, he would not have been able offer much to the classical musician who could only play music by reading from a score, but he could have helped those who wanted to improvise their own free-flowing style. Whether it was jazz, blues or reggae, they would all be working with the same twelve notes and laws of harmony, no matter how far those laws were pushed to their limits.

Using what Bruce called 'the three stages of cultivation' we can further compare learning a martial art with learning a musical instrument. The first stage – the 'primitive' or 'innocent' stage – is like learning basic scales and chords, which have no meaning on their own but are necessary building blocks. The second stage – 'sophistication' – means learning to play 'licks', copying phrases from other musicians or favourite records and stringing things together. The third stage – 'artlessness' or 'spontaneity' – is when you realize you have a vocabulary. From words to sentences you progress to expressing yourself in paragraphs or even poetry. You can make up your own solos around the chords that are given to you. You can write, play an instrument or fight without having to think about it.

Wayne Hawkins, a JKD instructor and the musician responsible for the music track on the documentary *A Warrior's Journey*, adds, 'I think the mindset of a jazz musician is very much like that of a JKD practitioner.' 'If people had four arms and four legs,' said Bruce Lee, 'then there would be a different kind of martial art.' And there would also be a different kind of music.

Bruce Lee's intentions have often been misunderstood by members of the mixed martial arts community who believe that he was accumulating every possible technique he could, as if to create an 'ultimate fighting' arsenal. But a good martial artist doesn't set out to compile an encyclopedia of techniques any more than a good musician does. To make a further analogy: would the ultimate musician be one who learned every jazz and blues lick, classical piece and pop tune he could, along with the folk music of Kazakhstan, and then tried cobble them together into one unholy fusion? Of course not. Both musicians and martial artists learn techniques, but ultimately this is done in order to identify the underlying principles of their art, such as harmony in music or pressure in martial art. Then, once a certain level of proficiency is reached, they can interact with others, as the spirit moves them.

Bruce once likened his approach to that of a sculptor. Some sculptors, he said, create their work by adding one bit of clay to another and building it up until they've accumulated what they want. But Bruce's approach was more like that of the sculptor who starts with a formless piece of stone, from which he chips away everything that's not needed until he's left with the essentials and with what works. Far from gathering the many flowers on its branches, Bruce was far more concerned with getting down to the underlying energetic root principles of the martial arts tree.

*

Bruce Lee's critics have made much of the fact that he never fought in competition and chose to have people like Chuck Norris and Joe Lewis as his unofficial representatives. One of the most vocal of these critics has been Joe Lewis himself, who on various occasions has said:

Angelo Dundee [Muhammad Ali's trainer] never fought, but he understood the science of fighting. And Robert De Niro looks good in *Raging Bull* – he throws some good-looking punches. I must've heard Bruce say a thousand times, 'You can't swim without getting in the water, Joe.' But here's a guy who never competed. We never really saw him get in the water.

Bruce had two agendas: one, to get in movies by working with big name directors, producers, writers and actors, and two, to build up his stature as an instructor by working with world champs like myself, Mike Stone and Chuck Norris. That was a smart move 'cos it paid off.

Were his skills as good as they've been written? No. But he hit really hard for someone of his size. I tried on numerous occasions to get Bruce to spar with me, but he never would. We did strictly limited drills. I believe he had the speed and power to become a world-class boxer, but the real questions were never answered. I've never stood in front of another human being who was as quick as him. And he not only had speed, he had the inner confidence to use it. He was like Ali. And I've stood before both of those men, so I know. On the plus side, Bruce was fast and he was coordinated and he moved very well on his feet. On the other side, he had a long, skinny neck, which means he wouldn't be able to take a big punch. Back in the mid Sixties, his kicks were a little weak and he sometimes over-lunged.

But asking how good Bruce Lee might have been in competition is like asking how good Mike Tyson might be as an actor. *Enter the Dragon* is the highest-grossing film in history. That's an accolade good enough to last ten lifetimes. Don't try and make him more immortal than he already is! He's a leading candidate for the greatest martial artist of all time, but that still doesn't make him a great *fighter*, just like being a great fighter doesn't automatically make me a great actor.

Ed Parker also believes that in a street fight Joe Lewis would have been too much for Bruce to handle, but others feel differently, and one of them is James deMile:

> I decided to show him what the reality of street fighting was, but he stopped me cold and tied me up, so that he could hit me at will and I could do nothing about it. I've read some of Joe Lewis's comments but I know Bruce would have blown him away, or anyone else for that matter who acquired their reputation by playing tournaments. Bruce was the best fighter I've ever known, not pound for pound, but against anyone.
>
> Bruce accomplished his fighting skills in the first few years, then began to explore the martial arts as an art. People assumed that he changed because he went on to explore many different concepts and techniques, yet I didn't see anything that was better than what he did in the beginning. He just didn't teach people everything he knew.

Jim Kelly was once asked who he considered to be the greatest tournament fighter, and he replied, 'I would dearly love to say Bruce Lee, but I can't because he never fought in competition. I've heard tales about martial artists he sparred against and there are people who aren't telling everything they know about his ability. There's a code of silence protecting their friends and their reputations and egos. It's not that they were no good; it's just that Bruce was incredible. I would stake my life on Bruce doing extremely well in competition. In fact, I doubt there was anyone in the world that could have beaten him.'

Ernest Lieb, a fifth dan karate black belt who won forty-two tournaments, didn't consider himself a match for Bruce. Another top karate man, Ken Knudson, said that when Bruce side-kicked him he felt as if his eyeballs were left where he'd been standing. Fred Wren, one of the top ten karate practitioners in the US when Bruce was alive, says that he never met anyone with more fighting knowledge and ability than Bruce. Louis Delgado, who once beat Chuck Norris in the Grand Championship, maintains that Bruce Lee baffled him totally, adding, 'I was completely in awe when I fought him.' When asked who would win a real fight between Bruce and himself, Chuck Norris commented, 'Why Bruce, of course, nobody could beat him.'

Though some consider Bruce a middle-class tough guy rather than a hard-core fighter, Dan Inosanto did see him fight on the streets of Hong Kong. 'We're talking street fights,' he says. 'I've seen him in what I don't even call fights. I've seen guys who wanted to break his bones, but they couldn't do it, so it turned into a lesson. They found out that he could just literally play.' Dan Inosanto adds two telling comments, firstly, 'A match in the ring is not a fight' – even Muhammad Ali once said that in a real street fight he wouldn't give much for his chances – and secondly 'Does a woman have to enter a beauty competition to be beautiful?'

It is thanks to Bruce Lee bringing kung fu to the West that, in recent years, monks from the Shaolin Temple have toured both America and Europe with a stage show. And it's because of this that the person who I believe is carrying on Bruce Lee's true martial arts legacy is now in the West.

While on the first ever Shaolin Temple Monks tour of the US in 1992, a thirty-fourth-generation monk called Shi Yan Ming defected to the West. On the last date of the tour in San Francisco, in the middle of the night, he slipped out of his hotel and escaped to the new world. Unable to speak English, he somehow managed to make his way to New York, where he hid out in a basement with only bread and cereal to eat, while the newspapers and TV announced that a Shaolin monk had escaped.

The rebellious monk eventually founded the US Shaolin Temple in New York and currently teaches authentic Shaolin martial arts and Chan (Zen) Buddhism. Like Bruce Lee, who rebelled against the traditionalists to teach kung in the West, so Shi Yan Ming has angered authorities in China. And just as happened with Bruce, students have flocked to him, including many celebrities from the world of music and film. Although Shi has embraced Western culture, married and fathered two children, there is no mistaking his ability, integrity and authenticity. On his website, Shi Yan Ming's story begins with the words, 'Before there are branches, there are roots.' While it ends, 'Believe in yourself, trust yourself and you will find all the answers to all your questions.' Bruce Lee couldn't have put it any better himself.

# 29

## ... and Blossoms

Thirty years ago, the explosion of interest in martial arts in the West was brought about almost single-handedly by Bruce Lee through his starring roles and iconic status as the world's first and best martial arts action star. His athleticism was a unique blend of Western physicality and Eastern fighting principles, which redefined the genre of action movies and the martial arts themselves for the modern era.

As a *movie* martial artist, Bruce Lee invented a new vocabulary. Rather than using methods that harked back to the Chinese theatrical tradition or the over-the-top action sequences that were standard fare, Bruce insisted on long, well-choreographed fight scenes played out in real time. His film work set new standards: no longer could fight scenes rely on a few lumbering haymakers, trampolines or slick editing.

As an innovative teacher, Bruce Lee defied his culture and fought with his own countrymen in order to reveal the Chinese fighting arts to people in the West. After breaking with tradition, rather than sticking with one particular martial art, he aspired to learn everything he could about every method of combat from every teacher he met or sought out. Through a natural genius for martial arts he transcended stale tradition and divisive styles to set martial arts on an entirely new footing.

Driven to become the best that he could be, he collected

techniques and information and met as many great martial artists as he could. At the same time he sought out cutting-edge methods of body conditioning, exercise and diet, also embracing the Western ideal of increasing his power in whatever way possible.

Because Bruce Lee never fought in open competition we have no way of knowing how good he might have been as a martial sportsman. Although there is a lot of anecdotal evidence about Bruce's street fights, or the way he dealt with challenges from young guns on his films sets, we have no way of measuring his abilities against any of his supposed equals – Joe Lewis for example. Yet even without actually taking part in competition, Bruce Lee was the trailblazer for the modern hybrid fighters who compete in what has become known as 'mixed martial arts'.

Within his first year of training with Bruce Lee, Joe Lewis became unassailable in tournament competition. Ten of the greatest karate men of the day fought Lewis, and all ten were knocked out before the end of the second round. Joe was the most successful competition fighter among those Bruce advised, and it was Bruce who suggested Joe try using boxing techniques in karate and who showed him how to use the angular attack principle found in wing chun. Encouraged by Bruce to try out more realistic forms of combat, Lewis became one of the pioneers of full-contact karate in the early 1970s. In effect, Bruce Lee devised strategies while Lewis tested them out in the ring.

> . . . Long-range kicks and swinging punches from an opponent would be frustrated through a system of jams. Straight-line deflecting strikes, simultaneous blocks and strikes and mobile adaptable footwork patterns . . .

It's interesting to compare the above description (from Chapter 2) of the Shaolin master martial art that evolved into wing chun with the description of Joe Lewis's title-winning contest against Greg Baines on 17 January 1970 in Long Beach Arena. Greg Baines was a kenpo karate stylist and California state's heavyweight champion. Most of the traditional karate men in attendance thought that the event was some kind of bizarre publicity stunt. They couldn't quite believe that anyone would step into a ring in front of thousands of people with the chance of having his face smashed by a back fist or his body buckled by a side kick.

Rather than relying on scoring points for touching his opponent, which was more like a game of tag, this bout marked the introduction of the full-contact fighting that was being pioneered by Lewis. Baines, the crowd's favourite, took a very traditional wide and deep stance, the kind that allowed karate practitioners to break bricks and boards. When Lewis started dancing around the ring, darting in and out on the balls of his feet, the audience could barely stifle its chuckles. Yet right from the bell, Lewis scored points against the less mobile Baines. Whenever Baines attempted to land a kick, Lewis intercepted and jammed it, countering with a left hook or combination punch. When Baines attempted a punch, Lewis trapped the strike and countered at the same time with what Bruce called a 'stop-hit'. Before the end of the first round, the audience was almost stunned into silence. This wasn't karate!

Baines fared no better in the second round. Each time he set himself to strike, Lewis moved away, and each time he withdrew his punching hand, Lewis flowed into the gap with a vicious hook. Although Baines had good karate skills, Lewis wasn't observing the traditional methods. His moves were quick and light and he kept his hands raised high, rather than held low. Instead of locking out in the usual karate-style punch, he snapped his fists in the whip-like way of the kung fu practitioner. The coup de grace was a move that had never been seen in a karate competition. Lewis faked a move, almost in slow motion, and switched leads, creating an opening for a double hook combination that sent Baines tumbling to the mat.

This knockout signalled the end for more than Greg Baines. People could no longer argue or boast of traditional karate's superiority. Some tried to argue that Lewis's performance wasn't really martial arts at all, while others said that Baines had fought without commitment or spirit. What had proved to be so stunningly effective was the insight of Bruce Lee's martial concepts allied with Joe Lewis's ability as a competitive martial artist.

Throughout the contest, the announcer kept referring to the bout as American kickboxing, and the mistaken terminology stuck. As a result, Joe Lewis became known as the man who pioneered kickboxing in America. For their part, most of Bruce Lee's followers have always looked at the 1970 Lewis v Baines contest as the birth of tournament jeet kune do.

Bruce Lee's skills extended to places even he wasn't aware of; in his June 1982 interview for *Playboy*, boxing champion Sugar Ray Leonard said:

> One of the guys who influenced me wasn't a boxer. I always loved the catlike reflexes and artistry of Bruce Lee and I wanted to do in boxing what he was able to do in karate [sic]. I started watching his movies before he became really popular in *Enter the Dragon* and I patterned myself after a lot of his ways. Lee was an artist and like him I try to go beyond the fundamentals of my sport.

The tae kwon do master Jhoon Rhee, who respected Bruce's skill and his rebellious attitude, devised and introduced the Safe-T equipment which was first utilized in the World Professional Karate Championships in 1974. Bruce's training methods were made public by Lewis's competition appearances, combined with the use of Jhoon Rhee's protective equipment. In this way, Bruce was at the root of the growth of martial arts into a competition sport in the West, which in its infancy was nothing less than applied jeet kune do.

Joe Lewis and his student, Tom Tannenbaum – the producer of *Longstreet* who had moved on to become head of Universal TV – were instrumental in producing a ninety-minute special out of the 1974 championships. This event established the sport of what became known as full-contact karate or American kickboxing. From this evolved the mixed martial arts (MMA) or ultimate fighting contests of today. At first MMA would simply pit one style against another, say judo against wrestling, or boxing against karate, before martial sportsmen began to cross-pollinate techniques as Bruce himself had done.

There is no doubt that Bruce's fighting methods emerged from having first fully embodied wing chun principles. This evolved into jun fan gung fu with the gradual assimilation of techniques drawn from various other styles of kung fu, such as praying mantis, along with techniques from Western boxing, Thai boxing, ju-jitsu and fencing, amongst others. Howard Williams was only fifteen when he began training with Bruce Lee and James Lee at their Oakland school, and he recalls that the transition from jun fan to jeet kune do was not a gradual one but happened almost overnight.

Williams recalls, 'Bruce was coming up to Oakland every other weekend with his family, between *Green Hornet* shoots. One day he said, "Listen, this is not jun fan; it's now jeet kune do." Bruce showed us this new stance. We thought it was boxing; it looked more like kickboxing at first but he still used the trapping from wing chun.'

Tim Tackett, a schoolteacher who trained with Bruce, says, 'There are different aspects to it – sensitivity, trapping, grappling, boxing, kicking, kickboxing – and putting all those together. Once you have experienced it all and can do it, then you have a core. This core is the thing that's going to come out of you when the guy steps out of a truck because you had an accident with him, or you accidentally ran him off the road, and he's just had twelve beers, and he's 260 pounds and couldn't care less if you're a black belt. Whatever comes out of you then has to be automatic.'

'Bruce could change in midstream,' says Dan Inosanto. 'One minute he could favour a kicking system, then at middle range he could explode like a savage street fighter or Western boxer. When it got in tight, it would look like wing chun. When he got to the ground it was like ju-jitsu. Bruce knew how to integrate techniques. If there was a common thread, then it was an understanding of range.'

Doug Palmer says, 'Although Bruce Lee was grounded in the school of wing chun, every time I met him he'd expanded the style to include not only the corpus of what had gone before but a whole new dimension that magnified the effectiveness and universality of his own school. This wasn't mere technique, jeet kune do transcended style. Jeet kune do was an approach, a philosophy, a way.'

Taky Kimura recalls, 'Bruce called me and said that chi sao was not the focal point any more, as we had thought earlier. I was shocked. He probably realized the limitations of certain aspects of wing chun when trying to practise sticky hands with someone like Kareem Abdul Jabbar. I have to say that at that time I didn't understand what Bruce meant, but now I do. I guess this was part of his liberation as a martial artist.

'He didn't mean chi sao was useless, only that it was not the nucleus of what he was teaching in Los Angeles. He realized that it was an important part of the totality in combat, but not the only part of it, as he emphasized during his days in Seattle where he taught wing chun.

'For a wing chun man, chi sao is probably the most important aspect of training and it dictates the student's approach to fighting. He didn't have the tunnel vision of the classical kung fu man. The wing chun that I know is the version Bruce taught me and I guess its structure takes away a lot of the impractical things that you can learn in other systems. But don't misunderstand me; I don't want to take away anything from anybody else.'

Unfortunately after Bruce Lee's death a lot of martial artists, believing that they were following Bruce Lee's philosophy, cast aside their systems only to discover that with no core structure, they were virtually useless. They simply moved away from being blindly traditional to becoming blindly non-traditional. This common misunderstanding of the philosophy of jeet kune do prompted many martial artists to take a 'salad-bar' approach that fell far short of what Bruce Lee intended. To 'absorb what is useful' doesn't mean simply to select, assemble and accumulate techniques from many different styles, thinking that your new mix-and-match hybrid will have the best of everything. To absorb what is useful first requires a core understanding that you can work from.

'However much people venerate Bruce Lee,' says William Cheung, 'this kind of thinking is mistaken. You *do* need forms, otherwise how can you break away when you have nothing to break away from? Otherwise what have you except an amalgam of styles which is claiming to be free of styles? I say that we are born without knowledge. We have to acquire it first before we can be free of it.'

Dan Inosanto echoes this: 'Bruce didn't want jeet kune do to have a blueprint; that was his whole philosophy at the time. I said, "Well, you've got to start from some place; even a child has to be taught something before he can express freedom."'

But Bruce would sometimes point himself in one direction and his students in another. He didn't teach forms to any of his students; he still preferred to teach people who had already been through formal training, since only they could appreciate what he had to offer. Bruce believed that novices needed to learn forms, but that once a certain level of understanding was reached the martial artist could go outside of fixed boundaries to where the true expression of the art is found. But a martial artist can't begin from no stance, no form or no technique, any more than a musician can go straight to being a virtuoso. Each must learn the fundamentals and forms of music or fighting, which he may eventually use as a basis for improvisation and creativity.

It is clear that Bruce Lee based his fighting method on wing chun, then went on to study other methods. This wasn't so much a process of adding and accumulating techniques, but of embodying them into core principles. For example, all boxers have the same basic style, but Muhammad Ali didn't fight like Joe Frazier, and modern boxers fight differently from the early champions. Western martial artists have a more powerful build while Asian martial artists are lighter and faster. In going beyond basic core skills, each fighter attempts to get the best from his or her particular personal attributes – temperament, speed, power, strategic awareness and so on.

Anyone who attempts to define jeet kune do runs the risk of being like those in the fable of the blind men attempting to describe an elephant: one felt the tail so thought the elephant was like a snake; another felt its leg and thought it was a tree, and so on. Human nature, being what it is, means that each person can relate only to what he already understands. Naturally a wing chun practitioner will readily identify the wing chun element of Bruce's art.

Before he met Bruce Lee, Jim Kelly had already applied jeet kune do principles to karate, resulting in a different understanding to that of most of its practitioners. Bruce recognized what Kelly had done and paid him the compliment of not choreographing Kelly's fights in *Enter the Dragon*, telling Kelly he understood his own art and should do what he wanted.

The real point of jeet kune do is that after a sufficient level of technical ability has been embodied there follows the possibility of further self-discovery and self-expression. Jeet kune do doesn't apply to those of us who are learning the root skills: it implies a level of mastery, or at the very least one of substantial competence.

At the heart of his teaching, Bruce Lee wasn't promoting a martial art: rather he was hoping to instil in his students a real sense of self-understanding. Anyone who identifies with or tries superficially to imitate Bruce Lee has become trapped. To be inspired to experience and understand for oneself is exactly what he intended. The real help that Bruce Lee offers is the inspiration to self-help.

The same truth was expressed by Jesus Christ, another teacher whose insights have given way to various dogmatic and fundamentalist factions, when he said, 'Follow me and you will lose yourself, but follow yourself and you will find both yourself and me.' In the same way, Bruce Lee did not believe that one should put one's faith in others or wait passively to be shown the way: he considered that each person must take some individual responsibility. Once, when asked if he believed in God, he replied, 'If there is a God, he is within. You don't ask God to give you things; you depend on God for your inner theme.'

As I once remarked about religion, 'Put every great teacher together in a room and they'd agree about everything, but put their disciples in there and they'd argue about everything.' Bruce anticipated that this might well be the fate of his own teaching and often commented on the similarity between martial arts and religions. He thought the classical arts were just as limited and out-of-touch with life as dogmatic and fundamentalist religions. He was more concerned with embodying the living spirit that's alive only at the very moment it's being experienced, not when someone later writes or reads a description of it. Bruce intended jeet kune do to reflect the nature of the Tao itself, to be a vehicle that could be *used*, not conveyed by words, grasped by the mind or fixed as a system.

# 30

## The Pathless Land

In a neatly typed fifteen-page essay, 'The Tao of Gung Fu', compiled in the University of Washington's campus library in 1962, Bruce Lee wrote:

> Gung fu is Tao; the spontaneity of the universe . . . The word 'tao' has no exact equivalent in English. The concepts of way, principle or even truth are all too narrow. Lao Tzu, the founder of Taoism, described it in the following words: 'the way that can be expressed in words is not the enduring and unchanging Way' . . . Tao is the principle underlying everything, the supreme ultimate pattern, the principle of growth . . . the way man should order his life to fit in with the Way the universe operates.

After his collapse in May 1973, Bruce Lee told his older brother Peter that he planned to live to be a hundred and told Chuck Norris, 'When I'm thirty-five, I'll stop working and spend the next ten years living quietly with my family and will see nobody. Then I'll come out again and see what I can do for my society.'

Years earlier, in a long letter explaining his hopes and ambitions to his girlfriend and dancing partner, Pearl Cho, he declared his intention of achieving 'impossible goals' before adding, 'People will say I'm too conscious of success.' He then went on to quote the late Charles Steinmetz, who when asked what branch of science would make the most progress in the next twenty years replied, 'Spiritual realization.'

On another occasion Bruce made two drawings of himself: the first was of himself as a young martial artist and action star, a square-jawed cartoon hero, not unlike the images found in modern Manga comics. The second image was of himself as a wise old master like Bodhidharma. Bruce Lee was well aware of the two divergent streams running through him, what George Tan has called the 'Confucian' and the 'Taoist' in him.

George Tan writes:

The common view of Bruce is that he was a sort of Taoist; he used the word *tao* over and over again. But in reality he was more of a Confucian. The basic precept of Taoism is that you accept things as they are and the world as it is. Taoists don't try and push the river. But Confucians manipulate the world. Bruce Lee was someone who had somewhere to get to, and he had to get there quick. And he wasn't about to let anyone stop him. Bruce was a Confucian in Taoist clothing ... Bruce's philosophizing came about when he needed to develop an image – a device to market his martial art. He realized that there was more to be made from philosophizing than from getting punched in the face.

Joe Lewis comments:

When Bruce was attempting to add substance and essence to his art, he constantly quoted Krishnamurti. He never used the name Krishnamurti in front of me, but all you have to do is read a few of Krishnamurti's books and you'll find not only similarities but direct wordings. ... I used to address the audience after I'd won a tournament and Bruce would have written out a little speech about jeet kune do. Only I could never get it right. I could never make sense of what he'd written for me. One time he said jeet kune do means the thus-ness of the techniques. Like we're all supposed to know what 'thus-ness' means.

It was in the teachings of Jiddu Krishnamurti in particular that Bruce Lee found the philosophical underpinnings of jeet kune do. Krishnamurti was born in 1895 to an impoverished family in southern India. His spirituality was recognized early, and at the age of ten he was adopted by an esoteric organization, the Theosophical Society, to be groomed as their future figurehead, and was sent to be educated in England and France. In 1929 he renounced his role of 'messiah', saying that religious sects and organizations stand in the way of truth. Though he continued to teach and lecture throughout the world, he remained unwilling to offer any ready-made system for approaching this truth. 'Truth is a pathless land,' he wrote. 'Man cannot come to it through any organization, through any creed, through any dogma, priest or ritual, nor through any philosophical knowledge or psychological technique.'

Bruce Lee took many of Krishnamurti's sayings on self-realization and applied them to jeet kune do. In *Freedom from the Known*, speaking of the traditional religions, Krishnamurti wrote, 'If you deny the traditional approach, as a reaction, then you will have created another pattern in which you will be trapped.' Referring to the classical martial arts, a sign on the wall of Bruce's school read, 'Do not deny the classical approach, simply as a reaction, or you will have created another pattern and trapped yourself there.'

Krishnamurti's message was that, by their very nature, all systems of thought and religion obscure the truth, which is a living force that cannot be named or pinned down. The core of his teaching was a dialogue with his students in which they were continually challenged to overcome ready-made concepts and come to a state of present attention, in the same way as the Zen master challenges his pupils. A great many of the aphorisms on jeet kune do attributed to Bruce Lee were taken directly, or adapted slightly, from writings and talks by Krishnamurti.

Truth is not something dictated by your conditioning as a
Hindu, or whatever religion you belong to. The man who is
really serious, with the urge to find out what the truth is, has
no concept at all. He lives only in what is.

*Krishnamurti*

Fighting is not something dictated by your conditioning as a
kung fu man, a karate man, or a judo man, or whatever. The
man who is really serious, with the urge to find out what the
truth is, has no martial art style at all. He lives only in what is.

*Bruce Lee*

Linda Lee's ex-husband Tom Bleecker writes:

What does Bruce Lee have to offer that qualifies him as a
philosopher? You're aware that Lee failed out of college? There
are college graduates working on philosophy doctorates that
are far more qualified on this subject. He was anything but a
philosopher. What he did was to occasionally play the Oriental
card at a party or interview. He was anything but a gifted
philosopher.

Ever since Albert Goldman put his poison pen to paper to
write his denigrating articles, much has been made of the idea
that Bruce Lee was no more than a fortune-cookie philosopher
who used the bits and pieces of knowledge he'd gained as a means
to market himself and create a certain aura, without understanding much of what he uttered.

Just because Bruce Lee dropped out of university doesn't
negate what he had to say. For the record, I dropped out of
school at fifteen, yet here I am a published author, speaking with
you on weighty philosophical matters. Since I wrote the first
edition of this book I have even seen *my* words and observations
attributed to Bruce Lee, but one can hardly blame *him* for that.

On the one hand there are those who openly dismiss the
philosophical aspect of Bruce's life and work, while at the other

extreme there are those who meticulously catalogue his shopping lists and letters that say no more than, 'See you next weekend, George,' as if they were laden with pearls of wisdom. Gone are the days when innocent fans used to sit around the Ouija board trying to contact Bruce. Now the Indian branch of the Master Lee Fan Club deifies 'Him' as a fully fledged messiah, fulfilling Bruce's prophecy that his art would one day be dogmatized as a kind of religion.

When Bruce Lee said that 'styles are parts dissected from the whole, divisive by nature, and keep men apart', he was referring to various systems of martial art: karate, kung fu, judo and so on. But if you take this aphorism and reapply it to life, it becomes even more valuable. Apply it to any religion or ideology, or any interest or habit, and 'style' can just as easily apply to a lifestyle, just as 'way' can apply to a way of fighting, way of thinking, way of voting, way of worshipping and so on.

It refers to anyone who believes that his religion is superior to another's, or that her race or nationality is better. It points towards anyone whose happiness depends exclusively on the results of a particular football team, or on having the right designer labels to wear. Most poignantly of all it applies to all those 'fan-tasists' who idealize or idolize Bruce Lee, just as much as it applies to those with an axe to grind, who criticize or disparage Bruce, ultimately at their own expense.

Stirling Silliphant believes, 'If he'd lived, I think Bruce would have become a genuinely great man. All my life I've known only idiots. I define an idiot as a person who makes less of himself than he could be by blaming his actions on something, or someone, outside himself. The only non-idiot I've known, the only person I've seen who exercised his abilities, whether physical or intellectual, to the highest possible degree, is Bruce Lee.'

# APPENDIX 1

## Bruce Lee Films, TV and Books

### COMPLETED WORKS

## CHILDHOOD FILMS (1941–60)

Bruce Lee's first screen appearance was at the age of three months, when he was carried on stage as a baby girl by his father in a Chinese picture called *Golden Gate Girl*, made in San Francisco. His first professional role was at the age of six in the Hong Kong-made film, *The Birth of Mankind* (1946). When he was six, Bruce also played his first role under the name Lee Siu Lung (Lee Little Dragon), appearing in *The Kid* (1950), which was based on a popular comic strip, and with his father, comedian Li Hoi Cheun, cast in a supporting role. Bruce Lee plucked audience heartstrings for the next decade as he portrayed a series of hard-luck orphans and abandoned heirs in dramas with titles like *A Son is Born* (1953), *An Orphan's Tragedy* (1955) and *Orphan's Song* (1955). His last film of this type, made just before he moved to the US, was *The Orphan* (1960, but shot in 1958). The teenage Bruce Lee played a juvenile delinquent redeemed by a teacher who is eventually revealed as his father.

The young Bruce Lee made several other films, playing street urchins and orphans in tragedies like *A Mother's Tears* and comedies like *It's Father's Fault*. Later he played juvenile delinquents and rebels in films such as *The Thunderstorm*, which imitated the *Blackboard Jungle*-style films being made in the USA.

Altogether Bruce Lee appeared in more than twenty pictures as a child actor, the best-known being *The Orphan*, a film about Hong Kong street gangs made when he was eighteen and which gave him his only leading role. It's certain that there would be no interest in any of these films today were it not for Bruce's participation in them.

**1941** *Golden Gate Girl* (aka *Tears of San Francisco*)
**1946** *The Birth of Mankind*
**1948** *Wealth is Like a Dream* (*Fu gui fu yun*)
**1949** *Sai in the Dream* (*Meng li xi shi*)
**1950** *Blooms and Butterflies*
— *The Kid* (aka *My Son, Ah Chung, Kid Chung*) (*Xi lu xiang*)
**1951** *Infancy* (aka *The Beginning of a Boy*) (*Ren zhi cu*)
**1953** *Myriad Homes* (aka *Countless Families*) (*Qian wan ren jia*)
— *Blame it on Father* (aka *It's Father's Fault, The Bad Boy*) (*Fu zhi guo*)
— *The Guiding Light* (aka *A Son is Born*) (*Ku hai ming deng*)
— *A Mother's Tears* (*Ci mu lei*)
— *In the Face of Demolition* (*Wei lou chun xiao*)
**1955** *An Orphan's Tragedy*
**1955** *Gu xing xue lei*
— *Gu er xing*
— *Love* (aka *Carnival*) (*Ai*)
— *Love: Part 2* (*Ai xia ji*)
— *Orphan's Song*
— *We Owe It to Our Children* (*Er nu zhai*)
**1956** *Too Late for Divorce* (*Zhia dian na fu*)
— *Wise Guys Who Fool Around* (*Zao zhi dang cu wo bu jia*)
**1957** *Darling Girl*
— *The Thunderstorm* (*Lei yu*)
**1960** *The Orphan* (*Ren hai gu hong*)

# The Green Hornet (1966–7)

Based on the popular radio drama *The Green Hornet*, created by George W. Trendle.

CAST AND CREW

**Britt Reid / The Green Hornet:** Van Williams
**Kato:** Bruce Lee
**Lenore 'Casey' Case:** Wende Wagner
**Mike Axford:** Lloyd Gough
**District Attorney F. P. Scanlon:** Walter Brooke

A Greenway Production in association with 20th Century Fox Television.
**Head of Production:** William Self
**Executive Producer:** William Dozier
**Producers:** Richard Bluel and Stanley Shpetner
The series had various writers and directors: mainly Jerry Thomas and Norman Foster.


EPISODE GUIDE

The following weekly episodes were aired by ABC TV on successive Fridays, between 7.30 and 8.00p.m.

1) 'The Silent Gun': 9 September 1966
2) 'Give 'Em Enough Rope': 16 September 1966
3) 'Programmed for Death': 23 September 1966
4) 'Crime Wave': 20 September 1966
5) 'The Frog is a Deadly Weapon': 7 October 1966
6) 'Eat, Drink, and Be Dead': 14 October 1966
7) 'Beautiful Dreamer, Part One': 21 October 1966
8) 'Beautiful Dreamer, Part Two': 28 October 1966
9) 'The Ray is for Killing': 11 November 1966
10) 'The Praying Mantis': 18 November 1966
11) 'The Hunters and the Hunted': 25 November 1966
12) 'Deadline for Death': 2 December 1966
13) 'The Secret of Sally Bell': 9 December 1966
14) 'Freeway to Death': 16 December 1966
15) 'May the Best Man Lose': 23 December 1966
16) 'The Firefly': 6 January 1967
17) 'Corpse of the Year, Part One': 13 January 1967
18) 'Corpse of the Year, Part Two': 20 January 1967
19) 'Ace in the Hole': 3 February 1967

20) 'Bad Bet on 459-Silent': 10 February 1967
21) 'Trouble for Prince Charming': 17 February 1967
22) 'Alias The Scarf': 24 February 1967
23) 'Hornet, Save Thyself': 3 March 1967
24) 'Invasion from Outer Space, Part One': 10 March 1967
25) 'Invasion from Outer Space, Part Two': 17 March 1967

Further crossover episodes were made to launch the second *Batman* ABC series:

'The Spell of Tut': 28 September 1966
'The Case is Shut': 29 September 1966
'A Piece of the Action': 1 March 1967
'Batman's Satisfaction': 2 March 1967

The Green Hornet and Kato characters also made a guest appearance on *The Milton Berle Show* in the fall of the 1966–7 season. Bruce Lee and Van Williams also made a personal appearance as themselves on a rock and roll variety show, *Where the Action Is* (episode 19 of 27, aired 1 September 1966). This show toured the US and featured popular music acts of the day, such as the Mamas and Papas and the Knickerbockers, playing games and interviewing celebrities.

## The Green Hornet (1974)

After Bruce Lee's death, 20th Century Fox couldn't simply re-release its twenty-five *Green Hornet* episodes for TV because, if they'd been aired on a daily basis, like *M\*A\*S\*H\** or *Frasier*, they would have been run in less than a month. So in late 1974, the studio released a movie called *The Green Hornet*, which was a sloppy compilation thrown together from three of the TV episodes ('The Praying Mantis', 'The Hunters and the Hunted', and 'Invasion from Outer Space'). It was so poorly edited that it made no sense at all, and to add to the confusion, random fight scenes from other episodes were thrown in to lengthen the action sequences. The film was billed as a 'Kato and the Green Hornet' film and stills from other Bruce Lee films were used to promote it. Ambiguous newspaper ads even implied that it was a new Bruce Lee movie.

In the summer of 2004, Kevin Smith was writing a screenplay for a new series of *The Green Hornet*, which was originally scheduled for release in 2005. It was rumoured that Jet Li would portray Kato and

Jake Gyllenhaal would play the Green Hornet. In 2004, Smith put the film on the back burner, then in 2006 he announced that he no longer had anything to do with *The Green Hornet* project, which has subsequently failed to materialize.

# CAMEO APPEARANCES (1967–9)

## Ironside (1967)

A wheelchair-bound Detective Ironside battles the bad guys on the streets of San Francisco.

> **Season 1, Episode 7:** 'Tagged for Murder': aired 26 October 1967
> **Writer:** Arthur Weingarten
> **Director:** Charles S. Dubin
> Starring Raymond Burr as Robert T. Ironside and featuring Bruce Lee as Leon Soo

## Blondie (1969)

A TV show based on the newspaper comic strip.

> **Season 1, Episode 13:** 'Pick on a Bully Your Own Size': aired January 1969
> **Writer:** Arthur Weingarten
> **Director:** Charles S. Dubin
> Featuring Bruce Lee as a karate instructor

## Here Come the Brides (1969)

To avoid losing their logging crew, the Bolt brothers bring in a hundred prospective brides from Massachusetts to Seattle.

> **Season 1, Episode 25:** 'Marriage, Chinese Style': aired 9 April 1969
> **Writers:** N. Richard Nash, Alan Marcus, Skip Webster

**Director:** Richard Kinan
Featuring Bruce Lee as Lin

## Marlowe (1969)

On what looks like a standard missing-persons case, detective Philip Marlowe (James Garner) meets a blackmailer (Jackie Coogan), who is later murdered. A set of incriminating photos of a sitcom star (Gayle Hunnicutt) and a gangster (H. M. Wynant), which the blackmailer was holding, leads Marlowe along a convoluted trail of dead bodies and uncooperative people, including a stripper (Rita Moreno), a TV executive (William Daniels), a kung fu hit man (Bruce Lee), a shady child psychologist (Paul Stevens) and a frustrated police lieutenant (Carroll O'Connor).

> A karate expert, Winslow Wong, is hired by Steelgrave to put the heat on Marlowe. He is played by none other than renowned martial arts expert Bruce Lee in his pre-star days. He offers Marlowe money to forget looking for Orrin, but when Marlowe refuses, Wong tears up his office karate-style in a hilarious scene. It's a classic in physical comedy.
>
> *Dennis Schwarz: Ozus' World Movie Reviews*

Based on Raymond Chandler's novel, *The Little Sister*
**Writer:** Stirling Silliphant
**Director:** Paul Bogart

The film was re-released in 1974 with Bruce Lee given top billing.

# FIGHT CHOREOGRAPHY

## The Wrecking Crew (1969)

Special agent Matt Helm recovers stolen bullion in a camp Bond spoof with flashy and fleshy production values. The film is both funny where it's supposed to be, and hilarious where it isn't – for example, in this film Denmark has huge mountains! The stars are Dean Martin, Sharon

Tate and Elke Sommer. Bruce Lee was hired as the fight arranger and is credited as the 'karate advisor'.

> Adapted from the novel by Donald Hamilton
> **Writer:** William McGivern
> **Director:** Phil Karlson

## A Walk in the Spring Rain (1970)

A middle-aged romance starring Ingrid Bergman and Anthony Quinn. While on vacation in the mountains, the wife of a college professor meets a simple compassionate handyman whose love of life is the opposite of that of her dry, boring husband. Not surprisingly a passionate affair ensues, which is broken up by their selfish children. Bruce Lee was hired to direct the fight scene that writer Stirling Silliphant contrived to fit into the story.

> Adapted from the novel by Rachel Maddux
> **Writer:** Stirling Silliphant
> **Director:** Guy Green

## Longstreet (1971)

Produced by Tom Tannenbaum for Paramount TV, *Longstreet* was aired weekly by ABC TV from 9 September 1971 to 10 August 1972, on Thursdays between 9.00 and 10.00p.m.

The starring role belonged to James Franciscus as Mike Longstreet, a blind investigator. Bruce Lee featured as Li Tsung in the pilot and opening episodes, written by Stirling Silliphant, and he also had small parts in episodes 7, 10 and 11.

1) **'Longstreet':** 23 February 1971
   **Writer:** Stirling Silliphant
   **Director:** Joseph Sargent

2) **'The Way of the Intercepting Fist':** 16 September 1971
   **Writer:** Stirling Silliphant
   **Director:** Don McDougall

7) **'Spell Legacy Like Death':** 21 October 1971
**Writer:** Sy Salkowitz, Mark Rodgers
**Director:** Paul Krasny

10) **'Wednesday's Child':** 11 November 1971
**Writers:** Howard Browne, Stephen Kandel, Mark Rodgers
**Director:** Jeannot Szwarc

11) **'I See, Said the Blind Man':** 18 November 1971
**Writer:** Sandor Stern
**Director:** Leslie H. Martinson

# The Big Boss (1971)

US title: *Fists of Fury*. Bruce Lee's first two feature films were muddled in transit to the US. His first movie, *The Big Boss*, was to be retitled *The Chinese Connection* for the US market, to link it to the hit drug-smuggling movie *The French Connection*. The cans containing Bruce's second film, *Fist of Fury*, were labelled wrongly as *Fists of Fury*. The confusion was complete when the films were then placed in the wrong cans. As a result, in the US Bruce's first film is known as *Fists of Fury*; while his second film is known as *The Chinese Connection*.

In *The Big Boss*, Cheng is a city boy who moves with his cousins to work in an ice factory. He does this with a promise to his mother never to get involved in fighting. However, when members of his family begin disappearing after meeting the management of the factory, he is forced to break the vow and confront the villainy of the boss.

**Writers:** Bruce Lee and Lo Wei
**Director:** Lo Wei
**Music:** Peter Thomas, Joseph Koo

**Bruce Lee:** Cheng Chao An
**Maria Yi:** Chow Mei
**James Tien:** Hsiu Chien
**Yin-Chieh Han:** Hsiao Mi (The Boss)
**Malalene:** Wu Maing (Prostitute)
**Tony Liu:** Hsiao Chiun (Mi's Son)
**Quin Lee:** Ah Kun

**Nora Miao:** Drink stand owner
**San Chin:** Hua Sze
**Chao Chen:** Foreman
**Chia Ching Tu:** Uncle

Filmed on location in Pak Chong, Thailand
**Released:** 3 October 1971

Of all of Bruce Lee's films, *The Big Boss* has the highest number of kills by Bruce Lee's character. In *Fist of Fury* the kill count is nine; in *Way of the Dragon* it is one and in *Enter the Dragon* it is five. *The Big Boss* has thirteen.

When the film was released in the US, the death of Hsiao Mi (The Boss) was cut down to show him simply being stabbed in the chest with a knife, in order for the film to receive an R rating. The original version of his death not only shows an explicit close-up of the knife in his chest but Cheng's fingers piercing the rib cage and blood flowing from under his shirt, which would have given the film an X rating.

When the movie was first released in 1971 in Hong Kong, it featured multiple scenes that have since disappeared from all mainstream edits of the film as a result of the 1972 Hong Kong movie-censorship crackdown. In the case of *The Big Boss*, this includes scenes of a body being cut in half with a circular saw, a blood vessel cut with a knife, causing blood to spew from a character's forehead and, most infamous of all, a man having his head split open with a hand saw. However, when these deletions were stipulated, editors also took the opportunity to cut out further sequences to increase the pace of the film. The deleted shots and scenes exist in the public domain only as still photos or quick snippets of footage in trailers, though there are private collectors who possess copies of the missing footage.

In the mainstream edit of *The Big Boss*, white 'splice lines' and jumps in the soundtrack often make it evident where scenes have been removed.

# Fist of Fury (1972)

Chen returns to China only to learn of his beloved teacher's death, which is being aggravated by continual racial harassment from the Japanese population in the area. While investigating his teacher's murder, Chen confronts the Japanese head on, with his mastery of kung fu.

**Writer:** Lo Wei (though Bruce Lee did much on-the-spot rewriting)
**Director:** Lo Wei

**Bruce Lee:** Chen Zhen
**Nora Miao:** Yuan Le Erh
**James Tien:** Fan Chun Hsia
**Maria Yi:** Yen
**Robert Baker:** Petrov (the Russian)
**Fu Ching Chen:** Chao
**San Chin:** Tung
**Yin-Chieh Han:** Feng Kwai Sher
**Riki Hashimoto:** Hiroshi Suzuki
**Jun Arimura:** Suzuki's bodyguard
**Lo Wei:** Detective

Filmed on location in Hong Kong and at Golden Harvest studios
**Released:** 22 March 1972

Sync sound was not widely used in Hong Kong cinema until the 1990s so the voices for this movie, even on the original Chinese track, were dubbed. On the Chinese track, the voice of the Russian fighter speaking English is Bruce Lee with added reverb.

In the training scenes, just before the Japanese spring a surprise attack on the school, Jackie Chan appears as an extra. He was also the stunt double for the Japanese villain, Mr Suzuki, in the final scenes. He can be seen flying through the air after Bruce's character delivers a flying kick. Chan fell much farther than originally intended, from a height of fifteen feet, and after the scene had been filmed, Bruce rushed over to see if he was OK.

In the scene at the park entrance, one of the Japanese men is played by Yuen Wah, who doubled Bruce Lee's acrobatic back flip.

The real Jing Wu School still survives with its headquarters in Malaysia and can be found in many major cities throughout the world. Due to the communist revolution, though, the Chinese ones are few in number.

## Way of the Dragon (1972)

Tang Lung (Bruce Lee) arrives in Rome to help his cousins with their restaurant business. They are being pressurized to sell their property to the mob, who will stop at nothing to get their hands on it. When Tang arrives he resists them and they are unable to defeat him, so the syndicate boss hires the best Japanese and European martial artists available to fight Tang, though he easily finishes them off. An American karate champion, Chuck Norris (Colt), has a showdown with Tang in Rome's Colosseum, in what is arguably the best fight scene Lee ever put on film. In the climax of the fight Colt, who is used only to the more rigid techniques of karate, is bewildered by Tang's broken rhythms – just as the Rhythm Man character was to have fought in *The Silent Flute*.

**Writer/Directors** Bruce Lee
**Cinematography:** Nishimoto Tadashi

**Bruce Lee:** Tang Lung (aka China Dragon)
**Nora Miao:** Chen Ching Hua
**Chuck Norris:** Colt
**Wei Ping Ao:** Ho
**Huang Chung Hsin:** Uncle Wang
**Bob Wall:** Robert
**Wong In Sik:** Japanese fighter

US title: *Return of the Dragon*. Because *Way of the Dragon* was released in the US after *Enter the Dragon*, it is known there as *Return of the Dragon*

Filmed On location in Rome and at Golden Harvest studios in Hong Kong
**Released:** 30 December 1972

The film was heavily cut in the US and UK, and was banned outright in Scandinavia.

After completing *The Big Boss* and *Fist of Fury*, Bruce Lee knew that he would never have to work for $7,500 a film again. He suggested that he and Chow form a partnership, Concord Productions. Unfortunately, at the beginning of 1972, Chow's first decision was to ask the inadequate Lo Wei to direct a new film to be called *Yellow-Faced Tiger*. Although Bruce went through the charade of several planning sessions, he was secretly planning to write, direct and star in his own movie, *Way of the Dragon*. *Yellow-Faced Tiger* was eventually made, starring Chuck Norris and retitled *Slaughter in San Francisco*.

## Game of Death (1972)

It was in 1972 that Bruce Lee donned his yellow catsuit and began work on what would surely have been a far better film than any of those he actually completed. Written and directed by Bruce, the film was to star him alongside Chi Hon Joi, Dan Inosanto, Kareem Abdul Jabbar and other notable martial artists. Further starring roles were intended for George Lazenby and Betty Ting Pei. At the time of his death Bruce had approximately twenty-eight minutes of film in the can at Golden Harvest in Hong Kong. Although there was a working script, the movie was essentially open-ended and improvised. All of the films Bruce made were changed during the course of filming and there is no reason to suspect that *Game of Death* would have been any different

Only three fight scenes from *Game of Death* have ever been seen by the public: the bako and nunchaka duel with Dan Inosanto; the fight with Korean hapkido exponent Chi Hon Joi; and, of course, the confrontation with Kareem Abdul Jabbar, master of 'no style'. Other planned fight scenes are said to have included a muay thai exponent and a room full of traps and battles with various other martial artists. These would have included some of the following: Bolo Yeung from *Enter the Dragon*, Wong In Sik from *Way of the Dragon*, James Tien from *Fist of Fury*, tae kwon do practitioner Jhoon Rhee, and possibly Sammo Hung and Chuck Norris. Bob Wall says that he was the intended opponent for level five, Taky Kimura was invited to play a role and declined and Wong Sheun Leung may have been a wing chun exponent.

Further scenes unseen by the public are said to exist, along with a hundred-page script. It is also reported that rather than having twenty minutes of film in the can, Bruce had more than four hours' worth. It's also speculated that the Lee estate may be holding on to further unseen footage from *Game of Death* with the intention of maximizing revenue by releasing it piecemeal, but it's hardly likely that they would have sat on this material for so long, other than for reasons of privacy.

Brad Kaup, editor of *A Warrior's Journey*, says that discounting alternative out-takes they used *all* of the scenes from *Game of Death* that they had access to and does not subscribe to rumours that there is any missing footage, yet he adds, paradoxically, that people should continue to search. According to the current research of Nick Clarke, along with investigations made in the 1970s by Don Atyeo and Felix Dennis for *Kung Fu Monthly* magazine, further footage from *Game of Death* definitely exists.

In 1975, *Kung Fu Monthly* claimed that a Toronto cinema showed 'unreleased footage from Bruce Lee's last film' in which a battle with a samurai played by Yasuaki Kitura was one of the unseen fights. In 1980, the Wometco Home Theater apparently showed a documentary about Bruce that contained previously unseen footage from *Game of Death*. In Malaysia a Seasonal Film video is said to exist, also featuring unseen footage. And in 1978, *JKD Hong Kong Club* magazine produced a special edition '*Game of Death* Extract' describing this missing footage. Similarly, the Philippine Film Archives are said to contain rare out-takes. Another eyewitness claims to have seen ninety minutes of continuous action back in 1975. One rumour claims George Lucas got hold of some of the film for inclusion in a future *Star Wars* project . . . and so the myths continue.

Bearing in mind that anyone who owns unseen footage of Bruce Lee would stand to make a lot of money from it, is it likely that they would have kept it hidden away for more than thirty years? Apart from the obvious out-takes, alternative takes and *mis*-takes that occur during the course of any film production, is there really any more genuine unseen footage of Bruce Lee in existence?

As a key player in the martial arts movie world and an expert of Mandarin cinema, one person who can shine a light on the situation is Bey Logan, who does believe that unseen footage of Bruce Lee exists somewhere in the Golden Harvest archives. But, he adds, 'it's unlikely that they know where it is, or are even aware that they have it. On the other hand, anyone with any idea of what to look for doesn't have access to it.'

## Fist of Unicorn (1972) aka Unicorn Palm

When Bruce Lee returned to Hong Kong in 1970, one of the first people he sought out was his old childhood friend and fellow child actor Siu Kee Lun, better known as Unicorn. And it was Unicorn who acted as the go-between when Bruce was sounding out the possibility of doing the 'Kuan Yu' project with Shaw Brothers.

At a meeting with representatives of the Sing Hoi Film Company, Unicorn was told quite plainly that he was no box-office draw and had no reputation, and that the proposed film, starring himself, could only be made if it somehow involved Bruce Lee. Bruce was always generous to his friends and had already given Unicorn the role of head waiter in

*Way of the Dragon.* Now he helped his friend further by arranging the fight scenes for this film, which Unicorn was putting together on a shoestring budget.

Footage of Bruce arriving on the set and coaching the actors was later contrived and manipulated into a new storyline, and when the film was eventually released, Bruce wasn't just credited with the fight arranging, but was given star billing as its leading actor.

## Enter the Dragon (1973)

Lee, a member of the Shaolin Temple, is recruited by a British agent, Braithwaite, to infiltrate a criminal operation run by a renegade Shaolin monk, Han. Lee is then sent to a martial arts tournament being held on Han's private island. He is also told that Han's men tried to abduct his sister three years earlier and that rather than submit to them she committed suicide. Also at the tournament are misfits Roper, who needs prize money to pay off gambling debts, and Williams, who is on the run from the police. All three soon find themselves pitted against Han's private army as he defends his underground labyrinth of narcotics and prostitution.

In almost every scene involving a large group of extras in white karate suits, there are a few who seem unable to stop grinning with delight at seeing their real-life hero in action.

**Writer:** Michael Allin
**Director:** Robert Clouse
**Producers:** Paul Heller and Fred Weintraub (Sequoia) and Bruce and Raymond Chow (Concord) for Warner Brothers
**Cinematography:** Gil Hubbs
**Editors:** Kurt Hirshler and George Watters
**Music:** Lalo Schiffrin

**Bruce Lee:** Lee
**John Saxon:** Roper
**Jim Kelly:** Williams
**Peter Archer:** Parsons
**Ahna Capri:** Tania
**Bob Wall:** Oharra
**Shih Kien:** Han
**Angela Mao:** Su Lin

**Bolo Yeung:** Bolo
**Betty Chung:** Mei Ling
**Geoffrey Weeks:** Braithwaite

**Filmed:** On location in Hong Kong
**Released:** 19 August 1973

Note: *Enter the Dragon* was Bruce Lee's fifth film, but the first to go on general release in the US. His fourth film, *Game of Death*, was incomplete at the time of his death and was released posthumously after much meddling.

After Bruce's unexpected death, the Warner Bros publicity department took a pragmatic view of circumstances. As one executive put it, Bruce's death was worth a two-million-dollar publicity campaign, and the box-office take was further augmented when Raymond Chow raised his admission prices by more than 50 per cent.

*Enter the Dragon* wasn't such a hit with his Chinese audience. They were upset that it had been released in the West first, as it added to the feeling that Bruce Lee had gone from being a Chinese hero to just another Oriental heavy in a Hollywood thriller. The Chinese preferred Bruce as the underdog triumphing over the odds, and it's true that there is little of Lee's natural charm in this film. The Chinese, who had come to look on him as a national hero, perhaps even something of a messiah, felt that he'd abandoned them and left them without a representative. The Japanese, on the other hand, had no trouble with the style of *Enter the Dragon* and the film was an enormous hit there. Raymond Chow hadn't even bothered to release Bruce's earlier films in Japan, knowing that they would never accept a Chinese star, but *Enter the Dragon* turned out to be an even bigger hit in Japan than it was in the States, prompting Chow to release all of Bruce's films there, further increasing their earnings.

> I had no illusion about *Enter the Dragon* being a great film, or even a good one. It was more of the same Bond-ish junk that I'd seen a thousand times and outgrown years before. *Enter the Dragon* itself hadn't affected me; it was Bruce Lee, who'd leapt, shining, from the screen.
>
> *Davis Miller*

The story is basically a mishmash of Bond plots, though in retrospect it also blends genres, which helps make the film a classic. Just as the later *Kill Bill* films combined elements of martial arts, spaghetti Westerns, samurai and yakuza films with the archetypal revenge plot, their predecessor *Enter the Dragon* does much the same thing. Already combining spy and martial arts films, *Enter the Dragon* also adds 'blaxploitation' to its content: from his first appearance on screen, Jim Kelly's Williams is a character who could have walked straight out of *Shaft*.

Even amid all the action and excitement of his life, Bruce maintained the hope of educating people through films with both a surface story and a deeper message, though he was never able to fully realize this ambition to educate people about the inner aspects of his art. The thousands of people that streamed into the cinemas weren't going to Bruce Lee movies to learn about awareness or discover freedom, but there are nonetheless lessons hidden in the films. The teaching sequence at the beginning of *Enter the Dragon* was added to the script on Bruce's initiative is unlike any other part of the film, and is a significant inclusion.

# OTHER MATERIAL

Many clips of relevance to Bruce Lee's life and work can be viewed on the YouTube website. These include his demonstration of the one-inch punch at the Long Beach International Karate Tournament of July 1964, his screen test for 20th Century Fox in February 1965, and his December 1971 television interview with Pierre Berton. Searches will also bring up other related material, including interviews with Dan Inosanto, who shows the viewer his unique collection of Bruce Lee memorabilia, including some of the signs that hung on the wall of Bruce's gung fu institutes.

# BRUCE LEE: BOOKS AND ARTICLES

## *Chinese Gung Fu: The Philosophical Art of Self-Defense (1963)*

This short manual was written by Bruce, using photographs taken in the parking lot of Ruby Chow's restaurant in Seattle, showing the jun fan gung fu (wing chun) techniques he was using at the time.

## *Wing Chun Kung-Fu (1972)*

This small book illustrates the basic principles of wing chun and was compiled while Bruce was working with James Lee in Oakland. It shows James demonstrating the first wing chun form, the sil lum tao. Bruce gave authorship and credit for the book to James as he believed he had already moved some distance from 'pure' wing chun, and because James was seriously ill. Bruce Lee is therefore credited only as 'technical editor'.

## *Bruce Lee's Fighting Method: volumes 1–4 (1977)*

These four volumes (1: *Self Defense Techniques*; 2: *Basic Training*; 3: *Skill in Techniques*; and 4: *Advanced Techniques*) show Bruce Lee's system evolving and feature photographs from his time working with Dan Inosanto in Los Angeles.

## *The Tao of Jeet Kune Do (1975)*

Not written for publication as such, this book was drawn from notes made for Bruce Lee's own personal study during the period he was laid up with his back injury in 1969. It has notes and drawings on various fighting systems including kung fu, boxing, wrestling and fencing. Much of the material was taken from other books on fencing and from the *US Army Boxing Manual*, as well as philosophical nuggets from various places such as *The Sourcebook of Chinese Philosophy*, D. T. Suzuki's essays on Zen Buddhism and the teachings of Krishnamurti. Although Bruce had no intention of publishing these notes, fearing they would be exploited, they were edited (mainly by Gilbert L. Johnson) and published in 1975 on the initiative of Linda Lee.

## MAGAZINE ARTICLES

Bruce Lee wrote several articles for various newspapers such as the *Hong Kong Standard* and also for martial arts magazines. One such article is 'Liberate Yourself from Classical Karate', written in 1971 for *Black Belt* magazine.

# APPENDIX 2

## Bruce Lee Films and TV

### POSTHUMOUS WORK AND
### INDIRECT INVOLVEMENT

## Kung Fu (1972—)

In the week ending 6 May 1973, around the time *Enter the Dragon* was being wrapped up, the *Kung Fu* TV series starring David Carradine was the number one show on US television, attracting a regular audience of 28 million viewers.

More than once Chuck Norris has admitted that his acting is a little pedestrian and that he's not blessed with great powers of expression. As Norris himself put it, 'David Carradine is about as good a martial artist as I am an actor.' Perhaps anticipating criticism of his limited martial arts abilities, Carradine once claimed that 'many of Bruce's moves were done by doubles'. In fact, in his entire career Bruce Lee only ever used a double on three shots. In the opening sequence of *Enter the Dragon* a gymnast did the somersault; this same gymnast later did the back flip in Bruce's controversial fight scene with Bob Wall. Bruce's back flip in *Fist of Fury* was also doubled by a stunt actor, Yuen Wah.

In 1986, a second *Kung Fu* TV movie was made featuring a young Brandon Lee playing Caine's son, Chung Wang. Towards the end of the film, Chung Wang asks Caine if he is his father. The question is more than ironic since, in real life, it was Brandon's father who came up with the concept for the series. In a second movie, *Kung Fu: The Next Generation* (1987), the action moves to the present day and centres on the story of Johnny Caine (Brandon Lee), who is now the great-grandson of Kwai Chang Caine.

Two decades after the first television series ended, a further related series followed the adventures of a descendant of Kwai Chang Caine and ran for four years from 1993 to 1997. Entitled *Kung Fu: The Legend Continues*, it again starred Carradine, whose character is now the grandson of the original Caine. As a tranquil, philosophical father, he leaves the fighting mainly to his detective son, played by Chris Potter.

In June of 2006, Ed Spielman and Howard Friedlander announced that a feature film, which would serve as a prequel to the original *Kung Fu* series and take place in China, was in development. They remarked that David Carradine would not be returning to the project and that it would not be 'an effects-laden project'.

## The Shrine of Ultimate Bliss (1974)

*The Shrine of Ultimate Bliss* was intended to be Bruce Lee's follow-up to *Enter the Dragon*, once he had completed *Game of Death*. The planned production budget of $10 million and worldwide marketing budget of a further $10 million were astonishing amounts at the time. By comparison, the 1974 James Bond film *The Man with the Golden Gun* had 'only' a $7 million production budget and a $6 million worldwide marketing budget. Forecasts that *The Shrine of Ultimate Bliss* was expected to gross around $400 million were not as ridiculous at it might first appear. *Enter the Dragon* cost just $850,000 to produce and by 2006 had earned more than $265 million at the box office. And with a mere $130,000 production budget, *Way of the Dragon* went on to gross more than $85 million.

But with the sudden death of 'the world's biggest star' the film's fate was sealed. On hearing of Bruce's death, Sonny Chiba refused to sign his contract and promptly flew back to Japan. There was bad press too for the film's other star George Lazenby, who, it turned out, was supposed to have dinner with Bruce, Raymond Chow and Betty Ting Pei the evening Bruce died. With no Bruce Lee, Warner Brothers dropped out and Raymond Chow immediately cut the film's production budget from $10 million to $850,000, as well as slashing the marketing and promotional budgets.

To try and keep the project alive, Chow brought in Asian stars

Angela Mao, Betty Ting Pei and Sammo Hung, as well as the Australian wrestler Roger Ward. He also invited rival studio Shaw Brothers to become joint producers in order to help pay for the film's still huge production costs – by Hong Kong film industry standards at least.

The British production, *The Man from Hong Kong*, was another attempt to hang on to the coat-tails of Bruce Lee's career. Director Brian Trenchard-Smith brought in Wang Yu, changed his name to Jimmy Wang Yu, and hired George Lazenby to play the villain. Jimmy Wang Yu was a good martial artist, as were others like Jet Li and David Chiang, but none of them was Bruce Lee.

# HIDDEN DRAGON: UNMADE PROJECTS AND UNSEEN FOOTAGE

In *Enter the Dragon*, the sequence in the Shaolin temple where Lee teaches a young monk how to kick with feeling and without thinking was not in the original script and was added at Bruce's insistence. But what was left out of the film is also of some importance. Lee's discussion with the head monk was much longer, before the following exchange was cut:

As Lee pays his respects to his teacher, the head monk remarks that Lee's skill has gone beyond mere technique and is now one of spiritual insight. The monk asks Lee the same question Lee has just asked the young monk: what was his immediate feeling towards his opponent while they were sparring? Lee replies that he experienced no separate opponent. There was only one fluid, spontaneous interplay of energy so that 'When the opponent expands, I contract, and when he contracts, I expand. And when there is an opportunity I do not hit; *it* hits by itself.'

Joe Hyams once asked Bruce, 'What if someone was to attack you and seriously meant to do you in? What then?'

Bruce answered, 'I would probably hurt him. If I did and I was on trial, I would plead not guilty, that I did not do it, *it* did it.'

At first Hyams didn't understand, so Bruce explained further. 'I throw a ball and you catch it. You walk into a dark room and without conscious thought you turn on the light switch. A child runs in front of your car and you jam on the brakes. You don't think about these things, they just happen. If someone tried to hit me, I wouldn't think about it, it would just happen. I would do whatever was called upon to be done without conscious thought.'

Due to the limitations of the budget there is no behind-the-scenes or out-takes footage from any of Bruce Lee's first three films. Bruce's first two films were made for the cost of a 30-second TV commercial in the US at the time, so often only one take and one print were made. Probably the only unseen Bruce Lee material that exists is the private film shot on set by actors involved in the various movies.

Bey Logan has mentioned a reel of film shot by Jon Benn, who played the heavy in *Way of the Dragon*, and there is also home-movie footage shot by Peter Archer and Ahna Capri on the set of *Enter the Dragon*. Bob Wall says that Ahna Capri has about ten minutes of 8mm film of him sparring with Bruce on the set. He adds that it may never be released because it can't be made public without obtaining the necessary clearances, which would have to be signed by Warners, Linda, et al., who would all want their cut. At one time Ahna Capri was asking $65,000 for her film from any private collector. Bob Wall claims to have two hours of film of Bruce teaching James Coburn and Steve McQueen, as well as footage of Bruce kicking the heavy bag, and of Bruce and Brandon on Hong Kong TV when Brandon was five years old. 'Why haven't I shown this stuff?' he says. 'We were getting ready to show it at the Imperial Palace in Las Vegas, but Linda killed it.'

During the making of *Enter the Dragon* cameraman Henry Wong shot five hours of 16mm film to be edited down to make a ten-minute behind-the-scenes documentary, which was to be used to promote the film prior to its release. Some of this footage featured Bruce's unscripted fights with film extras and intruders on the film set. The cameraman sent all this material to Warners, but on completion of the ten-minute film, and with the studio's approval, the New York editing company that assembled it destroyed the remaining film. Nobody realized at the time that they might have destroyed the most valuable Bruce Lee film of all.

Whenever the subject of cuts to Bruce Lee films comes up it usually concerns the censored nunchaka scenes from the various versions of *Fist of Fury* or *Way of the Dragon*, and similar missing scenes from *Game of Death* or *Enter the Dragon*. Now, thirty years on, much of that missing footage has been restored; the last time *Enter the Dragon* was shown on TV in the UK the scenes were intact. The film that has suffered most at the hands of the censors is *The Big Boss*. The infamous 'saw' scene is never there, while other missing scenes mainly concern violent knife fights, the 'bodies in ice' scenes and Bruce's scenes with the hooker. As mentioned earlier, it is often possible to see the white splice lines that appear on screen where these edits have been made and to hear jumps in the soundtrack.

## Green Bamboo Warrior

At the time of Bruce Lee's death he had completed only four films: *The Big Boss*, *Fist of Fury*, *Way of the Dragon* and *Enter the Dragon*. Once he'd gone back and completed *Game of Death* in South Korea he was also said to be planning a new project called *Green Bamboo Warrior*. It now transpires that he had a script for this as early as January 1972 and there are tapes of Lee explaining both the storyline and production ideas. He had approached *Enter the Dragon* co-star Bolo Yeung to appear with him. Confusingly, Lee had originally planned to make *Green Bamboo Warrior* as his third movie, and at first planned to call it, *Enter the Dragon*.

*Green Bamboo Warrior*, which in Chinese logic alternatively translates as 'Conqueror of the Golden Mountain', is set in San Francisco at the turn of the century. Bruce plays one of a group of Chinese workers who make the exhausting sea voyage from China in search of the proverbial mountain of gold in California. Soon after their arrival they are put to work in a mining town, where conditions are harsh and brutal. As a skilled martial artist, Bruce is elected the leader of the gang of workers, and before long he is using his skills to lead a rebellion against the cruel Western bosses. The foreman of the mine holds Bruce at gunpoint, as the rest of the bosses beat him, tie him up and leave him in the mine to die. Despite being badly wounded, Bruce escapes and finds refuge in the cabin of an old Chinese woman who also works for the mine. She tends to his injuries and nurses him back to health. Once he is recovered he vows to have his revenge with his weapon of choice: a length of green bamboo. Eventually he overcomes various challenges and becomes a hero to the Chinese workers.

While he was filming *Enter the Dragon*, a Hong Kong businessman, Andrew Vajna, who was making inroads into the film industry, approached Bruce. Bruce Lee made a pitch for *Green Bamboo Warrior* and Vajna was interested enough to seek out Golden Harvest executive Russell Cawthorne to begin work on an English version of the script. As things turned out Vajna's breakthrough eventually came as the producer of *Rambo: First Blood* and the later *Terminator* movies.

## Kuan Yu Project

Just before his death in July 1973, Bruce Lee was considering working with Shaw Brothers Studios, possibly as a tactic to put pressure on Raymond Chow. The rumoured Shaw project, to be called *The Seven Sons of the Jade Dragon*, was to have featured Bruce in period costume, playing the roles of all seven sons and their father.

The storyline is typical: Kuan Yu rescues the daughter of a peasant who has been kidnapped by a rich official on the eve of her wedding. Soldiers are sent to find and kill him and he takes refuge in a temple. The soldiers flush him out by burning down the temple, but when they are certain he is dead Kuan Yu bursts from the flames and defeats them before fleeing the country.

## Bruce and Elvis

After the filming of *Way of the Dragon* in Rome – and while Bruce Lee was working on *Game of Death* – film producer Carlo Ponti cabled Bruce from Italy with an offer of 'a large sum to be determined' to star in a film with Ponti's wife, Sophia Loren. Bruce was also offered $2 million to make two movies for a Hungarian producer.

He turned down an offer from MGM to make a picture with Elvis Presley in which the king of kung fu would meet the karate king of rock and roll. However, by this time the singer resembled a heavy training bag more than the karate exponent he's supposed to have been.

Elvis had picked up on karate while stationed in Germany with the Army in the late 1950s. Back in the US he continued training, first with Bob Wall and Chuck Norris, then later with Ed Parker. But because Wall and Norris wouldn't promote him through the ranks as quickly as he would've liked, and refused to train him when he was stoned, Elvis moved on. Ed Parker was more easily persuaded and rapidly promoted Elvis to an eighth-degree black belt. In return, Parker received $50,000 and a new Cadillac. Being the most famous celebrity to don a karate suit, karate circles knew what was good for business and were happy to give Elvis an inflated profile to go with his increasingly inflated size. Bob Wall and Chuck Norris continued to train Elvis's wife, Priscilla.

'Although he was supposed to be a high-ranking black belt,' says Bob Wall, 'Priscilla could kick the ass off Elvis.'

Elvis's tae kwon do ranking was equally questionable. Having given his Korean instructor a new car and $50,000 to start a new school – which the teacher promptly spent on a new house for himself – Elvis was suddenly promoted to a seventh-degree black belt. Soon, the singer had advanced even higher to the non-physical aspects of the fighting arts and, while others still sparred crudely, Elvis would keep an eye on them as he polished off another burger and meditated on the inner tranquillity offered by Percodan and Demerol. By now, Priscilla had taken up with a real karate champion, Mike Stone.

## Game of Death

### 'GAME OF DEATH': 1978 REMAKE

Scheduled for release in 1978, Raymond Chow heralded *Game of Death* as 'Bruce Lee's greatest film'. According to Chow, Lee had over a hundred minutes of film already in the can, and Robert Clouse was brought in simply to shoot a couple of 'bridging sequences' using Bruce lookalikes. As it turned out, only fifteen minutes of the original footage were usable, and a script had to be written to exploit it. Bruce's intended storyline of a martial artist attempting to retrieve a national treasure was now replaced with a formulaic plot in which an actor struggles against a criminal agent who's manipulating his career.

Even so, with Chow claiming that HK$4.5 million was being spent, this was by far the most expensive film Golden Harvest had undertaken. At one point, during the planning, Golden Harvest approached not only Steve McQueen and James Coburn but even Muhammad Ali and Pele!

In the promotional material for the film, Robert Clouse is quoted as saying, 'This electrically charged film contains the most spectacular footage of the Chinese-American superstar ever filmed. It is, we feel, a fitting memorial to Bruce Lee.' John Christopher Strong's deceptively classy opening titles are good enough to lead the unprepared viewer to think that he is about to enjoy an equally high-quality film. The Bond-style opening titles are accompanied by theme music from John Barry, the composer of the music for many of the actual Bond films. Once the film starts, however, the reality soon becomes apparent and a feeling of sadness descends on the viewer as dim shots of doubles are mismatched with snippets of the real Bruce Lee in action. In the film's most bizarre image, actor Hugh O'Brian talks to a cardboard cutout of Bruce. Yet, even this cardboard figure has more life and spirit than the pitiful affair that follows.

Despite its simplistic story, the film is agonizingly contrived to include several Bruce Lee stand-ins, along with footage from *Fist of Fury* and *Way of the Dragon* and the plot device of plastic surgery, which allows 'Bruce Lee' to completely change his appearance halfway through the story. The sense of betrayal and exploitation is complete when footage of Bruce's actual corpse is worked into the story. It's a devastating irony that the death of Bruce's character on the film set was a portent of the accidental shooting in 1993 of Brandon Lee on the set of *The Crow*.

The redeeming moments in the film are, of course, in the footage that Bruce shot before his death, the fights with Chi Hon Joi, Dan Inosanto and Kareem Abdul Jabbar, which have been later used to much better effect in the *Warrior's Journey* documentary (see below). In these scenes there's a surge in the quality of the action, but even these brief moments soon give way to inept, ham-fisted slugging. While one can hardly blame him for trying to dodge the bullet, in his own biography of Bruce Lee, the film's director Robert Clouse writes about *Game of Death* as if he had nothing to do with it:

> Several people close to Raymond Chow suggested, even pleaded, that the project be buried forever. But Chow argued that the film had already been pre-sold to the Japanese market, which had paid a great deal for the privilege. The final cut, with an attempt to use two look-alikes, was disappointing at best. There were even some embarrassing moments, such as the scene where a head shot, taken from a previous Lee film, was optically attached to the body of one of the doubles the head turning quite strangely and eerily. Yet the film was quite successful, as was almost anything about Bruce Lee, no matter how tasteless or fraudulent.

By the late 1970s, however, audiences were so desperate to see any new Bruce Lee material that *Game of Death* equalled the revenue generated by *Enter the Dragon*.

## GAME OF DEATH II: 1982 REMAKE (*AKA* TOWER OF DEATH)

Ng See Yuen's attempt to rework Bruce Lee's original footage for Golden Harvest is more exploitative dross made in a further attempt to perform the same tasteless trick. When the real Bruce Lee 'dies' halfway through, the movie rapidly descends into macho posturing and speeded-up fight scenes, which lead to an interminable Bond-style sci-fi climax. As the Chinese sage Lao Tzu put it, 'Wine may become so dilute that few will drink of it.'

## REWORKED MATERIAL

After Bruce Lee's death, there were many further attempts to piece together the incomplete footage of *Game of Death*. Throughout the 1980s and 1990s fan-based attempts involving edited VHS tapes were sold through martial arts magazines' small ads. The most well-known of these are the so-called 'Staycool' Internet edits, but more recently we've had the opportunity to see Bruce Lee's original footage edited into a more coherent form.

## A WARRIOR'S JOURNEY

The nearest we may ever get to seeing what Bruce Lee intended for *Game of Death* is John Little's documentary *A Warrior's Journey*, based on a twelve-page breakdown written by Lee. After assembling the footage in its intended form, Little then set about adding a score and dubbing the dialogue. Chi Hon Joi and Kareem Abdul Jabbar bridged the thirty-year gap and provided the dialogue for their respective Temple of Gold and Temple of the Unknown sequences. Considering that Little has watched *Enter the Dragon* over 500 times, he is probably both capable and entitled to have a stab at imitating the master, at least as far as dubbing Bruce Lee's voice. Meanwhile, Dan Inosanto chose to offer his services to the Japanese company Artport, who made a generally less successful, though occasionally superior, attempt at piecing together the same material.

*A Warrior's Journey* runs for around one hour and forty minutes, and is made up of an hour's well-structured documentary, including inter-views with the usual suspects, leading up to the *Game of Death* footage. Additional material is also taken from home movies released by Linda

Lee, which include Bruce presenting a trophy to Joe Lewis, along with clips from *Longstreet* and a selection of out-takes and bloopers. The documentary was premiered on Irish TV in 1999 and was seen again at a fan convention in Bradford in 2000. But by this time, before its official release, it had already been widely bootlegged.

## The Silent Flute (1979)

Like the unfinished *Game of Death*, the unmade *Silent Flute* was to be a pure martial arts film. But in 1978, David Carradine acquired the rights to *The Silent Flute* and a version of the film was made eventually in 1979 in Israel – not in Turkey as some have reported – with Jeff Cooper as the hero and Christopher Lee as Zetan.

Carradine considered himself 'perfect' for the role of Cord the Seeker, adding, 'With my reputation I was sure I could get the picture made.' In the end he opted to take the four roles Bruce would have played, commenting, 'That Bruce Lee, man, he's just too good. I must take over from him and carry on his work.'

According to the film's director, Richard Moore, the script was 'unfilmable', and Moore had further difficulties when Carradine insisted on using his old buddy, Jeff Cooper, in the role of Cord. According to the director, Cooper 'couldn't act his way out of a paper bag', so faced with trying to get a performance out of him and going way over budget, Moore elected instead to bring the film in on time.

Before the part of Cord had been offered to Jeff Cooper, it was offered to Joe Lewis, who turned it down because he was unwilling to work with Carradine. Joe said, 'They shot the film anyway and it came back a piece of junk.' In the end, Lewis had to supervise the re-shooting of several of the fight scenes and hire real martial artists to double for the actors used in some of the earlier sequences. Mike Stone doubled for Carradine, who considered it an insult. Joe Lewis ended up showing Carradine some slick easy moves, which they incorporated into the film, then Lewis doubled some of Jeff Cooper's flying kicks at the end of the film.

The film was released initially as *Circle of Iron*, and Bruce Lee's name appears no less than five times in the credits, although the film was far removed from anything he'd intended. To this day, James Coburn still refuses to see the film and has retained his copy of the original script, saying that the original had a 'higher aim' than the one that was made.

He was also less than impressed with Cooper as a martial artist and felt quite sad about the whole affair. Brandon Lee wanted to make a more faithful version of *The Silent Flute*, but died before he had the opportunity.

Although they were never filmed, a number of concepts present in *The Silent Flute* can be seen in later movies and television, such as the *Longstreet* episodes. In the pilot episode Li Tsung, played by Bruce Lee, teaches Longstreet to embrace his animal instincts and 'learn the art of dying', an idea borrowed from the Panther Man character, just as Rhythm Man's 'broken rhythm' technique features in the fight with Chuck Norris in *Way of the Dragon*. In addition, some dialogue is used in *Enter the Dragon* as well as in the uncompleted *Game of Death*.

In an ideal world, instead of the *Kung Fu* series and *The Silent Flute* being mangled into a vehicle for Carradine, Bruce Lee would have taken the leading role in *Kung Fu* at the ascendancy of his powers, working with quality scripts and direction.

In August 1972, Bruce wrote a letter to his wife Linda saying that he was working on a film script with the working title *Southern Fist, Northern Legs*: an obvious reference to two different styles of kung fu. In the Bruce Lee documentary, *The Man and the Legend* (1973), he speaks in Cantonese about elements of the storyline for this proposed film. But the storyline is so similar to that of *The Silent Flute* – a hero's quest in which he seeks out various martial arts masters – that they would appear to be one and the same idea.

# APPENDIX 3

## *Bruce Lee: Before and After*

### WING CHUN ANCESTORS AND
### JEET KUNE DO DESCENDANTS

William Cheung has always claimed that Yip Man practised and taught two very different versions of wing chun. Two generations before Yip Man learned the art, its grandmaster Leung Jan was spied on by a neighbour, Chan Wah Shun, while teaching his two sons. Knowing he was being observed, he deliberately modified what he taught. Although Leung Jan decided eventually to take his neighbour as a pupil, he continued to teach him a less effective version, fearing that the bigger, stronger Chan would claim the mastership after Leung's death. These fears proved to be well founded, since after Leung and one of the sons had died, Chan drove the remaining son away and assumed mastership of the wing chun lineage (see diagram p. 310).

From the age of thirteen to seventeen, Yip Man trained with Chan, before moving to Hong Kong to study at college. There he met an eccentric old man with a formidable reputation for kung fu. Yip Man challenged this old man and was defeated. The old man was Leung's surviving son, who then told Yip Man about the two different versions of wing chun, going on to teach him the more authentic or traditional method.

Yip Man returned home and worked for several years as a police inspector until he fled to Hong Kong during the Communist revolution.

When he was fifty-six, he revealed himself as the authentic master of wing chun and began teaching. In 1954, William Cheung joined the school and later brought along the pupil who was to become its most famous exponent, Bruce Lee.

William Cheung says that Yip Man taught the 'modified' version of wing chun to his students, and the 'traditional' version only to him. Although Bruce was a pupil of Yip Man's school, the bulk of his teaching came from the two senior students, Wong Sheun Leung and William Cheung. Because Cheung had been sworn to an oath not to reveal the authentic system to anyone during Yip Man's lifetime, he taught Bruce the modified form, but continued to drop hints about the lack of effectiveness of some of the techniques and how they could be improved.

My own teacher Derek Jones studied both the 'modified' system with Victor Kan, and the 'traditional' system with William Cheung. Whether or not Derek took William Cheung's assertions at face value is another matter, but he was in no doubt as to which was the more effective system. Just as the praying mantis master Gin Foon Mark told Bruce on his visit to New York, Derek Jones told us, 'The modified wing chun system lacks footwork, entry techniques and advanced strategy: it is very limited.'

Bruce Lee's teenage friend and fellow student, Hawkins Cheung (William's nephew), teaches what he calls 'classic' wing chun at his school in Culver City, Los Angeles. 'Modified, traditional, it's all bullshit,' says Hawkins. 'That's just William making mischief,' he adds, implying that William invented this historical divergence in the art, in order to promote his own teaching. If this is true, then William Cheung should take the credit for what he did in making it more effective, just as Bruce Lee and Derek Jones did.

As Bruce Lee, William Cheung and Derek Jones evolved as martial artists, each adapted and evolved wing chun in his own individual way, whether it was the 'mischief' of William Cheung's traditional wing chun, the genius of Bruce Lee's jeet kune do or the devastating common sense of Derek Jones's martial art of body, mind and spirit.

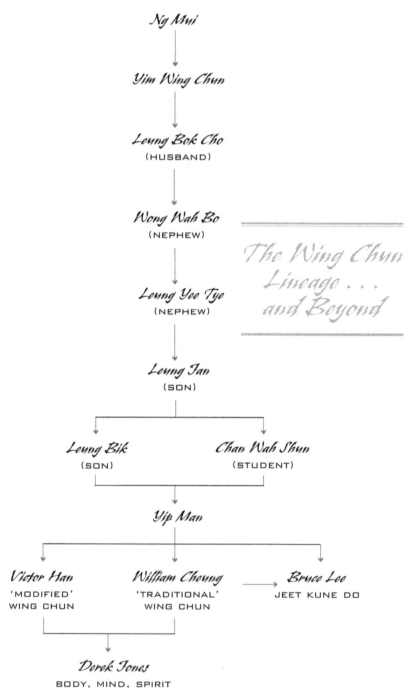

Ng Mui

↓

Yim Wing Chun

↓

Leung Bok Cho
(HUSBAND)

↓

Wong Wah Bo
(NEPHEW)

*The Wing Chun Lineage . . . and Beyond*

↓

Leung Yee Tye
(NEPHEW)

↓

Leung Jan
(SON)

Leung Bik
(SON)     Chan Wah Shun
(STUDENT)

Yip Man

Victor Han
'MODIFIED'
WING CHUN

William Cheung
'TRADITIONAL'
WING CHUN

→ Bruce Lee
JEET KUNE DO

Derek Jones
BODY, MIND, SPIRIT

This is a comprehensive, but by no means complete, list of Bruce Lee's students from his Gung Fu Institutes in Seattle, Oakland and Los Angeles.

## Seattle Institute

In October 1963, Bruce opened the first of his formal Jun Fan Gung Fu Institutes in Seattle – Bruce preferred the Cantonese *gung* fu rather than kung fu – at 4750 University Way. His students included:

**Taky Kimura** (assistant instructor): Still runs an import-export business in Seattle and treats all enquiries about Bruce Lee with patience, courtesy and good humour. He speaks of Bruce with undiminished respect and affection.

**Doug Palmer**: Now works as an attorney in Seattle. Doug spent the entire summer of 1963 with Bruce at the Lee family home in Hong Kong. Doug very generously gave me copies of, and freedom to quote from, his extensive journals on this trip and his other experiences as Bruce's student and friend.

**Linda Emery**: Became Mrs Bruce Lee and continues to guard jealously both his reputation and his marketing rights, which have now passed to Bruce and Linda's daughter Shannon. After Bruce's death, Linda married Tom Bleecker, with whom she co-authored the biography *The Bruce Lee Story*. After their divorce, Linda married entrepreneur Bruce Cadwell.

**Sue Ann Kay**: Was Linda's best friend, who originally introduced her to Bruce's gung fu class.

**Jesse Glover**: Met Bruce Lee in 1959 and was probably his first official student. He taught Bruce some judo and grappling moves and is now teaching what he calls 'non-classical' wing chun.

**Ed Hart**: Also teaches 'non-classical wing chun' after working for twenty years with Jesse Glover. He describes wing chun as 'the foundation of Bruce's art', adding that the resilience of its forms derives from the fact that tendons are twenty times stronger than muscles.

**Mike Lee**: Also aligned with the 'non-classical' wing chun faction.

**James DeMile**: Now teaches 'wing chun do'. He was hired by Richard Branson to teach Virgin Airlines cabin crew techniques to deal with violent and abusive passengers in air rage incidents.

**De Welle 'Skip' Ellsworth**: Now head of the Log House Builders

Association of North America. His website still contains a memorial to Bruce, who he describes as 'the greatest martial artist who ever lived'.

**Patrick Strong**: Based in Indianapolis, now teaches 'combative solutions'. A system with 'a core of JKD' to deal with street assaults and real-life situations.

Other Seattle students included Leroy Garcia, who taught Bruce to drive, and Joseph Cowles.

## Oakland Institute

The second Jun Fan branch opened in Oakland in August 1964. Personnel included:

**James Yimm Lee** (assistant instructor): When Bruce and Linda moved to Oakland in 1964, they went to live with James Lee's family. Because Bruce felt he was moving away from wing chun, and James needed the money, Bruce credited him as the author of his book on the first wing chun practice form, the sil lum tao. James died of cancer on 28 December 1972.

**Howard Williams**: Bruce nicknamed this student 'rugged'. He now teaches 'the JKD gospel pure and undistorted' at his school in San Pablo, California.

**Felix Macias Snr** and **Felix Macias Jnr**: Now teach 'the philosophical art of gung fu' emphasizing that 'we are not trying to exploit the teaching by turning it into a get-rich-quick gimmick, but as a constant evolution towards personal understanding and excellence'.

**Leo Fong**: Has teamed up with Joe Lewis and other Bruce Lee students to 'move Bruce's ideas into the new millennium'.

Other Oakland students included: Bob Baker, Ernie Benevidez, Gary Cagaanan, Richard Carney, Harry Chin, Dave Cox, Tom De Laurel, Jan De Laurel, Mike Fong, Dr Lloyd Freitas, Robert Garcia, Rodney Gee, Barry Hay, Gary Hum, Allen Joe, Jerome Lai, George Lee, Greglon Yimm Lee, Moon Ling, Allen Magdangal, Mario Magdangal, Bob Marshall, Fred Meredith, Al Novak, Jimmy Ong, Stan Paisak, Manuel Rodriguez, Gordon Toy, Alvin Wong, Dr Arnold Wong, Curtis Yee, Ed Kim Yee, Edward Yee, David Young, Hank Maguire and Gary Dill.

## Los Angeles Institute

The third Jun Fan School opened in LA's Chinatown district in February 1967 at 628 College Street, just a few blocks from the Dodgers' Stadium. Students there included:

**Dan Inosanto** (assistant instructor): Dan Inosanto still has a high profile in martial arts. His own teaching is based around a core of Filipino martial arts and his finest hour was in his weapons duel with Bruce in *Game of Death*.

**Ted Wong**: He was the first student to enrol at the Los Angeles school, but because of his natural talent he was soon invited to join the select group of private and celebrity students who trained in the garden of Bruce's house in Bel Air.

**Jerry Poteet**: Now teaches JKD 'pure and simple, exactly like it was given to me'. Poteet coached actor Jason Scott Lee for his role in *Dragon: A Life of Bruce Lee*. Poteet is also the likely candidate for the 'motion capture' images used in video games featuring 'Bruce'.

**Steve Golden**: Works with Patrick Strong who trained at Bruce's Seattle Institute.

Other Los Angeles students: Richard Bustillo, Dan Lee, Larry Hartsell and Bob Bremer all continue to teach martial arts. Further students include: Bill Bremer, Louis Delgado, Chuck Hill, Gary Fineman, Lee Hong, Melvin Kwan, Leo Duffin, Mike Cochrane, Herb Jackson, Pete Jacobs, Robert Lujan, Hayward Nishioka, Pete Rosas and Al Wolin.

## Private and Celebrity Students

During Bruce Lee's time as a teacher, as acting roles arrived, he had a number of private and celebrity students including:

**Kareem Abdul Jabbar**: LA Lakers basketball star and co-star in *Game of Death*, who is considered one of the greatest players ever, famous for his unblockable 'skyhook' shot.

**Steve McQueen**: The movie star who Bruce vowed he'd one day surpass.

**James Coburn**: Movie actor and probably the most serious of Bruce's celebrity students with a strong grounding in esotericism.

**Roman Polanski**: Martial arts dabbler and film director who once flew Bruce to Switzerland for a one-off lesson.

**Stirling Silliphant**: Oscar-winning screenwriter who wrote *Towering Inferno*, *In the Heat of the Night*, *The Poseidon Adventure* and many other successful movies.

**Joe Hyams**: Fellow screenwriter and friend of Silliphant, once married to Britt Ekland.

**Tom Tannenbaum**: Head of Paramount TV and producer of *Longstreet*. He later produced a TV special of the 1974 Karate Championships, which effectively began the sport of full-contact karate, and thus modern kickboxing.

**Mike Stone**: Karate champion who used Bruce's strategies in competition. He became Elvis Presley's karate instructor, taught him a few flashy moves, then made a successful move on Elvis's wife, Priscilla.

**Chuck Norris**: Karate champion who went on to co-star in *Way of the Dragon* and was Bruce Lee's adversary in arguably the best fight scene he ever put on film. Norris went on to enjoy a successful film and TV acting career.

**Bob Wall**: Karate champion and co-star of *Way of the Dragon* and *Enter the Dragon*. He is a now an entrepreneur whose company, Wall Street, is based in Tarzana, CA.

**Joe Lewis**: The most formidable karate champion of all time who used Bruce's strategies on his way to becoming 'the Muhammad Ali of karate' and who considers himself to be, at the very least, on a par with Bruce.

**Mito Uyehara**: Editor of *Black Belt* magazine and publisher of Bruce Lee's four-volume *Fighting Method*. Bruce Lee named Bob Wall's villainous character in *Enter the Dragon* 'Oharra' as a joking reference to Uyehara.

# EPILOGUE

## *The Way of Jeet Kyne Do*

## A PERSONAL APPRECIATION

In May 1994, while working in Seattle, I took the opportunity to revisit Lake View Cemetery. I found Bruce's and Brandon's graves situated beneath a pine tree at the crest of a hill. The area around the graves had been cordoned off so that nobody would walk on the recently seeded lawn, so I sat a short distance away. The azalea bushes were in bright bloom and there was a warm, gentle breeze. After I'd been there a few minutes a minibus entered the cemetery gates and wound its way up the hill to stop a short distance away from where I was sitting. A bunch of people got out, babbling excitedly, and immediately began taking photographs of each other. Each of them took their turn to climb over the cordon and pose for the cameras, trampling on the tender shoots of new grass. A few minutes later they were all back on the bus and making their way to the next stop on their itinerary. When the photographs were viewed later all would doubtless recall that they had been to Bruce Lee's grave. It's hard to believe that any of them had experienced actually *being* there.

I once remarked to one of my teachers about the inscription carved into the marble bench beside Bruce's grave: 'THE KEY TO IMMORTALITY IS TO HAVE FIRST LIVED A LIFE WORTH REMEMBERING'.

'No!' he replied, forcefully. 'That's not quite right. The key to

315

immortality is to remember your life at the very moment you are living it!' Many of Bruce Lee's words echo that truth.

In an essay 'The Tao of Gung Fu', written in 1962, Bruce Lee wrote:

> Concentration in gung fu does not have the usual sense of restricting the attention to a single sense object, but is simply a quiet awareness of whatever happens to be here and now . . . [The] mind is present everywhere because it is nowhere attached to any particular object because, even when related to this particular object, it does not cling to it.

Let's explore this idea further. Usually my attention is absorbed by whatever it is I happen to be doing – reading a book, watching TV, driving the car – and this kind of *automatic* awareness is where we live most of the time. But if I happen to shut my hand in a door, for a few seconds my awareness is diverted to the pain; this is an example of a second kind of *attracted* awareness, where something pushes or pulls it in a specific direction. This kind of attracted awareness may also have a more emotional aspect to it: for example, I see a picture of Bruce Lee, I hear a favourite tune, my team scores a goal and my attention is engaged.

But at certain times my attention can be intentionally held in one place for a period of time, such as studying for an exam, learning a new tune on the piano, or doing a martial art form. But even this kind of *directed* attention means that I only attend to one or two things at a time.

The kind of attention that we want to explore now is an *open* attention that includes everything, all at once. The word 'consciousness' itself means 'knowing all together'. We are talking here of something very practical.

So at the same time as one of us writes and the other one reads, I begin to turn my attention to my body and begin to include in my awareness the physical weight of my body, and the density of my bones and flesh. I taste the inside of my mouth and feel the temperature of the air and the touch of my clothes on my skin. I can now feel any sense of energy or space, tension or relaxation. And without losing this feeling and self-awareness, I might now focus on the tiniest detail of something in front of me, like the texture of the paper in my hands, and yet still be aware of my entire surroundings, in front, to the side, above and below.

I am aware of how my thoughts are stirred and want to follow their own direction, or at what point in this continuing process my awareness rebels, or gets stuck, or wavers. Through this simple process of meditation I can be aware of myself in the world at large. I can now even be aware of my awareness itself.

Maybe I think that not much has changed and that this is my normal way of being, but a curious thing happens whenever anyone hears or reads about this process. As soon as I am told that I am not as aware as I could be, this in itself generates enough self-consciousness for the reply, 'Of course I'm aware of myself!' But the attention soon lapses back into its more automatic or attracted states. The reality of the wider world is only true when I make a *conscious* effort and realize that at any given moment it is a completely fresh proposition that can only be present *intentionally*, and not *automatically*.

For some people, their sense of 'I' is located almost exclusively in the head: the body only gets any attention when something goes wrong with it. For such people the body exists mainly for the purpose of carrying the head around as it gets on with the important stuff. So how much, and how intensely, do I feel that I have a body – that I *am* a body. Does my awareness deliberately occupy and energize my human form, or is it *pre*-occupied with all the usual concerns? What can be the significance of anything that happens if I'm not fully present to myself? Am I always preparing for the next situation? If so, will I be present when it actually arrives? Will I be here and now, there and then?

When a magnet is passed over a metal bar, the bar itself gradually becomes magnetized. As every schoolchild knows, iron filings sprinkled around the bar reveal the newly created magnetic field surrounding it. In the same way, if I repeatedly pass my attention through my body, this gradually creates an energy field whose influence may ultimately extend far beyond my ordinary way of being, into 'a circle without limits'. And maybe even beyond the limits of time and space.

This is the meaning of the Buddha's saying that 'attention is the path to immortality'. There is also a Zen saying that the hero becomes enlightened with one thought, while the lazy man ploughs his way through books and scriptures. The 'one thought' is the same thought as the Buddha's. The simple process of opening the awareness to include everything that is happening, inside and out, here and now – remembering my life at the very moment that I am living it – *this* is 'the key to immortality' and the key to creating an energetic body of awareness that may survive the death of the physical body.

Don't think . . . *Feel!*

*Bruce Lee*

The purpose of life isn't 'to dare to dream', but to awaken. Bruce Lee counselled us to expand the circle of our personal limitations into 'a circle without limits'. As we know, jeet kune do applies not only to martial art practice but to all aspects of life. From this perspective we can all be considered works in progress. This work is our true priority in life, and no role model, saviour or hero can do the work for us.

Working on yourself doesn't mean continually analysing or thinking about yourself or your life; or trying to control yourself, force yourself to do better or become who you are not. All of that is self-defeating. Bruce Lee says, 'Don't think . . . *Feel!*' What he means is that, rather than projecting our ideas, fears or expectations onto the world, we should enter into the world of 'choiceless awareness' and direct experience.

True seeing, in the sense of choiceless awareness, leads to new discovery and the means to uncovering our potentiality.

*Bruce Lee*

Bruce Lee often quoted an aphorism that is used in Zen schools: 'At first a cloud was just a cloud, a mountain just a mountain. When I began studying the Way, a cloud was no longer a cloud, a mountain no longer a mountain. Now I understand the Way, a cloud is again just a cloud, a mountain just a mountain'.

At first, the cloud and the mountain are being seen directly, but as they would be seen through the eyes of a child or an animal. They are seen directly, but they carry little meaning. But after following the Way for a time, the cloud and mountain take on symbolic values. For instance, a cloud might be compared to a passing thought, or a mountain might represent stability or endurance, and so on. Eventually, when the third stage of the process is reached, they come to be seen as more than that. Now they are again seen directly, but this time through wiser eyes. Now they are seen as natural processes that reflect inner processes to which we were trying to give meaning in the first place. Now clouds and mountains are both real and symbolic, both symbolic and meaning-ful. The outer and inner worlds are connected and in tune.

The baby looks at things all day without blinking. That is because his eyes are not focused on any particular object. He goes without knowing where he is going, and stops without knowing what he is doing. He merges himself with his surroundings and moves along with it.

*Chuang Tzu (quoted by Bruce Lee in his 1962 essay,*
*'The Tao of Gung Fu'*

We all had to learn to see the world in the way that we do now, as a matter of habit. Children simply see a tree or a building, or hear a sound the way that it is, without adding anything to it. A child simply hears a bird sing; it's the adult who tells him that it's a canary. From the moment that we become more concerned with *what* things are than *how* they are, the world stops yielding to us directly, because a description of it begins to stand in between, so that we no longer see things the way *they* are but the way *we* are.

The way we are taught in school is to gather facts and concepts, so that, in the end, we grow up with a very fixed and unfluid sense of how things are. This is the problem with naming or labelling things: it makes us think of processes as things or objects. For example, we think of a chair as an object, but at what point exactly does a tree stop being a 'tree' and become a 'chair'? At what exact point in the process of cutting down a tree, shaping and assembling the pieces of wood, do we decide that it is 'tree' or 'wood' or 'chair', when it is essentially all the same thing shaped by time.

Language is completely inadequate to describe any of this because it always presents us with a linear arrangement of ideas, especially at times like this, when we are attempting to create a vision of something that exists 'all at once'.

In atomic physics, no distinction is made between matter and energy, since they are, in reality, two aspects of one indivisible whole.

*From Bruce Lee's notes, circa 1963*

The everyday world that we see around us appears to be one of solid objects in empty space. But there has been a shift away from the view that matter is made up of minute particles, to the view that the universe is understandable only through its underlying, interwoven patterns of energy.

In reality, there is no ultimately small particle or building block of matter in physical terms at all. Depending on how we observe and measure them, the so-called building blocks of matter – electrons, neutrons, protons and other sub-atomic particles – also display the properties of energy waves. And just as particles can behave in a wavelike way, so light waves can behave like particles, called photons. These wave particles come in packages, named 'quanta' by the scientist Max Planck, and the term has lent its name to the new science of quantum physics.

The physicist Jack Sarfatti describes the universe as a kind of 'quantum foam', where various patterns of vibration are set up. The idea that a chair is some kind of wispy fragile cloud of seething wave particles is pretty hard to appreciate when I bash my knee against it. It's a lot easier to see that a TV picture of a chair is formed by electromagnetic energy, but the actual wooden chair is formed in exactly the same way. Particles are like minute concentrations of energy that come and go like waves on an ocean. The bigger and slower the energy waves are, the denser the matter; the smaller and faster they are, the finer the matter. Jack Sarfatti further suggests that consciousness is the master vibration that holds all of this together, so that 'mind' and 'matter' are seen only as different-sized waves in the same sea.

The story of creation, whether told by present-day scientists or the Taoist philosophers, is essentially the same. In the view of modern physics, anti-matter (yin) collides with matter (yang) to form light. Light then forms the various energies of sound, colour and substance as some vibrations slow down and some speed up.

In the Taoist concept: in the beginning is the void. Out of the void emerge the two fundamental aspects of creation: yin and yang. The interaction of yin and yang produces chi – energy, or vibrations – and ultimately everything in existence. The interplay of yin and yang is a way of ordering and understanding anything that can be conceived: left and right, hard and soft, birth and death. Within any situation there may be an overall quality of yin or yang, but it can always be further subdivided into all its complexities until there are ten thousand divisions and comparisons.

To give another example, all of the words and ideas that you are reading are stored on my computer in the form of binary arithmetic, by which all information is recorded in combinations of 0 and 1 – a further example of combining the two to produce the many.

What the Chinese call *chi* – and physicists might call the 'zero-point energy field' – continually manifests as all of the different forms and processes that occur in time and space. To experience every aspect of this flow would also be to know that, ultimately, everything has the same source of arising and return, like waves rising, then falling back into the ocean. Between the beginning and the return to the beginning there appear all the interactions of life.

Bruce Lee depicted this process in a much more simple, graphic way. In the emblem of his gung fu institutes the first rank was a blank circle, the original state of freedom and potential a state of no'thing'ness, from which any 'thing' and every 'thing' might come into existence. The further ranks were represented by yin yang emblems of various colours, signifying every aspect of life. The highest grade was again the blank circle: the return to the source.

> Nobody wins a fight. Any victory is for the One.
>
> *Bruce Lee*

Despite appearances, all the various forms and activities of life are really one continuous flow of energy at various frequencies. Knowing this, Bruce often dismissed questions about the nature of yin and yang, not dismissing the concept itself, but trying to point out that, in reality, all apparent opposites arise out of one unified force. Perhaps we can now understand how Bruce Lee had mastered his art to the degree that he could say, 'Nobody wins a fight.' What did he mean by that? Simply that because everything arises and returns to the same source, any victory is for this One, even before any combat takes place. In this way, at the highest level, the martial artist develops a 'body feel' for everything in existence.

At the same time that Bruce was discovering all of this, Western body-mind therapists such as Wilhelm Reich and F. M. Alexander were also becoming aware that the revelations of the spirit take place in the body. Awareness of posture and balance, and feelings of gracefulness or awkwardness, all serve as a constant, accurate guide to our own psychological state. It's interesting that the English word grace itself implies both an ease of movement and the descent of spiritual energy. As the *I-Ching* puts it, 'By adopting a certain physical posture, a resonant chord is struck in Spirit.'

> The mastery of any art transcends the art.
>
> *Bruce Lee*

When movement and energy are intentionally brought into my awareness, not only do martial art techniques become more efficient, the whole of life is similarly affected. The level of the practitioner's outer skill and the inner state reflect each other. Understood like this, every art and skill *may* be a way to inner development. There is a Japanese saying: 'Archery and dancing, flower arranging and singing, tea drinking and wrestling – it's all the same.' From the ordinary point of view this makes no sense, but once the underlying principle is understood the meaning is clear.

The oneness of life is a truth that can be realized.

*Bruce Lee*

While he was a philosophy student at Seattle's University of Washington, Bruce Lee wrote an essay entitled 'The Relationship of the Organism to its Environment', in which he explained that there is really no such state as separateness or independence. For example: the paper this is printed on is made from a tree, and a tree only grows through soil, sunlight and rain. You don't have to be a mystic to *see* the sun and the rain in the paper you hold in front of you. In addition, there have been hundreds of people involved in bringing this idea to you: the lumberjack who cut down the tree, the publishers, printers and distributors and so on. If you look deeper, you'll see the food that gave everyone the energy to work and so on, all so that you can read these words, right now. If we take this process to its ultimate conclusions, we see that everything, everywhere, is connected and related.

The way I think of my 'self' is usually only symbolic. I can limit my sense of self to where my skin ends, or I can extend it to my home, my career, my family, my country, my race and so on. My 'self' is a concept that expands or contracts at any given moment, but my *felt* self – the dynamic experience of my body in life and the life in my body – knows, feels and senses that I can never be independent so long as I eat and breathe. And even when I'm 'dead', my material remains will be absorbed back into the earth, just as the traces of my spirit will continue to affect living people, beyond the limits of the time and space of my life on earth.

. . . Just as the spirit of Bruce Lee affects us now.

# Sources and Reading List

The author gratefully acknowledges permissions to quote copyrighted material from the sources listed below. Not all quotations in the text of this book are verbatim. However, care has been taken to retain their essential meaning and changes have only been made to maintain continuity.

The author extends special thanks to Doug Palmer for allowing total access and use of his personal diaries; and also to Bey Logan for carte blanche to quote from his comprehensive series of interviews with Joe Lewis.

## Works Cited

Beasley, Jerry, *In Search of the Ultimate Martial Art* (Boulder CO: Paladin Press, 1989)

Bleecker, Tom, *Unsettled Matters* (London: Paul H. Crompton, 1999)

Carradine, David, *The Spirit of Shaolin* (Boston MA: Charles E. Tuttle, 1991)

Cheung, William, *Wing Chun Bil Jee* (Burbank CA: Unique Publications, 1983)

Chow, David and Spangler, Richard, *Kung Fu: History, Philosophy, Technique* (Burbank CA: Unique Publications, 1982)

Clouse, Robert, *The Making of Enter the Dragon* (Burbank CA: Unique Publications, 1987)

— *Bruce Lee: The Biography* (Burbank CA: Unique Publications, 1988)

Dennis, Felix and Atyeo, Don, *Bruce Lee: King of Kung Fu* (London: Wildwood House, 1974)

Hyams, Joe, *Zen in the Martial Art* (Los Angeles CA: J. P. Tarcher Inc., 1979)

Inosanto, Dan with Sutton, Alan, *Jeet Kune Do: The Art and Philosophy of Bruce Lee* (Los Angeles CA: Know Now Publishing, 1980)

Jones, Steve, *The Intelligent Warrior* (New York: Harper Collins, 2004)

Krishnamurti, Jiddu, *Freedom from the Known* (New York: Harper & Row, 1969)

Logan, Bey, *Hong Kong Action Cinema* (Titan Books, 1995)

Miller, Davis, *The Tao of Bruce Lee* (Vintage UK/Random House, 2000)

Mitsules, John and Suddereth, Jake, *The St. Ann's Kid: A Seattle Memoir* (Seattle: King Street Press, 2001)

Palmer, Doug, 'A Summer in Hong Kong' (unpublished manuscript/diaries).

Pilato, Herbie, *The Kung Fu Book of Caine: The Complete Guide to TV's First Mystical Eastern Western* (Boston MA: Charles E. Tuttle, 1993)

Thomas, Bruce, *Bruce Lee: Fighting Spirit* (London: Sidgwick and Jackson, 2002)

— *Bruce Lee: Fighting Talk* (Henley-on-Thames: Bentwyck Henry, 2003)

— *Bruce Lee: Fighting Words* (Berkeley CA: Frog, 2003)

— *Immortal Combat: Portrait of a True Warrior* (Berkeley CA: Blue Snake, 2007)

Tzu, Lao, *Tao Te Ching* (various editions)

## Periodicals and Newspaper Articles Cited

Beasley, Ed, 'Joe Lewis Took Bruce Lee's Concepts into the Ring' (joelewiskarate.com)

*Black Belt*
   Howard, Arnold, 'Out of Nowhere Came Joe Lewis', August 1988

*Blitz*
   Cheung, William, 'The Bruce Lee Training Secret'

*Bruce Lee: The Untold Story* (Burbank CA: Unique Publications, 1986)

*Bruce Lee: His Life in Pictures* (Burbank CA: CFW Enterprises, 1988)

*Bruce Lee: 1940–1973* (Rainbow Publishing, 1974)

*Business Wire*
   'Bruce Lee Returns to the Screen', 2001

*Combat* (Walsall, England: Martial Arts Publications)
   Glover, Jesse, 'The Art of Bruce Lee', October 1991
   Logan, Bey, interview with Kwan Tak Hing, August 1987

*Fighting Arts* (Liverpool, England: Ronin Publishing)
    Noble, Graham, 'Bruce Lee: The Real Story' (date unknown)
*Impact Magazine*
    Logan, Bey, 'Green Bamboo Warrior'
*Independent* (London)
    Thomas, Bruce, 'Immortal Combat', 15 July 2003
*Inside Kung Fu* (Burbank CA: CFW Enterprises)
    'Bruce Lee Returns in the *Game of Death*'
    Cater, Dave, 'Jason Lee: The Part He Couldn't Refuse', December 1992
    Cheung, Hawkins, 'Bruce Lee's Hong Kong Years', November 1991
    — 'Bruce Lee Discovers Jeet Kune Do', December 1991
    — 'Wing Chun: Bruce Lee's Mother Art', January 1992
    — 'Cleaning Up Bruce's Classical Mess', February 1992
    Corcoran, John, interview with Tom Tannenbaum, January 1980
    — interview with Joe Hyams, April 1980
    Interview with Grace Lee: 'The One Who Knew Bruce Best', September 1979
    Painter, Dr John P., 'Will the Real Yin and Yang Please Stand Up?' December 1991
    Peters, Jennifer, 'Brandon Lee: Trying to Fill Some Mighty Big Shoes', November 1992
    Pine, Red, *The Zen Teachings of Bodhidharma* (New York: North Point Press, 1987)
    Poteet, Jerry, 'Single Direct Attack: Jeet Kune Do's One Punch K.O.', November 1991
*JKD Hong Kong Club*
    'Game of Death Extract'
*Kick Illustrated*
    'Up Close and Personal with Stirling Silliphant', August 1980
*K.O.A. Yearbook* (London: Paul H. Crompton)
    Crompton, Paul, 'William Cheung: The Best Fighter and No Apology', 1985
*Kung Fu Monthly* 1–76 (London: H. Bunch Associates Ltd, 1975–82)
    'Bruce Lee's Game of Death'
    'The Secret Art of Bruce Lee'
    'The Second Sensational Bruce Lee Scrapbook'
    'Who Killed Bruce Lee?'
    'The Unbeatable Bruce Lee'
    'The Power of Bruce Lee'

'Bruce Lee in Action'

*Kung Fu Monthly* (London: H. Bunch Associates Ltd, 1992)
    Special Issue 100

*Martial Arts Illustrated* (Huddersfield, England: Martial Arts Ltd)
    Bruce Lee Supplement, Vol. 1, March 1992
    Dragon Supplement, June 1994
    Johnston, Will, 'Brandon Bruce Lee: A Life Worth Remembering',
        June 1993
    Kent, Chris, 'Bruce Lee Gets His Due', July 1993
    Logan, Bey, interview: 'A Guy Named Joe: Part Two', June 1991
    — interview: 'A Guy Named Joe: Part Three', January 1992
    — interview with Richard Bustillo: Part One, November 1992
    — interview with Taky Kimura, January 1992

*Martial Arts Legends* (Burbank CA: CFW Enterprises)
    Corcoran, John, 'One on One with Stirling Silliphant', January 1993
    — and Shively, Rick, 'Elvis Presley: The Man and the Martial Artist',
        July 1991
    Imamura, Richard, 'Ed Parker: The First Twenty Years', July 1991
    — 'Daniel Lee: The Harmonious Jeet Kune Do/Tai Chi Synthesis',
        July 1991
    Maslak, Paul, 'The William Cheung Story: Bruce Lee in the Early
        Years', January 1993
    — with Don Wilson, 'The Fine Art of the Fight Scene', January 1993
    Tan, Rick, 'Who is Shek Kien?', July 1991

*Martial Arts Masters* (Burbank CA: CFW Enterprises)
    Montaigue, Erle, interview: 'Dan Inosanto: on Life After Bruce Lee',
        1992

*Martial Arts Movies* (Burbank CA: CFW Enterprises)
    'Dragon: 'The Life Story of Bruce Lee', 1992
    Rhodes, Scott, '25 All-time Great Movie Fights', 1992

*National Kickboxing*
    Miles, Mike, 'The Explosive Joe Lewis', April 1998

*People* magazine, Brandon Lee feature, Vol. 38, 10, 1992 (New York:
    Time Inc.)

*Playboy* magazine, Sugar Ray Leonard interview, June 1982

*The Times*, Mooney, Paul, 'China Claims Kung Fu King to Keep Legend
    Alive and Kicking', 11 April 2007 (London: Times Newspapers)

*Wrestling 101*
    Reilly, Joe, 'An Introduction to Mixed Martial Arts', October 2003

# Additional Reading

Anderson, Robert, *The Kung Fu Book* (Las Vegas NV: Pioneer Books, 1994)

Block, Alex Ben, *The Legend of Bruce Lee* (St Albans, England: Mayflower Books, 1974)

Campbell, Sid and Lee, Greglon Yimm, *The Dragon and the Tiger: The Oakland Year, Volume One* (Berkeley, CA: Frog, 2003)

— *The Dragon and the Tiger: The Oakland Year, Volume Two* (Berkeley, CA: Frog, 2005)

Chao, K. T. and Weakland, J. E., *Secret Techniques of Wing Chun Kung Fu* (London: Paul H. Crompton, 1976)

Confirmation Committee of the VTAA, *Genealogy of the Ving Tsun Family* (Kowloon: Hong Kong Ving Tsun Athletic Association, 1990)

DeMile, James W., *Bruce Lee's One-Inch and Three-Inch Power Punch* (Kirkland WA: Tao of Wing Chun Do Publications, 1975)

Deng, Ming Dao, *Scholar Warrior* (San Francisco: HarperCollins, 1990)

Draeger, Donn and Smith, Robert, *The Fighting Arts of Asia* (New York: Berkeley Medallion, 1974)

Gross, Edward, *Bruce Lee: Fists of Fury* (Las Vegas NV: Pioneer Books, 1990)

Hartsell, Larry, *Jeet Kune Do* (Burbank CA: Unique Publications, 1987)

— and Tackett, Tim *Jeet Kune Do: Volume 2* (Burbank CA: Unique Publications, 1987)

Inosanto, Dan, *Absorb What is Useful* (Los Angeles CA: Know Now Publishing, 1985)

— *Jeet Kune Do Guidebook: Volume 1* (Burbank CA: Unique Publications, 1987)

Kent, Chris and Tackett, Tim *The Jun Fan/Jeet Kune Do Textbook* (Los Angeles CA: Know Now Publishing, 1988)

— *Jeet Kune Do Kickboxing* (Los Angeles CA: Know Now Publishing, 1986)

Lee, Bruce, *Chinese Gung Fu: The Philosophical Art of Self-Defense* (Burbank CA: Ohara Publications, 1963)

— *The Tao of Jeet Kune Do* (Santa Clarita CA: Ohara Publications, 1975)

— and Uyehara, Mito, *Bruce Lee's Fighting Method, Volumes 1–4* (Burbank CA: Ohara Publications, 1977)

Lee, James Yimm, *Wing Chun Kung Fu* (Bruce Lee, technical editor) (Burbank CA: Ohara Publications, 1972)

Lee, Linda, *The Life and Tragic Death of Bruce Lee* (London: Star Books, 1975)

— *Bruce Lee: The Man Only I Knew* (New York: Warner Paperbacks, 1975)

— and Bleecker, Tom, *The Bruce Lee Story* (Burbank CA: Ohara Publications, 1989)

Meyers, Richard; Harlib, Amy; Palmer, Bill and Palmer, Karen, *Martial Arts Movies* (Secaucus NJ: Citadel Press, 1985)

Mintz, Marilyn D., *The Martial Arts Movie* (Boston MA: Charles E. Tuttle, 1983)

Needham, Joseph, *Science and Civilization in China* (Cambridge University Press, 1954)

Roote, Mike, *Enter the Dragon*, from the original screenplay by Michael Allin (London: Tandem Books, 1973)

Van Hise, James, *Video Superheroes* (Las Vegas NV: Pioneer Books, 1991)

Vaughn, Jack and Lee, Mike, *The Legendary Bruce Lee* (Burbank CA: Ohara Publications, 1986)

Wall, Bob, *Who's Who in the Martial Arts* (Los Angeles CA: R. A. Wall Investments, 1985)

Wing, R. L., *The I-Ching Workbook* (New York, Doubleday, 1979)

— *The Tao of Power* (Wellingborough, England: Aquarian Press, 1986)

## Periodicals and Newspapers

*Bruce Lee and JKD Magazine*, 1–12 (Hong Kong: Bruce Lee's Jeet Kune Do Club, 1976–8)
  'Bruce Lee Memorial Monthly No.1'
  'Bruce Lee: His Privacy and Anecdotes'
  'Bruce Lee's Nunchaka in Action'
  'Bruce Lee: The Secret of JKD and Kung Fu'
  'Bruce Lee: His Unknowns in Martial Arts Learning'
  'Bruce Lee Revenges . . .'
  'Bruce Lee: The Fighting Spirit'
  'Bruce Lee Combats'
  'Bruce Lee: The Immortal Dragon'
  'Great Dragon Magazine, 3'
  'Reminiscence of Bruce Lee'
  'Studies on Jeet Kune Do'

*Bruce Lee: King of Kung Fu*, 1–8 (Stanmore, England: Poster Magazine Publishing Co.)

*Exciting Cinema*: Kung Fu Special Issue, 1974 (Pennine Magazines)

*Farewell to the Dragon* (Philadelphia: The Cinema Attic, 1974)

*Fighters' Monthly*, Vol. 1, 1 (London: Fighters' Publications)

*Films and Filming*, 229 (London: Hansom Books, 1973)
    Bruce Lee's Jeet-kune-do Club, Hong Kong, 1976–8

*The Hollywood Reporter*, Alex Ben Block article on Dragon film, 7 May 1993 (Los Angeles CA: HR Industries Inc.)

*Karate Illustrated*, June 1977 and February 1979

*KO Magazine*, June 1984

Kung Fu Magazine Publishing Co., 1983–4 (Hong Kong)
    *Bruce Lee's Nunchaka Method*
    *Bruce Lee: His Eternities*

Kung Fu Supplies Co. 1978–9 (Hong Kong)
    *Bruce Lee in 'The Game of Death'* [sic]
    *Bruce Lee: Farewell My Friend*

Ochs, Phil, 'Requiem for a Dragon Departed', *Time Out*, February 15–21, 1974 (London: Time Out Publications)

*Official Karate*, July 1970

*Penthouse*, Albert Goldman feature on Bruce Lee, Jan/Feb 1983 (New York: Penthouse International Ltd)

*Popster*, 23 and 26 (London: Planet News)
    'Was Bruce Lee Killed by a Secret Death Touch?'
    'What Is Kung Fu?'

*Real Kung Fu*, Victor Kan interview, Vol. 2, 6, 1977 (Hong Kong: Comray Publications)

# Index